SILVER RIVER

Also by Daisy Goodwin

101 Poems to Get You Through the Day (and Night)
101 Poems to Keep You Sane
101 Poems to Help You Understand Men (and Women)
101 Poems That Could Save Your Life
Essential Poems for Britain and the Way We Live Now
Essential Poems to Fall in Love With
Essential Poems for Children
Poems to Last a Lifetime

DAISY GOODWIN

Silver River

A Family Story

FOURTH ESTATE · *London*

First published in Great Britain in 2007 by
Fourth Estate
An imprint of HarperCollins*Publishers*
77–85 Fulham Palace Road
London W6 8JB
www.4thestate.co.uk

Visit our authors' blog
www.fifthestate.co.uk

A catalogue record for this book is
available from the British Library

ISBN 978-0-00-225830-2

Typeset in Postscript Linotype Sabon by
Palimpsest Book Production Limited,
Grangemouth, Stirlingshire
Printed in Great Britain by
Clays Ltd, St Ives plc

All Fourth Estate books are printed
on Lettura Recycled paper with Blue Angel environmental
accreditation from the Hainsberg Mill in Germany.

Blue Angel is one of the world's first and most respected
environmental accreditation programmes. This high-quality
recycled paper, made from 100% post-consumer waste, has
been manufactured according to stringent controls.
For more information visit www.blauer-engel.de

For my mother Jocasta
and my daughter Ottilie
without whom this book could not
have been written

Acknowledgements

It has taken me eight years to write this book, so I would like to award a medal to my agent, Derek Johns, for not giving up on me or it. My editors, Clare Reihill and the incomparable Patricia Parkin, believed in the book when I had lost my way. I must thank all my Argentinian relations and friends who put me up, and put up with me, especially Derek Willans, whose own research into the family history spared me months of archive sifting. I must thank all the friends and relations who read this book and gave me their unvarnished opinions: Polly Astor, Jason Goodwin, Ann Elletson, Pippa Brown, Emma Fearnhamm, Tabitha Potts and John Silver, who gave me the real translation of 'Las Limpias'. My aunt Judy for the chance remark that set the book in motion, and my husband, Marcus Wilford, and my daughters, Ottilie and Lydia, who gave me the space to write this and the encouragement to finish it. And finally I must thank my mother for reading it with grace.

ONE

'But don't you want to be famous?' said Joe as he held me over the cliff. That was the first time I was close to the edge.

My mother, my stepfather Joe, my brother and I were walking along the cliffs at the edge of town. I was six and I had just switched from ballet dancer to film star when asked what I wanted to be when I grew up. Joe had heard this and found the idea of this plump scowling child wanting to be loved by millions irresistibly funny. He started to ask me what kind of films I'd like to be in.

'Action movies, Westerns, musicals?' I wasn't too sure about that bit as I hadn't actually seen many films. Joe bent down and pushed his face up against mine.

'Do you realize how many children want to be in the pictures? You've got to have something special going for you – a gimmick. Can you sing, can you dance, what's going to make YOU stand out from the crowd?'

I didn't know how to answer him. All the other grown-ups I knew told me how clever I was; I thought that would be enough.

1

'What you need is a stunt, something that's going to make you really famous.' Joe moved closer to the edge of the cliff and beckoned me to follow.

'You really want to be a film star?' I nodded. 'And you'd do anything to get there, right?' I wasn't quite sure what this meant.

'Come over here, Daisy, and look at that.' I looked over the cliff to the sea and rocks sixty feet below. Joe was smiling now, showing all his teeth, even the ones at the back. I could smell the shaggy fumes of his Afghan waistcoat. 'You are a very lucky girl. I am going to make you the most famous movie star in the world. What I'm going to do is to drop you here off this cliff and I'm going to film you falling down. Don't worry, you won't die – I'll put some cushions at the bottom. You might be crippled, but you'll be a crippled film star. The wheelchair will be your gimmick. And you don't like walking much anyway, so you wouldn't really miss your legs.'

Joe started to laugh his ogre's laugh, and a fleck of his spit landed on my cheek. I didn't know what to say. I did want to be a film star, but falling all that way would definitely hurt and I wasn't sure I trusted him to put out the cushions properly.

'Would I really be famous?'

'Definitely.'

'And would it hurt very much?'

'Not that much, and it would be worth it, wouldn't it? Why don't we try it now?' Joe picked me up and held me over the edge of the cliff. The rocks looked a very long way down. I realized that Joe was not serious about the cushions – but how serious was he about dropping me? I tried to wriggle out of his arms.

'But don't you want to be a film star? Are you scared

of a little drop?' He held me at arm's length over the cliff. I tried to kick him but I couldn't reach. My mother was laughing so much she couldn't speak.

I started to scream, 'Put me down, put me down, I don't want to fall down there, I don't want to be a film star, I just want you to put me down.' My brother was screaming too now and trying to pull Joe away from the cliff by tugging at his jeans.

The more I struggled and hit and cried, the more Joe chanted, 'Daisy the crippled film star, Daisy the crippled film star. See her amazing fall, watch her plucky struggle to walk again. Roll up, roll up, a chance to see film history in the making.' There was white all round his eyes like a horse. He started shaking me from side to side and I think he must have slipped a little because my mother came running over.

'Careful, Joe, I think she's really frightened. Put her down now.' Joe shook me again.

'You're not frightened, are you now, you're just acting, showing us what you can do when you're a famous film star.'

'I'm not acting, put me down at once,' I bellowed with such fury that my mother started laughing again.

'Oh, Daisy,' she said, 'you look so funny. I wish you could see yourself, you've gone bright red in the face.'

In the end Joe got bored with holding my solid six-year-old weight and put me down. I ran away from him as fast as I could down the cliff to the beach huts, which were empty now because it was winter. I sat in the porch of one of them and sobbed and sobbed and waited and waited for my mother to come and make things better. I was there a long time.

When she found me she said, 'Joe was only teasing you, darling. You shouldn't take yourself so seriously.' I hated what she was saying but I needed her too much to push her away. If I could sit on her lap and smell her smell then it didn't matter that I had to listen to her telling me how to be teased.

Back at the flat I sulked. I sat scowling in the corner. My mother laughed, 'You look like a grumpy Buddha,' but Joe didn't like it at all. He sat down and stared right back at me.

I heard him saying to my mother, 'She's like a negative force field, I feel like she's giving me the evil eye.'

'Oh, come on, Joe, she's only six.'

'She's like a black cloud hanging over us.'

My mother looked over at me. 'Oh, do cheer up, Daisy, you're making us all feel nervous.'

I picked up *A Little Princess* and let the book fall open to my favourite chapter, the bit where Sara Crewe wakes up to find her garret transformed by the kindly Lascar from the attic next door. I had read the book so many times that I skipped all the stories of Sara's humiliation at the hands of the evil Miss Minchin and went straight to the beginning of the happy ending. Books, unlike the grown-ups I knew, always did the same thing.

Years later I am reading this same chapter to my daughter. We are lying on her bunk-bed; I am squashed against the wooden board that stops her falling out of bed in the night. Ottilie's head lies on my shoulder. Every so often she burrows into my chest trying to push my ribs out of the way of a comfortable resting place. Like me, she is impatient with the 'sad bits', so by mutual agreement we go straight to the moment when Sara wakes up and can't understand why she feels so warm and comfortable. (While she slept, her Indian benefactor has replaced her ragged blanket with a sumptuous satin quilt.) We both sigh with pleasure as Sara runs her feet through the Turkish rug that the Lascar has put down over the bare splintered boards. But as I read on through the oh-so-familiar sentences my mind wanders.

My daughter is the same age as I was when Joe held me over the cliff in Swanage. Reading those familiar sentences takes me right back to the aggrieved little girl I was then. But, unlike me, Sara Crewe was improbably noble in the face of her tormentors. She didn't cry and run away in a huff. She didn't scowl like a grumpy Buddha.

My daughter senses my distraction and nudges me.

'Why have you stopped? You said you would read me the whole chapter. Read it properly.' I try to focus on the words, to do the different voices consistently. It is very important to me that I don't renege on our bedtime reading contract. My mother used to read Dickens to me, impeccably. Reading aloud is something I know that mothers do.

It was odd, really, given the way that falling has been such a theme in my family, that Joe should have chosen that particular way to torment me. I didn't know that then, of course. I only found out later, right about the time I became pregnant with my daughter.

It all started with a chance remark by a swimming pool. I was staying with an aunt, my mother's sister, in Normandy. The pool was black, the tiles were white limestone and the setting was a perfect rural landscape dotted with sheep. My aunt stood by the edge of the pool, hesitating. Somebody urged her to jump, but she teetered awkwardly at the side.

'I've got a thing about jumping,' she said, 'hardly surprising really when you think how many people in our family have died that way.' It was a jarring remark in that perfectly ordered setting. But when she told me the story I was only mildly interested. It was all a long time ago and in another country, Argentina, and what's more the money was all gone.

But when I became a mother everything changed. My pregnancy was euphoric, but shortly after my daughter's birth I tumbled headlong into a depression so profound that for the first time in my life I understood the lure of suicide. Afterwards, when I recovered my senses, the story of my mother's family began to resonate with me. My aunt's tale of missed footings and broken necks began to sound less like a series of unhappy accidents and more like a pattern.

Ottie is winding her hair round her finger, the sign that she is about to fall asleep. I slow the reading right down, leaving longer and longer pauses between the sentences describing the Little Princess's magnanimity to her former foes. At last with a little grunt I feel my daughter's body go limp. I lie there inhaling the faintly feral smell of her scalp. There is nowhere else I would rather be.

But, not for the first time, it strikes me that my mother had another place to go, somewhere with a more insistent rhythm than the steady breathing of a sleeping child. And, not for the first time, I want to push away the thought that this was the fault of the plump little girl who didn't like to be teased. I would like to find the reason somewhere in my mother's jumping, bolting family. Perhaps, somewhere in the past, there is a way to get us both off the hook.

TWO

I have only one memory of my parents together: a half-glimpsed scene at knee level. I am in the kitchen, which is painted red. My mother and father are shouting at each other. I am under the table. I can see my mother's feet stamping at the stone floor. Her boots have metal bits so when they hit the floor they make little taps. I know about this because I wear those boots when I am dressing up. My father has soft rubber on his shoes like the bottoms of my school sandals, so his feet do not make any sound at all. The feet move towards each other and then away again, finally settling on opposite sides of the room, but the shouting goes on. In the end someone, I don't remember who, finds me and takes me away.

But that scene is only a fragment. The sharp focus comes later when my mother has gone.

I don't remember the day my mother left, but I remember the moment when I noticed she had gone. Someone, not my mother, had left my brother and me alone in the bath with a Lucozade bottle made of glass. I was five and my brother was three so we were soon sitting in a tub of bright red water, crying. Someone, not my mother, came at last and plucked us out of the scarlet water and dried us and put plasters on my wounded knee. The someone may even have kissed it better; I don't remember, she was not my mother.

The next day, with the plasters still on my knee, my brother and I got into the back of the someone's car and were driven to my grandmother's house. This grandmother was my father's mother, who wore skirts and smelt of lavender and powder; not my mother's mother, who wore trousers and never let you win at snap.

This grandmother lived in a white house in the middle of a forest. My bed was in an alcove at the end of her bedroom facing a corridor. That night I listened to the rustle of my grandmother's newspaper and tried not to think about the murderers at the end of the passage. It seemed safe here in my grandmother's house but still I knew that something bad was going to happen. The next morning my knee was red and puffy underneath the plasters, so my grandmother put us into her car with the wood bits on the outside and the red seats that smelt of sherbet dips and drove us to the hospital. The doctor told me I was a brave girl as he pulled three needles of glass out of my knee. He sewed up the cuts with thick black thread. The wounds must have been deep because I still have three white scars on my left knee that burrow into the skin like maggots. I can feel them now: smooth and shiny and strangely comforting, but as a child I spent hours trying to rub them away, sometimes even to pick them off like scabs. I couldn't bear the idea that they would never go away.

I cried when we came back from the hospital, but not for long. My grandmother fed me boiled eggs and soldiers and I watched *Blue Peter* lying on her squashy pink sofa. I don't remember missing my mother or my father in the days that followed, but I do remember not knowing who to call when I heard what were definitely murderer's footsteps crunching on the gravel beneath my bedroom window. By the time the stitches came out of my knee I had quite settled into the pattern of my new life: school, pony club, climbing the twisted trees in the rhododendron thicket behind the house. My mother must have been to visit us then but I have almost no memory of her from that time, neither can I remember feeling any pain at her absence. All that is covered with thick layers of smooth white scar tissue like the gashes on my knee. I can only see my brother, small and blond, wrapping his arms round my mother's denimed knees, my grandmother trying to prise him away. I don't remember myself in this hot little memory. Where was I? Standing around waiting for my brother to leave off? Waiting for my mother to go, for things to be clean and comfortable again? Already I was beginning to associate my mother with discomfort – rumpled sheets, pillows with no pillowcases, funny food, butter used straight out of the wrapper. When we went to visit her in London about a year after going to live with my grandmother, she was staying in a basement in Blackheath. I remember how cold it was there and longing for my bed with the patchwork quilt at my grandmother's house. My mother had no children's drinks so she made us mugs of hot sweet tea which we drank reluctantly. At my grandmother's we always had Kia-Ora orange squash. Mummy clearly didn't know what was suitable for children.

In retrospect I can only imagine how painful this period must have been for my mother. While I was living with my grandmother, my parents were engaged in an acrimonious custody battle. Even in the sixties, the fact that my mother had left the marital home for another man counted against her. I don't think, won't think, that my mother knew when she left her Georgian house in Surrey Square that she was leaving her children too, but given my father's determination to keep us, that was the result.

When I was six my mother moved to Swanage with the man who became my stepfather. Joe had been around all along, of course, but I don't remember being aware of him until later. I think my mother must have kept him out of the way while the custody battle was going on. But in Swanage he was always there, bigger and louder than anybody I had ever known. Joe was another adult who didn't understand what was suitable for children. In the mornings my mother and Joe would never get out of bed. I remember waiting out those endless child hours for them to get up and start doing things for us. Sometimes in the afternoon my brother and I would be sent down the road to the beach alone, another flagrant breach of the suitable-for-children rules. We used to spend hours in the beach shop trying to figure out what the pickled walnuts were that seemed to feature on all the postcards set in nudist camps. When the shop-owner finally threw us out we would wander along the front enviously peering into the beach huts. I longed for one of these. All I could see past the fully clothed families drinking tea out of white china mugs on the porch were discreet tangles of sunburnt limbs and the odd deflated beach ball. I imagined my hut as a kind of Sara Crewe refuge, a palatial tunnel full of soft rugs and fur-trimmed mantles.

One afternoon we came back from the beach to find

my mother sitting on Joe's lap, feeding him toast. They
looked happy. The next morning, while we were waiting
for them to get up, my brother and I invented a game
which consisted of climbing up the banisters and then
jumping the six and then seven and then eight steps to
the floor. From the ninth step I misjudged the distance
and fell down the stairs. The impact was so great that it
shattered a large gilt mirror that was leaning against the
wall. The sound brought my mother rushing out of the
bedroom. She rounded on us for being thoughtless; I think
she was crying as she picked up the shards of mirrored
glass.

It was after this that I became officially clumsy, famous
for getting in the way of small tables and china ornaments. I was brilliant at breaking things; I even broke my
brother's collarbone. I suppose I was trying to take up
more space, be bigger than I was – an equal weight to
Joe. He seemed to succeed by crashing through things,
trampling on fragile rules about closing your mouth when
you eat, elbows on the table, leaving the last bit of cake
for Mr Manners, blowing your nose tidily.

At the time I had no words to describe him. My grandmother called him Joe Fame, which she used to sort of
spit out, but she hardly ever talked about him and we
knew not to mention him in front of my father. So my
memories of him at that time are all physical: the space
he occupied, his loud deep voice, his endless laugh. He
was like the giant in *Jack and the Beanstalk*, casting a
long shadow over the happy valley. He said words in a
funny way, 'book' to rhyme with 'puke', his hair was long
and had white flecks in it; he always helped himself first.
He was the child-eating ogre in the *Red Book* of fairy
tales. But no amount of spells would shift him.

Daytime was always best at my mother's. It was always more dangerous after dark. Mostly Mummy and Joe would shout at each other about something called D. H. Lawrence but sometimes Joe would turn round and start staring at me, looking for an opening. It could be the utter worthlessness of David Cassidy or table manners being a complete waste of time, anything really as long as it threatened something I thought I believed in. At least Joe never came the grown-up with me: I was as worthy an opponent as any adult, better perhaps because I was so easy to provoke, and the strength of my emotions matched his own. The thing we both lacked was perspective. He experienced everything as directly as I did. It never occurred to him that winning an argument against a child by shouting them down wasn't much of a victory. Joe needed an enemy. At some point he discovered quantum physics and he started to call me a black hole, a bottomless abyss where his life force would disappear for ever. I wasn't sure what life force was exactly – it sounded rather like a Roman candle – but I didn't altogether mind having the power to extinguish it. Joe may have destroyed my ambitions to be a movie star but he did give me a starring role.

Joe's father was a policeman in Newcastle. But his son had no respect for the law. In the early days he put a lot of his unquestionable energy into breaking the rules. Mostly he broke them without realizing: helping himself first, talking with his mouth full, breaking into 'Heartbreak Hotel' at full volume while walking down Swanage High Street, not taking baths. Foolishly, I let my disapproval show. From then on, Joe dedicated himself to poking at my childish notions of respectability.

The winter I was nine he told me that the best cure for chapped lips was the liberal application of earwax. It sounded disgusting but after an hour of Joe's glittering stare and booming voice I was ready to poke my fingernail into my ear and spread a little of the sticky brown substance onto my flaking lips. It tasted bitter and viscous. It certainly stopped me from wanting to lick my lips – the feel of the oily goo in my mouth made me want to gag.

Joe looked at me approvingly as I dabbed the gunk on my lips, his face serious with effort until he saw mine crumple with disgust. And then the cackle, which he had been suppressing until the moment the earwax actually went into my mouth, erupted.

I tried not to react, as I knew that would only prolong the knee slapping and snorting, the sprays of mirthful saliva; but the sense of having been tricked again was overwhelming. I felt my face going hot and red. I rushed out of the room, down the rickety wooden steps, and down the dog-turd-littered road that led to the beach. I was angry with Joe, but even angrier with myself for allowing myself to be taken in.

THREE

My father remarried quite soon after the divorce. My brother and I went to live with him and his wife in London and I suppose that was the moment I began to lead a double life. My stepmother, whose own mother had put nails in the back of her chair to stop her from slouching, had rules about everything: bedtime (eight o'clock), radio stations (Capital Radio was the devil's work), periods (Don't go near horses, they bolt). My stepmother drank coffee not tea, she abhorred garlic and never wore make-up. She wore baggy blue cord trousers, men's Hush Puppies and her hair in a bun secured with a biro.

My stepmother was diligent, disciplined and always there – everything, in fact, that my mother was not. But although my stepmother never stayed in bed, or teased me, or danced in public; even though she sewed on all my name-tapes, tested me on the characteristics of terminal moraine and made me a red plush velvet bedspread, she was not the woman I loved.

The transition from one parallel universe to another was awkward, confusing and occasionally painful. The first few days of the summer holidays were the worst. After arriving at my mother's flat in Swanage, my brother and I would open our suitcase, meticulously packed by my stepmother, and shut it again. As we usually slept in the sitting room – a room where one wall was covered by a poster of Che – there was nowhere to put our clothes.

By the end of the holidays the clothes that had been so neatly folded by my stepmother – the smug little balls of white ankle socks, the Colman's Mustard tin full of change so that we could phone home – had been scattered. Our clothes lay in heaps wherever we took them off. The socks lost their plump togetherness. The change was spent on ice lollies. (We learnt early on that ringing home was useless. The only reason to ring was so that we could come home early, but the answer was always the same: 'Let's just see how it goes. If you still feel the same in a week, we will talk about it then.' Like Persephone I had been allotted a time in the other world – every other weekend and half the holidays – and that spell could not be broken.)

And of course, after a few days the loss of a sock seemed less important. I stopped trying to pull the sheets straight like they were at home before I went to bed. I grew more tolerant of my new domain. I slept late in the morning and happily ate cold sausages for breakfast. There were even times when Joe stopped being the enemy; days when whole hours would go by when I forgot which side I was on.

For, much as I hated Joe, I had my price. The summer I was ten I sold my soul for a box of sweets. Actually, it was a cardboard crate full of Mars Bars, Kit Kats, Maltesers, Curly-Wurlys.

The betrayal began when I noticed a mistake in the

book I was reading: *Death on the Nile* by Agatha Christie. 'Corpse' had been printed in error as 'copse'. I pointed this out to my mother; I think I wanted to impress her with my spelling skills. 'Clever you, darling,' she said, her mind on other things, but Joe pounced. Did I know that if I wrote a letter to the publishers Fontana complaining about the mistake, hinting perhaps that my ten-year-old faith in the printed word had been undermined, they would have to send me a free book, maybe books.

Joe told me he did this all the time. But he thought that a letter of complaint from a little girl would be much more successful.

'You'll be able to start your own library with all the books they'll send you.' This was only a moderate lure; what I liked was the idea of correcting grown-ups' mistakes.

The letter was written that afternoon, largely at Joe's dictation, beautifully set out in my prize-winning handwriting.

He came with me to the post office and offered to lend me the money for the postage (I was sending my copy of *Death in the Nile* back as proof) in return for one of the free books. It was an offer I had no choice but to accept.

I was suspicious, of course, of Joe's intentions. Was this another earwax trick? But for once the whole exercise appeared to be genuine. Ten days later a parcel arrived addressed to me containing a rather slender apology and four paperback Agatha Christie novels. As I had read all of them already, it was no hardship to surrender one to Joe. And for the first time since he had arrived uninvited into my life, I felt that Joe might have his uses.

I spent the rest of the holidays reading: not for pleasure but for accuracy. I found mistakes everywhere from Baroness Orczy to Enid Blyton to E. Nesbit. Other publishers were not as generous as Fontana. Puffin sent me a letter congratulating me on my powers of observation but no free gifts. The thrill had gone. The holidays were almost over, my brother and I were taking the 5.20 to Waterloo the day after tomorrow. We started to look for the clothes that matched the list stuck to the inside of our suitcase.

But Joe didn't give up easily. Seeing my disappointment over the lack of goodies with the Puffin letter, he produced a Mars Bar from the pocket of his jeans. It was rather squashed, and as he peeled off the wrapper the chocolate coating looked white and crumbly in places. Not that I wasn't salivating – chocolate was chocolate in whatever condition – but this Mars Bar was not for eating.

'Look what it says here on the wrapper,' said Joe. '"*If this product is not entirely satisfactory please return it to us for a full refund.*" They say "*refund*" but if you sent them a Mars Bar with something really wrong with it they would have to send you lots of free sweets – especially if you are only ten or better still eight and you had been saving up your pocket money for weeks to buy this as a special treat. They would probably give you a year's worth of sweets, maybe even a lifetime's supply.' Joe bared his teeth and the greeny vein on the side of his head trembled slightly.

The vein and the grin would normally have made me wary, but I had just read *Charlie and the Chocolate Factory* and my head was full of chocolate rivers and the glories of confectionery.

The problem was that, apart from looking a bit tired, there was nothing really wrong with the Mars Bar. It didn't look bad enough to guarantee a lifetime's supply of free sweets. My brother and I puzzled over this until Joe suggested putting something in the Mars Bar which definitely shouldn't be there like a rat bone.

'And then you can write in your letter, "*Imagine my surprise*",' he did his squeaky little girl voice, '"*and horror after saving up for months for this Mars Bar that on taking my first bite, my teeth encountered something hard and bony.*"'

This seemed to be a splendid plan; the only problem was getting hold of a rat bone. In the end I made do with one of the little nuts from my brother's Meccano kit. I pushed it well into the layers of caramel and marshmallow with a pencil and carefully bit around it to make its discovery seem more authentic. Joe helped me compose the appropriate letter and together we parcelled up the dismembered Mars Bar and took it to the post office.

Standing in the queue I began to worry. What if the people at Mars spotted that the nut had been put there deliberately? If they found out what I had done they might send the police to arrest me. Worst of all I had given my address in London; I didn't trust Joe to care for my free sweets without helping himself.

Joe dismissed my fears.

'They will never know. And even if they did suspect, it's much easier for them to send you the sweets. They haven't got time to follow these things up.'

I allowed myself to be reassured, although I didn't quite believe that Joe would tell me if there was a real risk. But the anticipation of the free chocolate in what Joe enticingly described as novelty sizes was too much for me. I watched as the parcel was handed over and weighed, I stuck on the stamps and stood on tiptoe to drop it in the grey postal sack.

On the way home, Joe began to riff about the free things

that could come my way with a bit of application: shampoo, Coca-Cola, make-up, tights, more sweets. He was the Willy Wonka of Swanage High Street. I trotted along beside him, drooling at the thought of all that stuff. There was no more exciting phrase to my greedy ten-year-old self than 'free gift'. I used to spend many happy hours reading the promises of endless bounty that *Reader's Digest* would send my grandmother: 'a genuine treasure chest, containing the golden key of knowledge' was the sort of thing I coveted.

I did wonder, as Joe listed the potential spoils in his best baritone, why he didn't claim all this booty himself if it was so easy.

'Thing is, no one feels sorry for a grown man, but if a little girl like you writes to them they have to respond. No one wants to be swindling kids.'

This I felt was fair. In fact, I felt rather indignant on my own behalf: I was, after all, only ten. I had every right to have my Mars Bar delivered to me in a pristine condition. My genuine indignation at the sloppiness of paperback printing was recalled and used against Mars; the fact that I had engineered the whole situation, conveniently forgotten.

I had learnt from Joe more than just the mechanics of swindling multinationals; he had taught me to believe that I was in the right whatever the facts of the situation.

Such was the combined power of Joe's advocacy and my own greed that it never occurred to me that what I was doing was wrong. I worried about the consequences of being found out, yes; but I never questioned the morality of sticking Meccano nuts into Mars Bars. I had been led into Joe's ethical universe by my own sweet tooth. It was not such a difficult place to be; every ten-year-old could understand the power of free chocolate. That my thirty-four-year-old stepfather should respond to confectionery with the same intensity was more surprising. I think this must have been the closest I ever came to trusting Joe; when it came to chocolate, he was on the level.

The next day came and the summer was officially over. It was time for my brother and I to go home: brown, dirty, our suitcase full of lone socks. I had spent much of the holiday longing to be firmly tucked into my own bed with its smooth unrumpled sheets that never lost their moorings; but I woke that morning feeling less than happy. Partly it was the realization that with the smooth sheets came other things like homework, early bedtimes and protein requirements, and partly it was the awkwardness of saying goodbye. My mother used to hug me so tightly that she would bruise my cheekbone. I didn't know how to tell her it hurt. There were so many things I couldn't say.

When I got back to London, I found my school uniform – purple gymslip and tie, white shirt, grey socks – laid out neatly on the chair in my bedroom. Each item was clearly marked with its Cash's name-tape. Order had been restored.

When my stepmother came upstairs that evening to switch off the lights, she asked me how the holiday had been. 'Fine,' I said, compressing into that monosyllable all the impossible contradictions of my childhood.

The box arrived on a Saturday. It was so big that the postman had to ring the bell. I opened the parcel immediately; inside was a box bulging with Mars Bars, Twixes, Milky Ways, Marathons, Maltesers in adorable novelty sizes. It was like having my own sweet shop.

My brother looked at me in envy.

'Can I have a Kit Kat?'

'Not yet,' I said jealously. I wanted to keep all the sweets just as they were, shiny and abundant. I admired the purply sheen of the Mars wrappers, the martial red of the Maltesers, the noble protuberances of the Topics. It took me a while to find the letter.

Dear Miss Goodwin,
We read with regret your letter of the 16th August concerning an unsatisfactory product. Please accept the enclosed as a token of our sincere apologies.
Yours truly, etc. etc.

Apart from my name there was nothing personal about the letter. It was clearly the standard response to any kind of complaint. The scheme had worked.

For a moment I wished I was back in Swanage so that the triumph could be properly celebrated, but then I remembered that Joe would insist on his share of the spoils. The only person I could boast to was my brother, but he, infuriated by my selfish attitude to sweet-sharing, had complained to my stepmother about the injustice of my confectionery haul.

I was too excited by my own cleverness to take in the expression on her face when I told my stepmother how I had come by the sweets. Blithely I told her the whole story including the insertion of the nut, although I left Joe out of it. I knew from experience that mentioning his name was never a good idea in my father's house. Too late I noticed that my stepmother was making her cross face; when she spoke, her foreign accent became noticeable, something which only happened when she was really angry.

'How could you have been so wicked? Do you realize that someone will probably lose their job because you

21

have been so greedy and dishonest? Someone with children who won't get any presents this Christmas because a silly little girl decided she wanted some free sweets.'

I was astonished. The idea that my scheme had any consequences had never crossed my mind. I defended myself with one of Joe's lines.

'They probably know that it's a trick – people do it all the time – but they sent me the chocolates because I'm a child and it would look bad if they didn't.'

My stepmother blinked in fury.

'You are going to write to them today and tell them what you have done and apologize. And you are going to send back all the sweets.'

That was too much.

'But those sweets are mine. I got them. I'm not sending them back. You're a miserable old spoilsport.'

Thwack! My stepmother slapped me hard on the cheek. My brother, who had been cramming Maltesers into his mouth while he still could, put the packet back in the box and slunk away.

I appealed to my father. I blamed Joe. I knew it would be easier for my father to defend me to his wife if all the blame could be put onto Joe Fame (my father always referred to the man who had ended his marriage by his full name). My stepmother appeared to accept this version of events but I knew she thought I was guilty. In her world there were no grey areas. My stepmother as a ten-year-old would never have been tempted from the paths of righteousness by the likes of Joe Fame.

She insisted that I write to Mars confessing my sins and returning the sweets. When I pointed out that they might send the police to arrest me for fraud, she said that I had made my bed and now I must lie on it. She stood over me while I wrote the letter and as I taped up the box containing my short-lived booty.

I don't know what was worse: the shame of writing the letter or the loss of the sweets. I didn't feel remorse. My stepmother's moral indignation was as baffling to me as Joe's behaviour on the cliff.

A few days later I got a letter from Mars, hand-typed this time, deploring my deceitfulness. One phrase has stuck in my head.

'*Fraudulent behaviour of this kind costs our company thousands of pounds a year.*' There was no mention of anyone being sacked. '*In view of your age, we will take no further action.*' Relieved, I realized then that Joe was right and that my behaviour with the Mars Bar had been quite normal. It was my stepmother who was the problem; upsetting the balance with her refusal to play the game. This was quite hard to get my head around. Joe was not to be trusted, while my stepmother was clearly dependable – and yet he was right and she was wrong. It was too confusing. I stopped trying to reconcile my two worlds: all that mattered was the cover story.

FOUR

When I was eleven Joe became fascinated by the endless drama of little-girl friendships: the best friends who betrayed me, what Stella said about Natalie to Tammy and how horrible Fleur had been to Ashley. He identified with all the passion I put into these shifting alliances. He, too, had best friends who changed by the week and who stabbed him in the back on a regular basis. We both wore out our friends. We both wanted too much. My school life was not happy; I was a single in a class full of pairs. Sometimes established couples would allow me to tag along with them, but it was always a temporary arrangement. But even if I didn't have a friend at school, I could always be friends on the phone and I would spend hours every evening calling the girls in my class trying to write myself into the script.

Joe had friends who would come round every night for a month or so and then one night the parsnip wine would come out and things would be shouted and the friends never came back. It must have been after one such falling-out that my mother and Joe moved to London for a few months; there were too many people they had to cut in Swanage. So for a while, every other weekend I swapped the 5.35 to Swanage for the number 19 bus to the Angel. Joe, after listening in to one of my call marathons, a new experience for him as they did not have a telephone in Swanage, insisted that I ask some of these friends round to the house. I was dubious about this: the thought of Joe becoming part of my London life was troubling. I managed to cope with the huge differences between my two lives by holding them completely separate in my head. I was also apprehensive about what some of my friends who lived in big white houses in St John's Wood would think about Joe. He was not like anybody else they knew. But my mother and Joe were so keen on the idea of meeting my friends that I could not think of a coherent reason to refuse. And I wanted to prove that I did have a mother; maybe having a real mother would make me eligible as a best friend.

I invited the three girls that I most wanted to impress – Tammy who was the class show-off, Diana who had black nail varnish and a boyfriend, and Amanda who had waist-length blonde hair and platforms. My mother, whose only experience of little girls was the brief time she spent with me, thought the way to impress them was to prepare the most recherché meal she could devise. There can't have been many twelve-year-olds in the mid-seventies sitting down to home-made ravioli stuffed with shrimp. The ravioli took her hours to make so that when the girls arrived she was floury and fed up. We sat down, my friends, my mother, Joe and I, and the ravioli were passed round. Tammy, Diana and Amanda took two or three out of politeness but Joe, who never held back, helped himself to ten. As a result he was still chewing noisily when everyone else had finished. Tammy, Diana and Amanda stared at him as he reached out to help himself to the last of the food, despite the generous helping still on his plate and in his mouth.

My mother noticed just in time. 'Joe, offer some to the girls, they haven't had very much.'

'But they haven't finished what they've got.'

This was true; my mother's food was clearly too exotic for St John's Wood. She brought out the pudding which was a chestnut puree sweetened with whipped cream.

'Oh, just a little bit, please,' said Tammy, Diana and Amanda. I felt cross with my mother for not understanding about proper food.

Joe leant forward. He had the look I remembered from the cliff. His voice came out in a falsetto replica of my evening phone calls.

'"Did you hear what Tammy said about Diana to Ashley? She said that Diana's really selfish and she likes David Cassidy so she must be really stupid."'

Joe was just riffing, improvising on a few overheard notes, but to the stiff little girls round the table it sounded like recorded speech, evidence of what people really did say about you behind your back. I was rigid with shame. Any chance I had of becoming eligible had just been wiped out by that sentence. I could not think of a way to stop Joe from going on, short of putting my hand over his mouth. But Joe went on and on.

'". . . and then Amanda didn't ask Ashley to her party and Ashley was really upset but everyone was keeping it a secret but Tammy told her because she's really mean. I don't know why anybody wants to be her friend. She's always boasting about how she's got her own television in her bedroom."'

There was enough circumstantial evidence in this to convict. I may not have said those exact words but Joe had picked up the flow of my recent conversations well enough. I looked round the table. My mother and Joe were laughing but Tammy, Diana and Amanda were not. Joe paused for a second and I ran out of the room. I sat on the stairs and picked a large flake of paint off the banister. Tammy, Diana and Amanda followed me out.

'We think you're a really horrible person.'

'We don't want to be friends with you.'

'And we think it's really weird here.'

'I want to go home.'

Tammy rang her mother who arrived shortly afterwards in her baby-blue E-type and took the girls away.

My mother said, 'What a load of ungrateful wretches, after all the time I spent making those ravioli. I think you need to find some friends with better taste, darling.'

Joe was still doing his little-girl imitation.

I went for a walk along the canal. I had planned to take Tammy, Diana and Amanda there to show them the wall with all the rude words, but now I stared into the scummy brown water and wondered how I could throw myself in without actually getting wet.

The next day I woke up with a temperature of 105 and I didn't go back to school for another two weeks, which was long enough in little-girl time to wash away my sins. But as I lay sweating in my bed, I relived every excoriating second of that afternoon again and again. It did not matter how many times my mother said, 'Don't take things so seriously, Joe was only teasing you. And all those girls were much too silly for you anyway.' I knew another rule had been broken.

FIVE

Joe didn't have a job. Not a proper job like my father, who went away to make films. Joe was a novelist. He had two books with his name on the shiny orange covers. I don't know where they came from as I never saw him writing. He talked about it a lot, maybe he wrote at night. He would be fine, he said, if it wasn't for his problem with the life force. Sometimes he would stagger out of bed at lunchtime and say, 'The force, it's gone,' which meant that he would spend an hour describing his physical condition to my mother and the rest of the day doing nothing. Nothing, that is, except play the guitar and perfect his Elvis Presley impersonation. Joe had the build for Elvis and the voice and the sneer. I don't know whether his lip had always curled like that or whether he had trained it specially, but it was a perfect replica of Elvis's leer circa 'Jailhouse Rock'. At the time I had never seen Elvis and when I finally did see *Viva Las Vegas* on the TV, it felt as though the King was imitating Joe.

I recently found an old photo of Joe circa 1970. The picture is taken from a low angle and you can almost see his nostril hairs. His pelvis in flared jeans is thrust forward Elvis-like,

his hands are on his hips and the mouth is in the sneer. By
the seventies, Joe had found another alter ego to add to Elvis
– Jack Nicholson. After *One Flew Over the Cuckoo's Nest*
came out, Joe's smile, already alarming, became as wolf-like
as Nicholson's; the mad gleam was there already. I stopped
being a black hole and became Nurse Ratched, an even greater
threat to the life force. I am glad that he was no longer part
of my life when *The Shining* appeared. Looking at the photograph now I can still smell Joe, the horsey notes of his hair,
the acrid accents of sweat and something darker and deeper
which might have been his Afghan waistcoat. In the picture
a child, my half-sister, is clinging to his leg crying but Joe is
staring out into posterity. He doesn't look nice but he looks
unequivocally male, a great megalith of testosterone, a warrior
going into battle. As a child I saw him as grotesque, a character from Roald Dahl's *The Twits*, but now I realize how
sexy he was. My mother must have taken this picture; it's a
very accurate snapshot of what she wanted him to be –
Heathcliff, Mellors, Albert Finney in *Saturday Night and
Sunday Morning*, John Lennon, all rolled into one.

Always a trend-spotter, my mother had found a man who
summed up the late sixties circa *Revolver* – young, northern,
working-class, dirty, rude and sexy. She ran away from the
Connie Francis chart-topping world of my father for the
Swinging Sixties of the Beatles, Bob Dylan and Joe. Like
the rest of the family she had – has – a knack for creating
the perfect narrative, the two-line pitch that sells the movie
to the most cynical studio head. Beautiful young woman,
with nice husband, house and children feels there must be
something more to life. One day she meets rough diamond
with potential (played by Jack Nicholson) and she sets off
on her bicycle to start a new life with 'Blowin' in the Wind'
on the soundtrack.

It must have been hard for Joe to be hit with the full force of my mother's expectations. At first there would have been for him a terrific sense of triumph, of having struck right at the heart of the enemy, liberating this intellectual, southern woman from her bourgeois bonds. Joe didn't have much time for conventional politics, although I think he would have liked to be a dictator, but he liked a class war he could win. He used to mock the gentility of my mother's relations, their lack of life force; but he soon lost the Geordie accent of his childhood in favour of something richly RP. He had an actor's voice, rich and well modulated, convincing except for the occasional cackle which tipped the scale from warden to inmate. Sometimes, in moments of tenderness, particularly with his own children, some Geordie would slip back in, but most of the time he was Secret Agent Fame in deep cover behind enemy lines.

In the beginning it must have been everything my mother wanted – completely passionate, a life entirely in the present. At the time of the cliff-top incident their relationship must have been at its peak, my mother a lover not a mother then. Later, things cooled and the heavy knee began. Heavy knee would settle on Joe like a low-lying cloud. When Joe used to pick me up from the station in his Bedford van, he'd say as I struggled to load my suitcase into the back, 'I'd help you but the heavy knee's been very bad this week, very heavy.'

This I knew meant a weekend of home brew, late-night arguments and guitar playing. Joe accorded heavy knee with the gravity of a serious chronic illness, a sort of spiritual arthritis. Friends when they came round soon learnt not to ask Joe how he was. Even the most offhand enquiry would elicit at least a twenty-minute monologue on the exact status of the heavy knee: how long it took him to get out of bed in the morning, the fat slug that sat on his soul, the cancer at the heart of the life force. The first time people heard this they would sit in stunned sympathy imagining from the timbre of Joe's voice, the dejection of his body language, that he was suffering from something life-threatening, a man struck down in his prime. Sometimes they would ask, 'But what does the doctor say?' and Joe would look at them in amazement, turning his head to fix them with his most Nicholson-like stare.

'Doctors, what do doctors know about heavy knee?'

Regular visitors to the house were careful to step round the subject, but sometimes a milkman or one of the girls' teachers would say to Joe, 'And how are you today, Mr Fame?' and Joe would give them a fifteen-minute summary of his symptoms. The only person who managed to stop him in mid-flow was Sister Joseph, the headmistress at my half-sisters' school.

'Well, I'm sorry to hear you are feeling poorly, Mr Fame, but I think you'll find that fresh air and exercise are the cure for so many of life's ills.' Joe didn't take the girls to school for a long time after that encounter.

Joe found affirmation for his condition reading *Oblomov* by the Russian writer Goncharov. He didn't seem bothered by the story's satirical intent, he was just happy to find a literary role model. D. H. Lawrence, his usual hero, was after all really sick and made heroic efforts to escape from his illness. Joe, who was robustly healthy, was terrified of real illness. He only wanted illness as metaphor.

When my mother was pregnant with her fourth child, my youngest sister, she had a threatened miscarriage and was forced to spend a great deal of the pregnancy lying down. Joe was at once tender towards her and fiercely competitive when it came to symptoms. He would take the invalid trays of food in bed and then spend hours telling her about the war of attrition in his body.

In the end I think the heavy knee was too much for my mother. Although she occasionally suffered from it herself, her life was all about doing things. Every time I went down to Swanage for an alternate weekend or a bisected holiday my mother would be in the middle of some new project. I can remember her salting joints of pork, smocking, making parsnip wine, stencilling, quilting, stapling, gilding, glazing, drawing silhouettes, or creating collage screens, papier-mâché Christmas ornaments, *trompe l'œil* vistas. Eventually these projects became commercial, research for the books that she was beginning to write, but at the beginning I think she was looking for somewhere for all that energy to go. Her mother, grandmother and great-grandmother had all had actual physical frontiers to contend with. My mother didn't have to make her own clothes, even when she and Joe were living on twenty pounds a week, but she needed something to do. She was, and is, the most energetic person I have ever known.

Always ahead of her time at the beginning of the seventies, my mother put away the Che Guevara poster and the primary colours and covered her walls with hand-cut stencils. Goodbye *Avengers*, hello *Little House on the Prairie*. The white heat of technology was definitely extinguished in my mother's house. If something was worth doing, it was worth doing by hand. Part of her motivation was genuine poverty, but my mother clearly enjoyed being an artisan. She was also brilliant at improvising. Her first book, *The Pauper's Cookbook*, was a minor classic: delicious recipes written by someone who understood what it meant to be poor and passionate about food. When at the beginning of the eighties she published *Paint Magic*, it became an instant best-seller

because it made the top-drawer world of aristocratic deco-
rators accessible to anyone with a stencil brush and a tube
or two of raw umber.

No matter where she was living or how much money
she had my mother always had the most delicious food and
the most exquisitely decorated, if not always the most
comfortable, house. She cared intensely about detail, whether
it was getting the edges of a stencil perfectly crisp or the
brawn unimpeachably translucent. It wasn't a fussy thing
– she just saw no reason to compromise. She didn't want
or need an easy life. And I think it was this conscientious-
ness, besides her fluid prose style and perfect taste, that
made her books so successful. As an adult I can appreciate
what a fairy-tale feat it was for her to pull herself out of
poverty and relative exile to become a leader in her field.
I can't help but swell with vicarious pride when I meet
people who tell me that Jocasta Innes stopped them from
starving as students or that she liberated them from swirly
carpets.

When Joe used to mutter much later to me that my
mother had sucked him dry, he had a point. After meeting
her he never published another novel, but she began to
publish books that became very successful. My mother
had diverted the life force to her own ends. Heavy knee
was Joe's answer to this siphoning-off of his creativity. I
don't think it ever occurred to him that my mother had
no choice, that without her enterprise they would be destitute. Part of Joe's strength came from his inability to see
anybody else's point of view. He blamed her for his writer's
block and she in turn began to resent the burden of
supporting him and the children and the endless demands
of the heavy knee.

Appropriately, it ended as the seventies drew to a close. I

was seventeen. It was April and unseasonably hot. The train journey down was stifling, the moquette pile of the seat dug into my bare legs, there was no buffet car after Bournemouth so I sat hot and thirsty for the last third of the journey trying unsuccessfully to read *The Winter's Tale*, my A-level set text. I had other things on my mind, though, like the recent acquisition of my first real boyfriend.

For some reason, this time when Joe swaggered out of the Bedford van, I didn't have that mixture of dread and embarrassment that usually washed over me on first seeing him. He looked somehow smaller – less threatening. For once he seemed free of heavy knee – in fact in the forty or so minutes it took to drive from Wareham to Swanage I don't think he mentioned his health at all. Instead he talked about the book he was writing – a complicated erotic farce, in which an uptight, upper-class woman with life-force problems swaps bodies with a brutish working-class lout whose primal urges are in perfect working order.

'Imagine this, Priscilla the woman wakes up one morning to find that she's got a hard-on.' Joe had got about halfway through a bang-by-bang explanation of the plot when he suddenly broke off.

'Do you realize what an amazing woman your mother is?'

'Er . . . Yes, I suppose so.' I waited for Joe to follow up his remark, but he was silent for a moment and then launched into a description of the working-class hero of his book discovering what it is like to be penetrated by his own enormous member when trapped in the body of a frigid woman. We were halfway through the acrobatic climax when we arrived at the house.

My mother was in the middle of doing something complicated with pork fat. She, too, looked remarkably cheerful, excited about her new book on country kitchens. A young man had come down from London to do the illustrations.

'He's so chirpy, darling. He's always springing around cracking jokes.'

I didn't pay too much attention to this as I was looking for a way to tell her about my boyfriend. This was difficult as my mother was so fizzing with all her new projects that it was hard to find an opening.

I couldn't get her alone that day or the next. Joe was always around, being uncharacteristically attentive. 'Would you like a cup of tea, darling? Shall I make lunch?' I had not seen him like this for years. He was always touching her, talking about her, rushing in to read her things he'd written. It was completely different from my last visit when heavy knee had settled over the house like smog and Joe and my mother had barely spoken to each other except to argue about whose symptoms were worse.

Finally, I got my mother alone. I think she may even have engineered it. We went for a walk on the cliffs, the same cliffs that Joe had once threatened to push me off. My mother was walking ahead of me, springing along in her plimsolls and boy's jeans. From behind she looked younger than me. I lumbered along after her, looking for an opening. But just as I'd found the words she turned round.

'There's something I want to tell you.' She paused. 'I shouldn't really, but I've got no one else. It'll have to be our secret.' My mother and I had never had a secret before.

'The thing is, darling, I've fallen in love. My life feels brand new again. You don't know how exhilarating it feels.' But of course I did know the feeling, I knew exactly what falling in love felt like.

'He's younger than me, of course, but it's so great to be with someone who's so enthusiastic about life, someone who smiles all the time. He's got so much energy . . . He calls me Jock, can you imagine? He's so cute.' Her words were coming out in a rush now, but her face was turned away from me out to sea.

'It happened up here on these cliffs. We went for a walk one day and I just felt myself come alive again.' She paused, not sure how much I could understand. I wanted to say, 'What about Joe, the children, everything?' but I also wanted her to go on confiding in me, to stay this close. At the same time I was wondering who she was in love with; none of the bearded potters or diminutive poets that made up Mum's circle of Swanage friends sounded likely.

'I can't wait for you to meet him. He's so talented, his drawings are really wonderful.' It could only be the springy illustrator.

'How old is he?' I blurted out.

My mother winced a little. 'Oh, I don't know exactly – in his late twenties, I think. But that doesn't really matter.'

Late twenties. I did some sums in my head. The springy one was at least seventeen years younger than my mother, much closer, in fact, to me in age. I couldn't quite work out what this meant.

'Oh, don't scowl like that, Daisy. Aren't you glad that I'm happy, I've been miserable for so long. I can't tell you what a relief it is to have some fun again.'

Once more I did know what she meant. Securing my boyfriend had been the light at the end of the tunnel; suddenly stepping out into colour after years of black and white. *I* was entitled to some Technicolor, after all those years of exams and knee socks; but was my mother? I wasn't sure.

'He's just a brilliant natural draughtsman. The stuff he does is so vivid, so charming. I mean, he's not an intellectual,

I don't think he reads much, but he's got such a fresh take on everything.'

'Does Joe know?'

'No, of course not. In fact, these last few weeks he's suddenly become much nicer to me, much more loving. It's ironic really. I spent years waiting for him to get over the heavy knee, and now he has, it's too late.'

I thought of all the eager glances, the cups of tea, and began to feel a little sorry for Joe.

'Are you going to tell him?'

'Honestly, darling, you should be a lawyer. I don't know yet.'

She gestured out at the sea.

'It all seems so light-hearted at the moment. It's more of a relief.'

She turned back to me. 'But you won't say anything, will you?'

'No, of course not . . . Actually, Mum, I was wondering if I could have a friend to stay, a boy.'

'A boy . . .' She turned and looked at me full on. 'Are you sleeping with him?'

I mumbled something.

'Well, I don't think you can share the same room, if that's what you had in mind. The girls would think it was very odd, and I don't think Joe would like it. But if he doesn't mind sleeping on the sofa.'

I was scarlet now but also relieved. I wanted to have her lay down rules, not hear about her breaking them.

We walked back to the house, which seemed smaller somehow. Joe started offering to make dinner and I noticed that he looked smaller too.

The next day my mother had to go somewhere. London? To meet Mr Springy? I don't know. I stayed behind with

Joe and the girls. Joe was happy, to me unbearably happy. He took the girls to the beach, he made chips, he even offered me the last piece of bread.

Later I tried to shield myself from him with a book: reading was my way of blocking out the unwelcome, but Joe was no respecter of limits. He sat down next to me on the sofa and picked up his guitar.

> *'Well, since my baby left me,*
> *I've found a new place to dwell.*
> *It's down at the end of Lonely Street*
> *At Heartbreak Hotel.'*

He got up and started singing the chorus with the full pelvic-rotation shimmy. He hadn't done Elvis for a while. Elvis was for those life-force-enriched days and there hadn't been many of those lately. There was no way I could carry on reading without earplugs. When he got to the end of the song, he sat down and gave me the full-on Nicholson stare.

'You know, Daisy, I feel my life is coming together at last. I'm beginning to realize what's really important to me. And do you know what's the most important thing in my life?'

I looked at the floor. I had a pretty good idea.

'Your mother, that's the most important thing in my life. She's an extraordinary woman. I've been ignoring this for so long, she's been depressed, and I've had the heavy knee, but what we have is vital. I can't believe I didn't see this before. I wish I hadn't wasted so much time.'

So did I.

'I thought she was sucking me dry but actually she was supporting me – but I couldn't see it. And you know, now I feel so much better. I feel like a new man. You'll know what I mean some day.' He picked up the guitar again.

'*Lay, lady, lay,*
Lay across my big brass bed
Lay, lady, lay.'

This, I knew, was my mother's favourite song. I think Joe was practising for when she came home. There was nothing I could say. I had felt honoured when my mother had chosen to confide in me about Mr Springy but now I felt like a double agent, a spy in the house of love. I had spent so much of my life hating Joe and now he had turned into someone I felt sorry for. All I'd ever wanted since I first met Joe was for him to vanish completely from the face of the earth and to have my mother all to myself. He was my rival, my enemy, the man who had humiliated me more often than I could remember. I should have felt triumphant that at last I held the balance of power, but all I felt was emptiness. I didn't want to win this way.

The next day my boyfriend arrived. The sofa rule did not last beyond the first night; I don't think my mother could stand the sexual tension. It was easier to have us both up in the attic out of the way. I was too high with the skin-burning excitement of being with my boyfriend twenty-four hours a day to think much about what was happening to my mother and Joe. The boyfriend read Joe as a comic eccentric, and could not understand why I had been so frightened of him. I was beginning to wonder myself. Could this affable Elvis impersonator really be the ogre I had imagined?

My boyfriend and I left Swanage together so I didn't talk to either my mother or Joe alone before I left. When I got back to London I started working for my A levels – I had a revision schedule to follow. I was diligent, even the boyfriend couldn't distract me from my timetable. It was all very organized: Stuarts in the morning, *Winter's Tale* in the afternoon, boyfriend at the weekend. Everything had a place and everything was in its place. It was about the only time in my life when everything seemed perfectly ordered. Both halves of my existence were balanced. I didn't want to be anywhere else. I was moving on.

But then one day, I rang my father from the phone box outside school to say that I would be late home. I was just going into a long excuse when my father interrupted me, his voice sounding as if someone had their hands round his windpipe.

'You need to come home at once. Your mother's here. With the children. Joe Fame tried to attack her with a carving knife.'

I got into a taxi.

My mother had told Joe about Mr Springy late the previous night. He picked up the biggest knife in the kitchen and chased her down the street, my mother wearing only a nightgown, Joe wearing nothing at all. A neighbour had to restrain Joe. I think the police may have been called. In the morning my mother called a taxi and took my sisters on the train to London and my father's house. 'I just couldn't think of anywhere else to go, darling.' She stayed for about three months. It was the only time, apart from that dim scene with the shoes under the table, that I can remember my parents living together.

Joe was in my life for ten years or so; I was six when he appeared in my life and seventeen when he went up in smoke like the Fairy King. After my mother jumped, there was no attempt at reconciliation. She started a new life in Brick Lane with Mr Springy and Joe booked the Mowlem Theatre in Swanage to give an *Evening of Elvis*.

I wasn't there, of course, but I've been told it was spectacular. Joe was not an impersonator – there were no white suits with rhinestones – Joe simply *was* Elvis, although he might have felt he was improving a little on the original. At the time of the concert Elvis was still alive. I am sure Joe hoped that Elvis would somehow hear of this alternative self playing in the Isle of Purbeck and let him take over for a bit. As far as I know the long-distance operator never got Joe Memphis Tennessee, but what a way to mark the end of his marriage.

Joe still lives in Dorset. For a while he made earrings and lived in a caravan, but now he has a house and works as a faith healer. He never published another book.

I saw him once as an adult. He was smaller than I remembered, but his voice was the same. Small flecks of spit still flew out of his mouth when he laughed at his own jokes. He had come to visit his daughter, my sister, who was staying with me. I had spent the whole day on imaginary errands hoping to miss him, but when I got back he was still there in my house, drinking my tea, noisily. He greeted me as if I was the guest. I knew better than to ask after his health.

Inadvertently, I caught his eye and looked back at him reluctantly. Neither of us wanted to lose face by turning away. I could still see white all around the irises of his eyes.

And then I realized that he was as scared as I was. Perhaps he had always been. I stood up and offered him a biscuit.

We had spent ten years wanting the same thing; and she had left us both.

SIX

Ever since I can remember I have told stories, some of them more truthful than others. I'd like to say that my penchant for embroidering the facts was a skill I had to learn in order to cope with the inconsistency that surrounded me, but deep down I know that truth has never been my friend. Much easier to tell stories, at least they made sense.

I lied about my mother relentlessly. Starting a new school when I was eleven, I told my classmates that she was Chinese (she was in fact born in China). I was believed, at least for a while. Eight years later, at university, I told my fellow students that my mother had been the mistress of Fidel Castro. Again, I was believed, at least for a while.

I suppose I told these lies to impress new people, but I think it was also a way of explaining how utterly exotic and different she was. My mother's real life was too confusing to explain truthfully in those days, so it seemed easier to make her the heroine in a fiction of my own making.

This is how my relationship with Argentina began. I

knew my mother's family came from there. I knew nothing about the country – but it sounded like the sort of place the mother I was creating would come from. My real mother was to me a rare and exotic creature glimpsed on weekends and in the holidays, but never when we came home from school. I loved her tight gypsy-skirt ruffles, her chokers made from velvet ribbons, her gold hoop earrings. My mother would find that articles of clothing and jewellery would sometimes disappear at weekends and in the holidays and then reappear magically the next time we came to stay. I just wanted a bit of her. Everything about my mother was precious to me, and Argentina was a place where we could be together in my head. Somehow Argentina explained why my mother was so different from other mothers, from my stepmother, why she wasn't there.

At the time I never resented her absence. I found different ways of being close to her. Other children had imaginary friends; I had a fictional mother, a siren from the southern hemisphere. When I was nine I won a prize for my eerily freehand drawing of South America. I had traced that tapering-out line so often in my mind that I could reproduce it effortlessly.

In my family it was always called 'the Argentine', pronounced to rhyme with 'spine', a big solid sort of place, that was far away and full of cousins playing polo. Eileen, my mother's mother, had been born there on an estancia in the pampas, two hundred miles from the nearest town. She would tell stories of her childhood filled with tennis parties and friends called Bunny and Pookie. Whenever my grandmother had to use Spanish words like 'Las Limpias', the name of the estancia in which she was brought up, her normally clear voice became quite pellucid. Although she must have grown up surrounded by Spanish speakers, there was no hint of this in the way she spoke. The only aural clue to my grandmother's origins was the slight drawl, a reminder that her mother tongue had been imported to the land of her birth in the late nineteenth century. Her voice was a perfectly preserved echo of the accents of the Victorian adventurers who had made their way to the Argentine several generations before.

When I was about eight or nine I connected the Argentine of my grandmother's stories with Argentina, a country on the bottom left-hand page of my children's illustrated atlas whose symbol was a dusky man in baggy trousers straddling a bull with horns. I learnt that the capital was called Buenos Aires, the chief export was beef, and the principal language Spanish. I found in another book about children from foreign lands that José's father was a gaucho who spent all day herding cattle on a horse and that José always looked forward to the *asado*, a kind of South American barbecue, every year on his estancia. This Argentina was an enticingly foreign place, infinitely more intriguing than the Latin-tinged version of the Home Counties where Eileen used to live. It gave me a reason for having such dark hair and eyes. And Argentina sounded romantic in a way that the Argentine had not.

Shortly after I discovered Argentina I changed my name. My grandmother's maiden name had been Traill, Alice Eileen Traill, and in an attempt to appropriate the glamour of her history I started calling myself Daisy Georgia Traill Goodwin. To make it sound more glamorous still I added an e. 'Traille' had a real swish to it. To a nine-year-old it sounded like a Baroness Orczy sort of name, a hint that I had a history, that I came from a family full of secrets. I recently discovered some school exercise books from about this time, all of them carefully inscribed in purple ink with my new name. My handwriting changed too, from neat schoolgirl script to florid squiggle, as if to express this new swashbuckling family history.

At that time the exotic past I boasted of to my friends was completely fictional, since the facts as presented by Eileen were too mundane to be the stuff of fantasy. Her childhood seemed to consist of long periods without incident punctuated by tedious long journeys to nowhere. It was a monotone beginning which only burst into colour when my grandmother sailed to England to be educated at Bedford High School. But Argentina was a great backdrop for the sort of family history I aspired to. I decided that Eileen's mother must have had an affair with one of the gauchos working on the estancia, and that the black hair I shared with my mother and grandmother was a genetic reminder of that illicit love. And of course there was Lloyd Webber's Argentina. I remember sitting in my Dad's Mercedes bus and hearing Julie Covington singing 'Don't Cry for Me, Argentina'. The lyrics were baffling, since I now realize I misheard her as singing, 'Don't cry for me, Argentina, the truth is I never loved you.' A heartless jade breaking the heart of a whole country. I was a bit put out, since, after all, Argentina was my idea. I had never heard of Evita or Perón – they were definitely not part of the Argentine. I became vaguely aware of Evita's story, and made the connection to its rather curious sequel, the return of Perón and his new wife Isabelita to Argentina, which happened, at least the way I remember it, around the time that the song was number one. I hummed the tune for about a year; but it never became the music for my own Argentina, it didn't have the passion I was looking for.

Looking back, it seems clear that even as a child I was filling in the gaps, trying to construct a narrative out of a story that seemed curiously patchy, attempting to make sense of the relationship of the Argentine to Argentina. It is only now that I can read the signals that my nine-year-old self was trying to decipher. One of the clues to the fact that my grandmother's version of her childhood was heavily edited was her relish for the macabre. One of her favourite stories, indeed the only one from her childhood that has any kind of flavour, involved a picnic by a river. My grandmother and her two sisters, who were all keen swimmers, had new bathing costumes made up specially for the occasion. Eileen was showing off as she climbed onto the bridge and executed a perfect swan dive into the water. But after the first delicious coolness of the water she encountered something soft and horrible. At first she thought it was mud but as she struggled free she saw what was left of a donkey's head. My grandmother loved telling us about how long it took to get the rotting donkey flesh out of her hair and fingernails. She certainly enjoyed telling the story more than my brother and I enjoyed listening to it. (Even now I am reluctant to dive into water where I can't see the bottom.) This wasn't quite the Argentina I had in mind so I mentally filed it far away from the country of gauchos and promise.

SEVEN

With the blessing of hindsight it seems almost inevitable that Argentina would change my life. At the time it was just a place to go. I left school when I was seventeen, with nine months to fill before I went up to Trinity College, Cambridge, to read history.

Public-school girls and boys traditionally filled their gap years with travel to distant lands, a rucksack version of the Grand Tour. Most people went to India. But South America was both further away and closer to my boyfriend, who had gone to Los Angeles. And of course I had family there. I wrote to Robin Willans, my first cousin once removed, inviting myself and my friend Kate to stay. It never occurred to me that he might say no. His address was Los Olivos 935742, Provincia de Buenos Aires. It seemed incongruous to me even then; a remote, bureaucratic, foreign-sounding address coupled with his very English name. The Argentine and Argentina on one envelope. The reply came back months later – so many months later that I had begun to believe he didn't exist. It was the briefest of notes, telling us to ring him with our flight details. He would meet us at the airport and then take us to camp. Camp was puzzling. I'd hoped of course that he was rich and living in splendour. Camp sounded ominously frontier-like. When I eventually got through to him on the phone he sounded crackly and anachronistically posh, with the accent of a forties film hero. Camp was pronounced 'kemp'. It was a voice that was both quintessentially English and completely foreign. I realized for the first time that I had no idea where I was going.

I earned the money for the trip working in a stockbrokers' office. It was a job obtained through a favour. I spent most of the day adding up columns of figures incorrectly in an office full of men in dandruff-speckled suits. Occasionally one of the partners would take me out to lunch and with much hand-patting would explain to me the mysteries of the stock market. It was either much more simple or much more complicated than it seemed. Occasionally Argentina would be mentioned as part of some tale of cornering some product, silver maybe or beef. It was not one of the countries that anyone much bothered with, a dusty desk in the back office. Thinking about it now I realize that the historic firm I was honouring with my presence was probably one of the conduits through which money flowed into Britain from Argentina and trickled out again. Although never officially colonized, the Argentine was subject to Britain at least economically. The British did not settle there in the same numbers as the Spanish or the Italians, but they took up a lot of space. Until they were nationalized by Perón, the Argentinian railways were owned and largely run by the British, who had built them to carry the beef to the canning factories. All that was juicy and sanguineous in the beef was extracted and boiled and boxed into Oxo cubes or pressured into Bovril jars.

Fortunes were made pulping the bloody Argentinian beef into the triangular cans of Fray Bentos corned beef that were shipped to London and re-exported to district magistrates in the Punjab and colonels' ladies in Burma. The Spanish, so the Whig theory of history I had learnt for A level went, were fatally weakened by the endless supply of silver that flowed into Cadiz from the New World in the seventeenth century. But the tins of protein that came into Britain from Buenos Aires at the beginning of the twentieth century acted on the stunted Bob Cratchits of Britain like a tonic. Huge doses of aggression-boosting B vitamins coursed round the country in the Edwardian era building up the kind of men who fought for King and country in 1914. The Argentines, who ate nothing but beef, had wars on a regular basis until the Peróns introduced meatless days as an austerity measure and they had to make do with killing each other instead.

I prepared for the trip by studying the *South American Handbook*, an encyclopedia of rucksack wisdom printed on India paper and weighing about four pounds. Every speck of population on the sea-horse-shaped continent of South America was rated for comfort, cleanliness and authenticity by Northern Europeans and Americans looking for local colour.

Argentina was not a favoured destination for *Handbook* travellers. The authors disapproved of the way the first settlers had exterminated the indigenous peoples of the pampas. There was concern about inflation and rumours of a military government with nasty habits including unwarranted aggression to long-haired gringos. I dismissed most of this as referring to a foreign country I was not likely to encounter whilst enjoying the comforts of my family's ancestral estates. We might run into a little trouble in Bolivia or Peru but Argentina seemed as safe as Surrey. My only concern was that distance was not quite on the Home County scale: it took days to get from one part of the country to another. I had marked all the places I wanted to go to on the map and it was going to take weeks to see them all if we travelled by bus, 'the only way to see the country' according to the *Handbook*. (It was only when we arrived that we realized that anybody who could afford to travelled by air, even the Indians, which was why there was always room on the buses for *Handbook* travellers.)

Before I left I did a little research into the family. I was not all that curious. At eighteen I felt that they should be preparing for me, rather than the other way round. The most helpful member of my family was my Aunt Judy, who, unlike my mother who had difficulty remembering her own children, had a photographic memory for family nuances. Robin, her first cousin and our prospective host, was *sweet*, a word that for Judy meant a number of things. 'He's a brilliant polo player, married to a very rich woman called Ray. I think she's an Oxo heiress or something like that. Very long-suffering.' Robin, I later found out from my mother, had apparently been in love with Judy when they were both at Cambridge in the late fifties. Robin was at Magdalen, then a college for thick aristos, reading ag sciences, and Judy was at Girton reading history. Judy, who then looked like Shirley MacLaine in *The Apartment*, had Zuleika-like quantities of admirers. Robin, it seemed, came quite low in the pecking order. There was little that was exotic about Robin. He came from the Argentine in the way that people come from Herefordshire. His most distinguishing feature was a passion for polo.

I also wrote to Robin's mother Daphne, my grand-mother's eldest sister, who was famous in our family for her toughness. Her husband had been killed in the war and she had brought up her two sons and ran the estancia completely alone. I assumed that she would be overjoyed to welcome her great-niece from across the water. My friend Kate, it turned out, also had connections with Argentina. Her mother and grandmother had for some reason spent part of the war in Buenos Aires. Her mother arranged for us to stay with some friends called the Von Rottmeyers, who were Swiss. I discovered later that there are an extraordinary number of Swiss Germans living in Argentina, certainly more than in Switzerland. The Von Rottmeyers lived in a suburb of Buenos Aires called Hurlingham.

We flew to Buenos Aires on 21 May 1980. We had no idea just how unsafe Argentina then was. South American military dictatorships were at that time the stuff of comic opera. But I found the place to be both sad and sinister. There was a burden of things left unsaid, of actions never referred to, of emotions suppressed. The air was heavy with the tension I knew so well from my childhood, when my parents would pack away their rage to leave space for family life. The people were like wary children. Who knew what would happen if you walked down the street the wrong way, looked up at a window at the wrong moment, accidentally knocked into a lumpy stranger. If they were careful then perhaps things wouldn't be their fault. But as all wary children know, it always is your fault – if you had laced up your shoes in the right order and put all the pencils back in the Caran d'Ache box in the sweep of colour starting with white and ending with indigo then the shouting might not have started. No wonder Buenos Aires has more psychoanalysts per square inch than any other city on earth.

Men and women dressed with an old-fashioned care: four-buttoned cuffs, neatly knotted scarves, gleaming brogues, matching shoes and bags all in greys and browns and blues. 'Pass me by,' their clothes said, 'I'm minding my own business.' Thirty years earlier Eva Perón had a pink evening coat from Christian Dior embroidered with five miles of silver thread, enough to shock the world into noticing her and her country. But at the beginning of the eighties the *porteños* – as inhabitants of Buenos Aires were known (meaning literally 'of the port') – dressed to disappear (or rather not to disappear). The Avenida 9 de Julio is nearly half a mile wide, conceived like Evita's opera coat to impress the world; but it had itself grown dingy, like a woman putting a shabby cardigan over a party dress. The pavements were cracked, the paint was peeling, the shop windows covered in yellowing cellophane. The Paris of the southern hemisphere was ashamed of its own exuberance, in retreat from its former glories. The sumptuously laid-out boulevards had become run-down. By now the cracks have been filled with Sheratons and Citibanks, smoked glass and chrome replacing Corinthian pilasters and wrought-iron balconies; but when the junta was in power it was a city in denial, not daring to look into the future or to acknowledge its past.

We saw Robin, my first cousin once removed, just after we negotiated the heavily armed customs officers. He was beautifully dressed in the lightest of cashmere sports jackets and perfectly pressed trousers, his shoes gleaming. His clothes were English, his face could have been found in Norfolk, his accent was Edwardian in timbre, and yet he was clearly foreign, an Argentine wolf in mild English clothes. His drawl affected every part of him; he spoke and moved with a kind of controlled languor, a deep current flowing through the eddies and swirls of the Spanish speakers around him. If I had been ten years older or he had been ten years younger I might have found him sexy. As it was the whiff of the predator that came from him was disturbing and slightly embarrassing. I had not had much experience of men. My world then was full of wispy boys.

'I've put you girls into an hotel for tonight and tomorrow I thought we could go to camp.'

I wondered why we were not staying at his apartment in the city. Maybe he didn't like the look of us. We agonized about the cost of the surely expensive hotel. The whole point was to have a free holiday. In fact the hotel was both cheap and nice but I felt wrong-footed. I think that while our visit was something of an obligation for Robin it may have given him a welcome excuse to be in Buenos Aires on his own. Whatever the reason, Robin's air of distraction was both strange and familiar.

'You look a little like your Aunt Judy . . .' but not enough, said the dying fall in his voice. 'And how is your mother? She was always so . . . energetic.' Energy was clearly not one of Robin's favourite qualities. The drive to the camp was punctuated by these conversational forays. I chatted in what I hoped was a winning way for a while but I was checkmated so often that I gave up. The trip took six hours through scenery of such monotony that no matter how far we drove it never felt as if we were getting anywhere. The land was quite flat and the sky was bulbous with rain. It was neither cold nor hot, just dank and humid. We were squeezed along the road by the great grey rollers of the earth and clouds.

Robin's wife Ray looked as though she had sat under that grey sky for some time. She was more gracious than her husband, the echo of the heiress in her manners, but she was trapped behind a transparent veil of civility. Her three children were away being educated in a boarding school in Buenos Aires and she had too much money to be really busy in camp. Her days were spent devising menus that attempted to add variety to the staple diet of beef. The house was not the estancia of my imagination. It was indeed a camp – a bungalow built of red brick surrounded by thickets of evergreen shrubs, dusty laurels and rhododendrons; a little pocket of Aldershot in the great flat sheet of the pampas.

But if her house was defiantly British, Ray herself was a more complex mutation than her husband. Her voice was clearly on the cusp of Spanish and English. Her vowels too had the strange Edwardian contortions of her husband's – 'keyemp, hyet' – but there was a softness, a lushness in her r's and l's which spoke of siestas and hot dark nights. I suspect that it was the same in Spanish, although I rarely heard her speak it. She was a linguistic half-caste; never quite belonging to either language, always the intimate stranger. I wonder which language her sadness felt most at home in, her compressed English or her slushy, Argentinian Spanish. She certainly spoke faster in Spanish, but whether the difference lay in the rhythm or the meaning it was impossible to tell.

At one point Ray's father had owned three million sheep in Patagonia. Not bad for an orphan from some rocky islands at the other end of the world. And to have a daughter who looked like a discount version of Jackie Kennedy with the same sweep of cheekbone and chin and the same watchful brown eyes was, I suppose, the seal of his success.

*   *   *

My prevailing memory of that visit was of a menacing stillness. The air was heavy, the ceilings were low. We spent the evenings listening to the World Service. The clock chimes were cues for enormous gin and tonics. As the drinks were downed the air got stiller yet. The gin bottle was half-empty when the radio announced that American troops had carried out an unsuccessful mission on the American embassy in Teheran. President Carter came on the air sounding stricken.

'The man's a fool,' said Robin. 'The Americans look ridiculous. Everyone will be storming their embassies now.'

The radio started playing Richard Strauss and we all had another drink. Dinner was always meat, but in deference to British inheritance of the house, it was served with overcooked vegetables. We stayed there for what seemed like weeks, getting fatter and sadder. Sometimes we'd go riding on reckless polo ponies whose ambition was to get you knocked off by a low branch. There are very few trees in the pampas, but these ponies would head for them with purpose. The New Forest chapter of the pony club had not prepared me for this. The ranch hands thought we were a huge joke. Not being able to ride was worse than being illiterate. They rode like centaurs, welding themselves to the animals. You almost never saw them walking. All their work – cattle herding, repairing fences, fixing salt licks – took place on horseback. The relationship between the gauchos and their horses was intimate and yet banal. To my cousin Robin, horses meant polo and escape. He pronounced the word 'polo' with uncharacteristic relish. Everything from the location of Los Olivos to his choice of wife followed the game. He even sited his estancia within hitting distance of the Media Luna polo club. It was the rubric of his life.

*　　*　　*

I came back to England in September, and started reading history at Trinity. Argentina shrunk once again from a state of mind to a place on the map. The sort of history I was doing, the politics of the eighteenth-century hustings, birth rates in seventeenth-century England, even the Indian mutiny, bore very little relation to the passions, the illogicality of Argentina. In the world according to the Cambridge Modern History Tripos, the southern hemisphere was negligible, a black hole of a place whose only act of significance was to drain the lifeblood out of Hapsburg Spain. But apart from opening the Pandora's box of inflation in seventeenth-century Europe, South America had no role.

My teachers at Cambridge were too busy looking east-wards. India was the hot subject, a focus for national nostalgia and guilt. Even within my own family, my paternal grandmother's memories of India were in direct contrast to the aridity of my grandmother Eileen's stories of the Argentine. My Indian grandmother used Hindi words all the time – ayah, chota peg, tiffin – while Eileen hardly ever used Spanish except to swear in. This was an attitude clearly shared by the Falkland Islanders, whose corrugated-iron and warm-beer existence felt very familiar to me when they entered the national consciousness during my second year at Cambridge.

I had heard the Malvinas mentioned by Robin while I was in Argentina, usually with derision. They seemed a very insignificant footnote to Britain's role in this part of the world, a much less tangible reminder of the British presence in Argentina than the Harrods on the Calle Mayor. I never felt during my trip that Britain was hated or resented. I remember being amazed at the first news of invasion of the island by the Argentines: it seemed to be the action of a country completely different from the one

I had visited. But I had been in the Argentine not Argentina. This dramatic world of juntas, gold-braided uniforms and Exocet missiles seemed miles away from the muffled gloom of Buenos Aires and the monotony of the pampas. In 1982 my sepia-tinted Argentina was replaced with the lurid full-colour version that appeared on the six o'clock news and the front pages of the tabloids. At the time I was sharing a flat with a girl whose father was a major-general in the Black Watch regiment and whose brother was serving in the Task Force. To her, the Argentinians were the enemy, as brutal as the Nazis if not quite so efficient. Even amongst Cambridge undergraduates, whom one might have expected to feel some qualms about this resurgence of imperialism, the Falklands Factor was potent. I remember going to a party in a house whose hosts had hired a television specially to watch the news. There was cheering as Brian Hanrahan counted the planes coming back in to the *Canberra*. I wish I could say that I felt ashamed of the jingoism that raged around me or that I was somehow more sensitive to the sufferings of the other side, that I bravely booed the sinking of the *Belgrano*; but I'm afraid I cheered just like everyone else.

Now that I'm writing about it I feel that my sympathies are with Argentina. I suppose I feel attracted to precisely the thing my family couldn't handle – the fragile, touchy ego of an arriviste state, a gawky Latin teenager spoiling for a fight, a country with something to prove. I feel attracted by their lack of indifference.

But the Falklands were a long way from Cambridge. I found it difficult to imagine that this hiccup in the South Atlantic would disturb very much, certainly not the chilly calm of Los Olivos. It was only much later, at a dinner party at Judy's house in the Cotswolds, where I was the youngest person present by at least twenty-five years, that I got a whiff of the real war. Judy was talking to the master of an Oxford college about Argentina. I was only half following the discussion, being distracted by the idle rehashing of thirty-year-old gossip, intelligible only to a keen student of Evelyn Waugh's diaries. Through a haze of Duffs and Buffys I heard Judy say, 'They surrounded the house and threw stones at the windows. People she had known for years. She came out of the house with a shotgun, can you imagine? She must be well into her eighties by now.'

I realized she could only be talking about Daphne, Eileen's sister. I could picture her standing on the porch of her corrugated-iron house, shotgun akimbo. It would have been immaterial to the jeering mob that Daphne had been born in Argentina, had lived there all her adult life. She was English to them and I'm sure also to herself. There were probably men in that crowd whose parents had been born in Galicia or Naples, whose families had spent less time in Argentina than the Traills. But they had become Argentinian in a way that my family never had. By some skewed logic those teenagers were right to identify Daphne as the enemy, not the solitary eighty-three-year-old woman, but the state of mind she represented. She was still a pioneer defending her territory against enemy depredations, nearly one hundred years after her grandfather had fought off Indian raids in the same territory.

Daphne was the only one of my grandmother's sisters to stay in the Argentine. My feeling, gleaned from scraps of conversation through the years, was that Daphne was the plain one of the family, the Masha of these particular three sisters. From the way in which my grandmother lost no opportunity to promote rivalries between her children and grandchildren I assume that her notion of family came from a childhood of intense sibling competition, of which she, as the most beautiful and the most intelligent, would have been the undoubted winner. Daphne must have sensed that she would do better on her own. When I met her in 1980 during my gap-year visit to Argentina, she struck me as cruder but kinder than my grandmother. Daphne did not have the same talent for damning with faint praise that distinguished Eileen. Unusually in my family, she appeared to have quite uncomplicated feelings towards her own children, although I sensed she was fiercely jealous of Robin's wife Ray. In those days she was living alone on the remnant of the once vast Traill estate. Her house, Las Limpias, was largely built out of corrugated iron. It felt rather like the Nissen huts I learnt geography in at school – a temporary measure that had ossified into unsat-isfactory permanence. My aunt still had the jerky gestures and clipped way of talking that belonged to the tomboy she must once have been. She had spent the long years of her widowhood breeding bulls, an occupation which seemed more than a little symbolic. Her husband Tom had enlisted in the British army despite having a wife and two children, to fight a war on the other side of the world. At this distance it seems like a heroic, almost Quixotic, act but it could also have been the ultimate escape. Strong women can be uncomfortable to live with. I remember my stepfather telling me that my mother had devoured him, and I can see now what he meant. By the time they split my mother had consumed all the things that had attracted her to Joe in the first place.

I remember riding around camp with Daphne in her old open Land Rover (a British vehicle of course). She would occasionally stop to talk to the workers in a

Spanish which sounded so English in its intonation that even I could understand every word. The roads were terrible, mostly mud and littered with enormous potholes. Daphne drove extremely fast, moving up through the gears like a racing driver. About twenty miles from home we crashed into the most enormous crater. The jeep just sank down and we could hear the hiss of the air escaping from the front wheel. Even now I can remember how scared I felt.

My great-aunt was pushing seventy. Kate and I were young and strongish but we knew absolutely nothing about changing tyres. I could not even drive. There was absolutely no one in sight apart from a few of Daphne's bulls. The sky was full of threatening black clouds. I felt utterly helpless. But Daphne jumped out of the jeep and with a lot of swearing started pulling tools out of the back. In seconds she had got the jack in and whipped off the bolts. She was clearly in some pain: I think she must have had arthritis in her hands. Kate and I stood about listlessly as Daphne worked away. As so often in adolescence I felt irrelevant to the adult business of getting on with things. We knew we should be helping but we did absolutely nothing. I feel quite hot with shame now to think how we just stood by. Clearly I was not displaying what is a predominant trait among the women in my family, being good in a crisis. The tyre was changed and we were back on the road, or rather track, in about fifteen minutes. Daphne's manner to us was a shade brisker now. Supremely self-reliant herself, she must have found these two spoilt eighteen-year-olds very hard to understand, let alone like. She, after all, had run a farm, brought up two sons and looked after her ageing mother for years with no help at all.

She had long ago mastered the art of losing. But in a lifetime of being alone, the night the mob came must have been the loneliest of all. Brandishing her shotgun at the crowd was her last independent act.

EIGHT

Daphne's sister, my grandmother Eileen, lived in a house that was, on the outside, typically East Anglian, white-washed with patterns etched into the plaster. It was neat and monochrome, standing trimly against the flat sky, a half-timbered silhouette which was repeated all over the county, a familiar unchanging punctuation to the landscape that, apart from the aluminium tints of the double glazing, had remained constant for hundreds of years. Once inside though, the precise Tudor geometry was overwhelmed by the remains of my grandmother's life in China.

The drawing room with its half-timbered ceiling was full of rosewood nesting tables and vases whose glaze was so intricately cracked that as a child I pictured my grandmother patiently gluing the fragments of broken pottery together. On one wall hung a portrait of my grandmother painted during her reign in Shanghai. I assume the painter was English: certainly my grandmother poses in the languid hand-in-lap manner of pre-war society portraits, but she is wearing some kind of high-collared red silk jacket which together with her black hair and jutting cheekbones makes

her look like some fierce Manchurian chieftain. I don't
know whether the painter was particularly good, but there
was something about my grandmother that had clearly
jolted her out of her usual wispy portraits of society ladies
to produce something urgent and imperious. She had
turned my grandmother's awkwardness and angularity into
strength. Her hazel eyes look out almost belligerently; her
hands rest in her lap like coiled springs; on one finger she
wears a huge ring made out of carved jade – a ring to
kiss, to genuflect before. It was a portrait that demanded
respect rather than love. As a child I felt similarly wary
of the portrait's original. My other grandmother was indul-
gent and adoring, Granny Eileen was a challenge. Unlike
most of the adults I encountered at the time of my parents'
divorce, she didn't make allowances. Life was tough and
my grandmother saw no reason to disguise this. She
assumed that, just as her life was full of the Women's
Institute, Meals On Wheels and bridge evenings, all my
brother and I needed was sufficient activities. Staying at
her house was an incessant round of painting and model-
ling and very competitive card games.

Sometimes on rainy afternoons, my grandmother would
set us to polishing the silver: an eclectic assortment of odd
candlesticks and numerous cups and trophies, the remnants
of a fiercely competitive life. There were cups for diving,
for lacrosse, for the Nanking club mixed doubles, for the
Saffron Walden mixed fours. My grandmother could have
stepped straight from the pages of the Angela Brazil stories
which were my favourite reading at the time. It was an
impressive tally and one that I, being short-sighted and
lamentably uncoordinated, had no hope of emulating. So
it was with a kind of vicarious pride that I pushed my
thumbnail in to dislodge the dirt from the grooves of my

grandmother's names. First Alice Eileen Traill, and later Alice Eileen Innes. I can only imagine that she wanted to impress us with her achievements as nothing else in her house was ever cleaned with such thoroughness. I never liked to walk in the kitchen without shoes in case my bare feet encountered something sticky on the yellow-and-black vinyl tiles. But her silver was quite worn by furious polishing.

The last thing she would give us to work on was her set of Apostle spoons which lived in a blue velvet case. On the end of each spoon was the faint impression of a lighthouse. This, my grandmother told us with gloomy relish, was the Traill family crest, a memento of the days when her family had been wreckers and had lured ships to their ruin on the rocky Irish coast. Then one of the Traills had repented of his wicked ways and had become a priest, but had kept the crest as a reminder of their infamous past. 'They used to hold up lanterns to make the ship's captain think they were coming in to harbour. The ships would run aground on the rocks and the wreckers would wait until the last cry of the drowning sailors had faded away before going down to the shore.' My grandmother particularly enjoyed the part about the anguished cries of the mariners. My brother and I accepted this story as yet another one of my grandmother's collection of unhappy endings. We had no difficulty in connecting her with the wicked wreckers of the past.

The old country was echoed in her name, Eileen, which she preferred to her original Christian name of Alice. I don't know whether the name she chose had any significance but polishing the Apostle spoons was the only time that my grandmother ever referred to her family's Irish past. It was much later, after my grandmother's death, that one of my aunts told me the story of the Rector of Skull. The tale she told me seemed so neatly turned that I felt that it had been much polished like the Apostle spoons. This Traill was the Rector of Skull, a small town in the west of Ireland, during the Great Potato Famine. According to the story he had been so shocked by the suffering of the people that he had set up a soup kitchen. But the soup itself was as rotten as the potatoes and it killed the starving even as it fed them. The Rector of Skull (what a name) with his misguided philanthropy had finished off what the famine had begun. My grandmother never told me this story and yet it had all her hallmarks – the optimistic beginning, the grotesque pun in the name Skull and the compulsory unhappy ending. I liked the story a lot – it was the perfect starting point for the story I wanted to tell about a family whose misfortunes ricocheted from one generation to another. What did it matter if it was not strictly true?

It was with some surprise then that I discovered the actual town tucked away on the south-west coast of Ireland. The town's name was spelt differently from the way I had put it together in my head, a soft 'ch' replacing the death's head 'k' – which it turns out, however, was the old way of spelling the name, and the way it would have appeared in the Rector's day. It was enough to send me there in search of him. I had little hope of finding anything, putting the felicities of the story down to the fine embroidery of my family's storytelling, but I wanted to see the place where the Traills had made their first jump into the unknown. I entered 'Schull' into my Internet browser, and it came up with a page of hotels and holiday cottages and a picture whose pixels blurrily composed themselves into the outline of a lighthouse. I am by inclination resistant to the power of coincidence but it would have been churlish to ignore this. I booked my ticket content to stand on the cliffs and look out over the sea to Argentina, since nothing got in the way of the pencil line I drew in my atlas between the south-west coast of Ireland and the sea-horse shape of South America. I hardly expected to find an impression of the Traills themselves; any dent they may have made would have been worn away like the lighthouse on the Apostle spoons.

Schull itself is the kind of place that was 'discovered' in the seventies: people drifted here looking for a new life. As a result the High Street's ten pubs are interspersed with aromatherapists, galleries specializing in modern ceramics, a holistic healing centre and delicatessens that sell sourdough ciabatta made from organically grown Irish wheat. The estate agent's window was full of pictures of ruined cabins for sale at inflated prices. '*For those with more money than sense,*' read one hand-written caption underneath a blurry photograph of a derelict tower, '*only accessible by helicopter, but it has magnificent sea views and there isn't another soul for miles.*' Another read simply, '*We've been offered 80,000 for this,*' (a charmless bungalow), '*but we'd like more.*' All the properties for sale were either the sorry remains of peasant huts or spanking new bungalows designed from an American memory complete with aluminium siding and baseball hoops above the garage doors. There was nothing in between, none of the substantial farmhouses or charming vicarages that would have dominated the window of an equivalent estate agent in, say, the Cotswolds. This omission puzzled me as my picture of the Irish countryside was conjured up from the novels of Somerville and Ross and Molly Keane, in which there were no shortage of big houses. The only imposing buildings I had seen on the drive down from Cork were the Victorian edifices of the Church of Ireland, some spruce, some derelict, that seemed to occupy the pole position in every town or village I passed through. Where, I wondered idly, were all the Catholic churches? Eventually I discovered them in back streets well away from the main drag, but by that stage I had come to understand why they were so unobtrusively sited. It was a coded landscape, contoured with grievances, the naming of a street, the placement of a church.

I drove to Schull on the day that Ireland voted on the Good Friday Agreement, furious Unionists and Nationalists on the radio invoking the past as casually as the present: nothing was forgiven or forgotten.

The Crocus bookshop, prop. Deirdre O'Driscoll, had a display of books on local history in its tiny window.

'Do you have any books about the Famine?' I asked.

'We've got the odd one or two.' Without looking round, the bookshop owner gestured to the shelf behind me, four solid shelves of books about the Famine, followed by another four on how to trace your Irish ancestors. I picked up one of these latter books and flipped through the pages of Kennedys and Murphys and O'Learys to the T section, but there was no entry under Traill. In my ignorance I didn't realize that looking for a Traill in a book of this kind was the equivalent of a well-off white from South Carolina looking for their name in a book designed for blacks to trace their African roots. At the time I attributed the absence of Traills to their insignificance – they were simply too obscure to be traced.

I looked through the shelves of books on the Famine. I picked up a thick one and looked up Traill in the index: again nothing.

'Would you have anything dealing specifically with Protestant clergymen?'

The bookshop owner finally looked up. 'What is it exactly that you're after?'

'I'm trying to trace someone who lived here.' The bookshop owner went back to her accounts.

'I think he was the Rector here during the Famine.' That made her look up.

'Oh, you mean Traill?' She spoke of him as one might of an acquaintance living in the next street, an acquaintance for whom one had mixed feelings. 'And why would you be interested in him?'

'Well, I think he's my great-great-great-grandfather.' I felt foolish saying this; it seemed like such a presumption. Traill belonged here in Schull, not to me. But the bookshop lady seemed to find nothing odd about my claim.

'Well, I've always said that he was a good man really, he did the best he could. Even if he did keep a horse right the way through the Famine.'

The 1840s were closer than I thought. I had found the Rector all right, not just a worn-down name on a tombstone but a person capable of arousing strong feelings. From the way the bookshop owner was picking her words I guessed that she was not one of Traill's supporters. I asked her if she had any information on him.

'Oh no, you'll have to go to Cork for that,' but then she appeared to relent a little. 'Well, there was a most interesting article in the *Mizen Head Historical Society Journal* by Father Padraig. You'd most likely want to read that. I'm the secretary, you see, and we brought out a special edition for the Famine anniversary.'

Could I buy one of these special editions?

'Well, I'm afraid that's totally impossible. They were

that popular I very much doubt if there are any spare
copies lying around.'

What kind of secretary, I wondered, failed to keep back
copies? What about the priest who wrote the article? Might
not he have a copy?

'Oh, I very much doubt it.' We appeared to have reached
an impasse.

Just then an elderly man walked in.

'Donal, you'll never guess who this is. Robert Traill's
great-great-great-granddaughter.'

'Is that right?'

'Yes, she's here to find out about him.'

'Well, good luck to you. Traill wasn't a bad soul, not
compared to some of them.'

He gave me a commiserating look, as if to say that it
wasn't my fault. I didn't need to ask if the Rector had
really poisoned the whole village. Whatever he had done
was bad enough.

The bookshop lady rummaged through a pile of papers by
the till. 'I've got a picture of Traill here somewhere. Oh,
yes, here it is.' She pulled out a yellowing page torn from
the *Illustrated London News*. 'That's himself there.' She
pointed to a sketch of a gentleman in full Victorian regalia,
stovepipe hat, frock coat and cane, sitting on a chair in
some kind of hovel with a huge hole in the roof. Behind
him was a bundle of rags, which on closer examination
proved to be a woman huddling over two small children.

I don't know if it was just a quirk of the engraving but
my great-great-great-grandfather appeared to be gazing
out into the middle distance, completely unaware of the
human misery behind him. The caption underneath read,
Mullin's Hut at Skull.

'Of course in this picture he is visiting the poor, but he told that "do-gooder" Trench when they came to set up a soup kitchen that he, Traill, had never set foot in a Catholic home before, and that was when the Famine had been going for a full two years and this a parish of 18,000 souls. Can you imagine that? He'd never set foot in a Catholic home, when they were dying all around him.' Deirdre O'Driscoll looked at me balefully.

'And how many Protestants were there in the town then?'

'Not as many as there were after the soup kitchen opened. Traill wasn't as bad as that souper parson down in Goleen, but none of them could resist it. Of course some poor devils were always going to convert. It was that or starve to death. Some people still won't have anything to do with the souper families, but I'm from Co. Wexford myself, so I'm no part of that.'

I wasn't sure what she meant by 'souper', but I didn't want to betray yet more of my ignorance.

She pointed at another engraving of the main street, deserted save for two small figures carrying baskets. 'And that's Traill's daughters carrying food to the starving villagers. Small, aren't they?'

'The daughters?'

'No, the baskets.'

I was in dangerous territory. It was just becoming clear to me why it had been so controversial for the Rector to have kept a horse in 1847. Hoping to divert her a little I asked her where the Rectory was.

'And what a splendid house that was, overlooking the harbour with a great lawn stretching down to the sea. Sir John Moore camped there you know, before the battle of Corunna. Of course it's all gone now, they pulled it down to build some holiday cottages.'

'What a shame. Don't they have any planning restrictions here then?'

Deirdre O'Driscoll gave me an old-fashioned look. 'I don't think there were many people here with any particular affection for that building.'

It was time to leave. I paid for the engravings of Traill and his daughters. Mollified, perhaps, by the money Deirdre relented. 'I expect you'll be wanting to see his grave. Take the Goleen road past the holiday cottages and you'll come to the old church. He's buried there. You'll know that he died of famine fever, a couple of months after that picture was drawn.' Her tone implied that nothing had acquitted Traill so well in life as his leaving of it.

I took the Goleen road out of Schull, past the orderly ranks of Celtic Holiday Cottages which stood on the site of the Rector's house, past the Michael Collins Community College, till I came to the old church, ruined now, but, like all the Church of Ireland buildings, magnificently situated on a hill overlooking Schull Harbour. All that remained of the Rector's church was the outer walls and the arched window at the end of the nave which framed the view of the sea. The church must have been in ruins for some time because the original Protestant graveyard was now completely lost under a carpet of shiny granite tablets commemorating dead Maloneys and MacCarthys, Twiskes and O'Driscolls. There were Catholic graves everywhere, even in the nave of what had been the church. They were immaculately kept, these usurpers, the granite gleaming, the inscriptions crisp. Some of the graves were adorned with goldfish bowls sporting aquatic crucifixes and Madonnas.

It took me an hour to find the Rector's grave, which was completely hidden by the funeral-wreath flora of this spot – outsize chrysanthemums, enormous marguerites. The tomb itself was an altar-like slab with a lengthy inscription carved into the stone.

Sacred to the memory of Rev. Robert Traill who for a period of 17 years that he presided over the parish of Skull as Rector with his Blessed Master 'went about doing good'. Till at length he died in full sacrifice to his superhuman efforts in relieving the prevailing distress in the Famine years of 1846 and 1847.

Behind me a pair of old ladies were tending to a grave, plucking out the infant weeds that were poking through the green glass chips, caressing the granite tombstone with a yellow duster, adorning it with a bunch of stiff yellow chrysanthemums still in their shiny cellophane wrapping. Rather self-consciously I began to pull at some of the burgeoning plants that embraced my great-great-great-grandfather's grave, but they had put down deep roots and no amount of tugging would dislodge them. I sat on the tomb tracing the inscription with my fingers. It was a plain text but for the '*superhuman efforts*'. I wondered who had chosen those words. His wife? Finding Traill's tomb had made me think of him as a person, someone who had actually lived and died here on this green Irish hill. He was more now than just a name on the family tree or a grotesque family story.

The light was going. The old ladies had gone home. I lay back on the slab, which smelt of salt. Traill's tomb was untended and unloved, but it still had the prime position in the churchyard, below the ruined altar, a peak of mouldering limestone jutting out from the neat shiny graves that ran down to the sea.

I had to wait until the next day to visit the Schull Public Library, which opened on alternate afternoons. I asked the librarian who was busily putting Wilbur Smith paperbacks into plastic jackets whether she had any copies of the *Mizen Head Historical Society Journal*.

'I hope it's not Volume Three you're after.'

I suspected that it was.

'You and everybody else. And that would be the one volume that we're missing. I'm not saying anyone took it deliberately but we certainly did have a full set. Have you tried Deirdre in the bookshop?'

I explained the situation. The librarian sighed.

'I don't know why this Volume Three is such an issue. I went to the meeting of the historical society where they were all up in arms about it. I'd only gone because I fancied one of the men on the committee, so I wasn't really following what was being said, but they were making such a commotion that I stood up and said that I got quite enough of this sort of behaviour at home with my three children and I walked out.'

She showed me into a kind of office at the back filled with books on local history.

'If you like I can ring Jenny on the committee. She's sure to have a copy of Volume Three and I'm sure she'd be only too happy to help a descendant of Robert Traill.'

I picked up a history of the parish. Flicking through it I came across a crudely drawn picture of a coffin with *Robert Traill RIP* written on the lid, and *'Go Home You Bloody Orangeman'* underneath. As I had spent the morning listening to Gerry Adams and Ian Paisley denouncing each other on the radio, it was a jolt to find the same hatred coming from the page of a parish history of the 1830s. I wasn't quite sure which side I was meant to be on.

The librarian gestured for me to come to the telephone. A brisk English voice asked what I wanted with Volume Three. I told her about my connection with Traill and my encounter with the lady in the bookshop.

'And Deirdre wouldn't give it to you. Well, she can be a bit funny about these things. Not to worry, I'll photocopy it for you myself. To my mind if Robert Traill were alive today and working for the starving in Africa, people would be falling over themselves to call him a saint. I suppose you know about the diary . . . I don't have it myself but I think Patsy Shepherd knows where it is. You can't miss her house, it's the one past the cemetery with the green balls in the garden.' I could hardly believe what I was hearing, it was as if the Rector had only recently departed from Schull, leaving his belongings behind him, among them his diary.

The balls that Jenny on the committee had mentioned, turned out to be defused landmines arranged in a kind of ballistic rockery outside a bungalow with plate-glass windows looking over the ruined church. Patsy Shepherd answered the door in her pinny, being of the generation that wears a pinny when cooking her tea. I gave her some preamble about being Robert Traill's great-great-great-granddaughter, which she accepted calmly.

'I expect you'll be wanting his diary then.'

I followed her into an immaculate parlour. There was no crucifix in the room, and I spotted a photograph of Patsy and what must have been her husband flanking a man in a dog collar. It seemed likely that this was a Church of Ireland household.

'I've lent this diary to three other people, but never to a descendant before. It's a shame they pulled down the Rectory before you could see it – such a beautiful building it was too.'

Patsy had been given the diary by her father, the Rector of Bandon. She must have decided that my genetic credentials were good enough security and I walked out past the bombs with the diary in my pocket.

I had come to Schull expecting little more than atmosphere. A footnote or two to a tall tale of my grandmother's. But the past seemed much closer here than it did at home. At every turn I had encountered people for whom Robert Traill was part of their everyday landscape, someone they had an opinion about, a position on. I had expected history, records, concrete things, not the shifting nuances of opinion and hearsay. I had thought to find Robert Traill safely buried, not living on as a symbol both of callousness and heroism. A man who fed his horse oats which could have kept a starving family alive, or a martyr who died as the result of his superhuman efforts to fight the Famine, depending on your point of view. I had expected the case of Robert Traill to be closed, all passion spent, only to find the jury divided and no verdict in sight.

NINE

Robert Traill and I were both thirty-five when we arrived in Skull (or Schull) but there the parallels end. I found it charming, he found it 'primitive and half-pagan'. I went there out of curiosity, he went there out of a sense of duty. He inherited the living from his father, who had never lived in Skull; he stayed in Lisburn living off the income it brought him and employing a curate to fulfil his pastoral duties. But his son was part of the evangelical movement which campaigned against absentee clergymen. Robert Traill felt he had a moral duty to take up residence in his new parish, even though his recently acquired wife Anne preferred to stay with her family in Dublin. As the sister of a well-to-do baronet she probably had mixed feelings about Schull. It was hardly fashionable and it must have felt like a daunting place to bring up small children – they already had one child, a daughter, and Anne was expecting another.

Perhaps in order to placate his wife, Robert immediately started fixing up the Rectory. In his diary he writes that *'my improvements have made it a very comfortable residence, but the expense has been great . . . about 1500 pounds. The world talks grandly about good livings, but it will be long, even if my days are spared, until mine repays the expenses it has entailed.*' Money was a constant worry which grew worse as anti-tithe riots spread through the south of Ireland. It was an awkward situation: Traill was dependent for his livelihood on rates paid by the Catholics.

The new Rector had finally persuaded his wife to join him in Skull when he was attacked by anti-tithe protesters. After the rock-throwing incident Traill sent his family back to Dublin. 'My wife says, she never could sleep there another night in peace.' The difficulties of living in Skull must have put a considerable strain on their marriage. Anne Traill spent as little time as possible in the Rectory. On 12 January Traill writes that '*I shall have been thirteen weeks separated from my dear partner and the children whom the Lord has given us. Looking over a late letter of Mrs Traill's I observe a pretty little anecdote. On the morning of Christmas Day, she asked our second little girl now approaching three what this day meant. She thought for a while, and then replied, "It was the day Papa used to come home."*'

I read the Rector's diary with a mixture of fascination and irritation. The historical background is intriguing but I found it really hard to sympathize with a man whose diary is one long moan. Every page is a catalogue of one misery or another. Traill complains constantly in his diary of the horrors of travelling back and forth to Dublin, '*for it very rarely happens that I have not to contend with ungodliness on the way*'. In one Pooteresque incident Traill tells off a fellow passenger, a Roman Catholic, for swearing. The man threatens to '*throw him off the bl—dy coach*' and has to be forcibly restrained by the other passengers. Traill certainly seemed to have a knack for causing trouble wherever he went.

The only sympathetic part of the diaries is when he writes about his family. He talks constantly about how much he loves his wife and children and how much he misses them when he is alone in Skull. It is heartening to discover that though Traill's religious and political views are difficult to understand – virtually incomprehensible except perhaps to a member of the DUP – he is capable of human feeling. Despite their long periods apart, Robert and Anne managed to produce eight children who survived infancy. Five daughters and three sons. In 1835, when Anne gave birth to a son who died three days later, Traill writes, '*Our dear little baby has breathed its last . . . It came up like a flower, and has been cast down when its bud had scarcely been formed and almost ere our eyes could behold it. For it we cannot mourn. It had just entered on a world, which all, who have passed through it have found strewn with thorns.*' But while Traill attempts to comfort himself with the idea that his baby has gone directly to heaven, his wife is unconsolable: '*My Poor Anne feels the stroke acutely, for a mother's tenderness will not sleep. Time, however, that softens affliction, and the assurance that our God doeth all things will I am confident allay her sorrows.*' I can't believe that Robert can have been much comfort to his grieving wife.

I suppose it is churlish of me to complain of the moroseness of Traill's diary as the eight years from 1835 to 1843 were full of deaths – his father, his infant son, his curate's wife, his sister-in-law, his mother. Of all the deaths he describes in his diary, his mother's is the one that he writes about most bitterly: '*Oh how deeply shall I feel, and how bitterly I shall mourn your loss. Seldom did I see thee, removed to the other extremity of the island, but it was sweet to me to think that I still had a parent in the land of living.*' He describes sitting at his mother's deathbed whispering the 23rd psalm in her ear as she breathed her last. After his mother's death he writes that for the first time in his forty-five years he feels utterly alone. It is the last entry in the diary.

I wonder why Traill kept his diary so assiduously. (I'm assuming that there were other later diaries that have been lost.) It is not considered enough to be intended for posterity. His writing has an urgency about it which suggests it was written in an emotional swirl. On every page Traill is angry or sorrowful or afraid. In eight years there is not a single day which he records as being happy. Admittedly, in the years that Traill kept his diary an awful lot did go wrong. He took on a job that was not only difficult but dangerous. His life was under constant threat not only from the anti-tithe rioters but also from diseases like cholera which regularly decimated that part of Ireland. He is constantly worried about money as he has two house-holds to maintain. Worst of all he has to spend long periods of time away from his family, without knowing whether he will ever see them again. In one entry he writes, '*nine weeks tomorrow morning have past since I parted from Anne and the children. When I bade her Adieu, the thought flashed across me, that we might never meet again on this side of the grave.*' It is a perfectly legitimate sentiment given the situation and yet I can't help feeling that Traill's outlook is almost comically bleak.

The tone of the diary reminds me of the journals I kept as a teenager: a minutely detailed catalogue of the wrongs that had been done to me, the staggering unfairness with which I was treated. Like Traill's my cup was always half-empty. I constantly expected the worst. Later, when I had left home and found a future that went up instead of down, I stopped keeping a diary. But Traill's life seems to have had no such respite.

It is possible that Traill enjoyed being miserable. In 1840 he was offered a comfortable living in England which he refused. He justified his decision to stay to himself, and presumably to his disappointed wife, by consulting the Bible. Traill used the Bible rather like the I Ching, letting the book fall open randomly and then interpreting the text as it pertained to his current predicament. On this occasion he found a passage that met his needs: '*Go ye into all the world and preach the gospel to every creature, intimating, as it seemed to me, another sphere of labour in the vine yard. Whether I have formed an accurate estimate of the subject, time will decide in the development of the divine purpose.*'

Anne Traill must have been horrified by her husband's decision not to take the job in England. Living in a fortified rectory miles away from the sort of company she was used to, surrounded by a local population who bitterly resented everything she stood for, cannot have been an enticing prospect. It would be fascinating to read Anne's letters to her husband. The only hints at her state of mind come from the occasional comment in her husband's diaries: '*My poor partner is very low from worrying about her mother/ Anne is full of grief after the death of our poor baby/ Anne refuses to spend another night in this house.*' There is one telling entry in which Traill is making up his mind whether he should go back to Dublin with Anne for her confinement: he agonizes about where his duty lies, with his wife or with his parish which is raging with cholera. After a great deal of deliberation he decides to go to Dublin and records that, '*Anne's mind is much at ease since we finally determined on going to Dublin. My acquiescence, she states, was a most marked answer to prayer.*' Anne clearly had her own channel to the Almighty.

At the front of the diary there is a rather poor engraving of the Rector, looking surprised and stiff in his white clergyman's stock. He looks more delicate than I had imagined – all cheekbones and angles. He has the beginnings of a receding hairline, a sharp nose and a slightly startled look, the face of a man with ideas who lacks the physical strength to carry them out. There is something febrile in his portrait and in the tone of his diaries – emotions sweep through him like fevers. His temperature is always raised, his dander is always up. But despite the seriousness of his situation there is an element of bathos to the diary. Sadly it finishes in 1843, three years before Traill finds a subject worthy of his anger.

Nowhere in Ireland was more severely affected by the successive potato failures of the 1840s than the south-west. Subdivision of land and the lack of any local industries had resulted in almost total dependence on the potato, which until the 1840s had been a blessed crop, easy to grow even in the most unprepossessing conditions and nourishing enough to support large families. The average Irish labourer ate between ten and twelve pounds of potatoes a day. West Cork had very few of the cottage industries such as weaving, which in other parts of Ireland added a layer of cash to an otherwise subsistence economy.

As a result, when the blight was discovered in the potato

harvest in 1846, it meant that famine followed almost immediately in Skull. There were no reserves of food to fall back on, no other crops to replace the potato apart from seaweed. Still more unfortunately, given the British government's avowed intention of forcing Irish landlords to take responsibility for their tenants, there were no powerful magnates in the area, only the poor Protestant planters whose resources were hardly greater than those of the Catholic peasants.

There was simply no food to be had. But the British government was reluctant to intervene. There was a Malthusian train of thought that held that to help the Irish would be to encourage them in their fecklessness. In May 1846 an article in *The Times,* clearly influenced by Whig spin doctors, described the Irish as '*a people born and bred from time immemorial, in inveterate indolence, improvidence, disorder and consequent destitution.*' At the end of 1846 the situation in Skull and the town of Skibbereen further down the coast had become so dire that Routh the Relief Commissioner wrote to London requesting permission to open up the government food depots. Trevelyan the Chief Secretary of the Treasury refused, explaining that, '*You must draw out the resources of the country before we make our own issues. In the execution of this duty you must be prepared to act with great firmness and to incur much obloquy.*'

Although I studied the Victorian period at university, I had never realized the level of what we can only call racism that existed towards the Irish in Victorian England. Reading contemporary sources it is clear that for men like Trevelyan, the Famine was a punishment rather than a natural disaster. This callousness has not gone unnoticed in Ireland, of course, hence my reception in the Crocus bookshop. I can understand now why the grievances are kept burnished and bright.

Trevelyan's sentiments were ones which the Robert Traill who became Rector of Skull in 1830 would probably have shared, but in the sixteen odd years between his incumbency and the onset of Famine the rebarbative evangelical had mellowed into a man whose compassion exceeded the bounds of his beliefs.

When the first signs of blight were discovered in the potato crop of 1845, there were many different theories as to how to treat it. Traill thought that the blight could be kept at bay if only the potatoes were stored in clean well-ventilated pits. Clean living and fresh air would surely drive away this disease born, he assumed, of negligence and slovenliness. Unfortunately for Traill the virus refused to be anthropomorphized. No matter how carefully the pits were dug, how meticulously they were lined with ash, the potatoes when they were dug up emerged black and putrid. As the scale of the disaster began to emerge in the winter of 1845–6 Traill put aside his ailments and became chairman of the Skull Relief Committee, which consisted of landowners and other men and women of influence in the area including the Roman Catholic priest. This was the first time that Traill had sat in the same room as a Catholic priest, let alone have a conversation with one.

Traill's decision to cooperate with the Catholics shows how profoundly the threat of famine had shaken him. This was not a situation in which God would help those who helped themselves. He realized that intervention was unavoidable. But the act of intervention was particularly hard for an evangelical Protestant like Traill. How could he be sure that he was acting with God's approval, for if the Famine was the rod of a wrathful God then any attempt to mitigate its effects would be flouting the divine will. The Traill of the diaries who derided the Catholics for their deluded half-pagan ways might not have intervened, but the Traill who had seen the deaths of his baby and his mother could not bear simply to be a spectator. He needed to act.

Traill's response to the British government's indifference was a modern one. He invoked the media. In a series of letters to the Cork Constitution, which were later reprinted in *The Times*, he tries to alert the public to '*the situation of one of the most miserable spots in this afflicted, famine-stricken land*'. He describes the conditions he was living under at the time:

> *How or where to begin the tale of horror, I scarcely know. My house is more like a house besieged than anything else – literally a beleaguered fortress. Ere the day has dawned the crowds are already gathering: nor do they retire until long after the shades of night have fallen. My family one and all are perfect slaves worn out with attending them; for I would not wish, were it possible, that one starving creature should leave my door without something to allay the cravings of hunger or the means of purchasing some means of sustenance.*

To reassure his Protestant readers that this charity was not being squandered on the feckless Roman Catholics, Traill is at pains to point out that his situation is '*marked by a character of peculiar difficulty . . . because I have the charge of a Protestant population – one of the largest rural ones in the kingdom and one of the most miserable and impoverished that can be conceived – a flock that has been an increasing and heavy tax upon me from the moment of my coming among them'.*

Traill must have felt that his message would be more effective if he could show that the Famine was ecumenical in its effects. This was not a Roman Catholic problem but an Irish one. A situation so extreme that *'I cannot refrain from stating that, on one occasion, without a cessation for a moment, Mrs Traill weighed out, and distributed with her own hand, 200 weight of rice alone; and I do not think she has been well since. But as she remarked to me the situation is hopeless.'*

Traill's prose style is more than equal to the horrors he is describing: he had after all spent years becoming fluent in the language of disaster. Here he is describing the changes that famine has brought to Skull:

> *Formerly the eye was cheerful, the cheek bright and the step buoyant, but now all is changed. The haggard eye, the pale sunken cheek, the emaciated frame, and these meet you in every passer by. One poor creature came up to me this forenoon as I was returning from my weary rounds, and literally staggered like a drunk man. I charged him with intoxication – but alas – it was starvation and I cannot describe the regret that I felt that my purse had been emptied before I met him, and thus I was prevented from ministering to his wants on the moment . . . Not one, not one is there that has the look of bygone days. A deep settled dejection – a gloom unbroken reigns around. It seems as if a mighty wave has rolled over our people and swept the former race away.*

'*Our people*' is significant. Despite his references to the size of his Protestant flock, the use of '*our*' shows that the Rector of Skull recognized that starvation did not observe religious distinctions.

In his letters to *The Times* Traill speaks in the voice of an Irishman who seeks to pierce English indifference to his country's plight: '*Let England therefore learn a truth which those who live, as I long did, amidst the comforts and amenities of that favoured land cannot form a conception. There, all is enchantment compared with the rocks and wretchedness amidst which I dwell.*' Traill's moral centre of gravity has shifted due west from the man who railed against the poor deluded Roman Catholics and complained of living in this '*barbarous country*'. In the eight or so years since he stopped keeping the diary he has left behind his twitchy exile to become the champion of '*our people*'. His letters could be delivered straight from the pulpit with their resonant, alliterative crescendo: '*Famine is advancing with strides so fearful that I verily believe, that if some superhuman efforts are not made to relieve us, half of our population will ere long be blotted from the book of being.*'

As the Famine continued, starvation was replaced by disease as the main cause of death. Two years of malnutrition affected the young and old principally but the famine-associated diseases of typhus and typhoid – '*famine fever*' – affected everyone. Ironically, the very poor had over the years built up a resistance to typhus, but the better-off, who had been protected from it in the past, were now coming into daily contact with these deadly illnesses. Traill writes on 5 February 1847, '*This very day I did visit no fewer than twenty three persons in twenty different houses labouring under fever and dysentery . . . more than double the number I ever had on my sick list at any one previous period. Hitherto, I am thankful to say no Protestant has*

86

died; the deaths among poor Roman Catholics average twenty five daily, an average which is hourly increasing.'

This last sentence was underlined in the article about Traill in the *Mizen Head Historical Society Journal*, not I think by its author who is generally sympathetic to Traill, but probably by a more resentful hand. Though Traill's distinction between a Protestant and a Catholic reads uncomfortably today, his physical efforts to relieve the suffering around him were impartial. A government inspector, Major Parker, wrote that Traill was *'exerting himself to the utmost. He employs about fifty men on his own premises in every way he can; has soup kitchens constantly at work, sells meal at reduced prices in his own house but all will not do. Individual charity will not go far; his doors and windows are beset by miserable wretches, and Mrs Traill and family are exhausted by their incessant exertions. The people now drop off very fast and deaths increase daily.'*

The setting up of a soup kitchen recalls the family story about the hapless Rector of Skull. Where did the notion that he had poisoned his flock come from? Or was that a malevolent flourish of my grandmother's, conjured from the stark rise in the mortality rates? In fact, there might be some strand of truth in it.

Soup kitchens were considered by the government to be the best way of relieving the starving, better and cheaper than giving them money (not to mention how politically unpopular it would be). The famous chef Alexis Soyer came over to Dublin to demonstrate how a delicious and wholesome soup sufficient for the sustenance of body and soul could be made with a few readily available ingredients.

Unfortunately, the pioneers of the soup-kitchen movement tended to be not chefs but evangelical clergymen who were more interested in saving souls than in filling stomachs.

For soup was hard for the people to stomach. Literally. For bodies wasted, as the inhabitants of Skull were, by years of famine, 'stirabout' – a mixture of imperfectly ground Indian maize, oats and water – was a nutritional disaster. To a population used to eating only potatoes, this lumpy mess of half-cooked grains (Alexis Soyer having returned by now to his usual station at the Ritz) meant dysentery and diarrhoea. Moreover, as neither corn nor rice, unlike the potato, were complete foods providing all the nutrients necessary for health, an unrelieved diet of soup led to scurvy and pellagra. The Irish, who previous to the Famine had been one of the tallest peoples in Europe, literally shrank as the diseases of vitamin deficiency like rickets kicked in. Soup wasn't much of an alternative to starvation.

Certainly the mortality rates in Skull were increasing daily, soup or no soup. On 5 February 1847 Traill writes, '*Our medical friend, Dr Sweetnam, informed me that if he stated mortality in my parish to be thirty-five daily, he would be within the truth. The children, in particular, he remarked were disappearing with awful rapidity and to this may be added the aged who together with the young – neglected perhaps amidst the widespread destitution – are almost without exception swollen and ripening for the grave.*'

Soup could be hard to stomach in other ways. Next to Skull in the neighbouring parish of Altar, the Church of Ireland minister had set up a soup kitchen to bring spiritual as well as actual nourishment to the poor Catholics in his parish, offering them sustenance if they would convert. This kind of religious blackmail, proselytization through starvation, became known as 'souperism'. This was what Deirdre O'Driscoll had been referring to darkly in the Crocus bookshop. In Altar, there are to this day families worshipping in the Church of Ireland with Catholic surnames, still distinguished by people with long memories like my friend in the bookshop as 'soupers'. The way in which Deirdre employed the term suggests that death by starvation would have been preferable to accepting this particular mess of pottage.

Souperism does not figure largely in the official histories of the Famine; the evidence for it seems to be supported by a century and a half of local grievance rather than by documentary evidence. It is enough though to make the Church of Ireland perpetually suspect, dividing small-town historical societies one hundred and fifty years later.

I was relieved to find that there is no evidence to suggest that Traill was guilty of souperism. Indeed, the article from the *Mizen Head Historical Society Journal* written by a Catholic priest, Father Hickey, states categorically that Traill never was and never could be accused of it. But for the sort of people who can and do spot souperist surnames Traill is guilty by association. A man who kept a horse during the Famine, giving it food that could have gone to poor Catholics, a man who had been Rector of Skull for seventeen years without once setting foot in a Catholic home, a man who is '*thankful*' that so far there have been no Protestant deaths, could not be blameless.

Even a favourable epitaph from a Catholic priest cannot clear the Rector of Skull's name. There are wrongs that no amount of rational historical analysis can ever right. The scars of the Famine are still raw in the town even after all this time. Before the Famine the parish had a population of around eighteen thousand; ten years later it was only eight thousand. Some of that missing ten thousand had emigrated to America, but a horrifying number died of disease and starvation. Catholic deaths far exceeded Protestant ones even in proportion to their relative sizes. Whatever spin revisionist historians now put on the severity of the Famine, I can now understand the heat of resentment in that bookshop when I announced that I was the Rector's great-great-great-granddaughter.

In March 1847 a typhus epidemic was in full swing, the spread of the disease made much easier by the crowds waiting for food. A brush in passing was enough to transfer the fever-transmitting louse or its dustlike excrement to a new victim, and one fever-stricken person could pass the disease to a hundred others in the course of a day. The captain of the ship that brought the corn into the village saw a mass of bodies buried without coffins, *'simply a few inches below the soil; when warm weather comes and they decompose there must be a pestilence'*. Bodies half-eaten by rats were an ordinary sight; *'two dogs were shot while tearing a body to pieces.'*

'Never in my life,' wrote the captain, *'have I seen such wholesale misery.'*

At the end of March, Traill came down with famine fever, a typhus variation from which the sufferer could seemingly survive a terrible attack of high fever and vomiting, only to relapse again and again. Traill had become such a key figure by this point that when the news of his illness reached London, Trevelyan, the Secretary to the Treasury, wrote to him enquiring after his health. The Rector wrote his last letter in reply:

> *My health having suffered from anxiety and fatigue, I feel myself almost unequal to the exertion of writing.*

Unless a gracious God sustain me and a generous public continue their aid, I must sink, and those around me perish. I need not say how numerous are the claims of a starving population of 18,000 – now thinned by the hand of death – of whom 2,000 are Protestants and whose destitute condition weighs heavily on my heart. My weekly expenditure has reached the alarming amount of nearly sixty pounds, nor do I see the slightest prospect of its diminution; my fears apprehend me to the contrary.

Sixty pounds a week was an unbelievable sum for the Rector to be finding from his own resources, about six thousand pounds in today's money. The size of his contribution is extraordinary if you consider that fourteen years earlier Traill was railing bitterly against those poor deluded Catholics *'who are caballing to deprive me of my tithes'*. Tithes that came to around eight hundred pounds a year.

His letter to Trevelyan was his last. Traill died a few days later on 21 April 1847.

Traill was buried by his church; the gravestone cost three hundred and fifty pounds. He could have gone to England, he could have left Skull to his curate like his father did, but he stayed on to fight. Despite the horror of life in Skull during the Famine, I feel sure that Traill had never felt more alive. If you compare the querulous self-absorption of the diaries with his robust full-blooded letters during the Famine, it is clear that he has found his voice.

Traill spent his life looking for a cross to bear. He leaves the order of his life in Lisburn for a parish in the poorest part of Ireland, full of what he termed *'half-pagan, deluded Catholics'*. He loves his wife and his children and yet he persists in living in a place which his wife hates, and so they spend much of their early married life apart. Traill records his misery at being away from his family, and yet when after much pleading he is eventually offered a living in England, he turns it down. Traill is a man who when he arrives in Skull is so vehement in his beliefs that the local Methodist minister challenges him to a duel. When a clergyman friend of his in Dublin is sick and Traill is given the opportunity of preaching there for a month, he prepares a series of sermons of such blistering evangelicism that the Archbishop himself is forced to intervene. Traill's enemies are everywhere, real and imagined. In his diaries people are always threatening to strike him.

But when the first signs of the blight appeared in 1846 Traill, for the first time in his life, was in a situation where his talent for making trouble was an asset. His metamorphosis from the evangelical crank who arrived in Skull in 1830 to the man who gave his life trying to save the people he once despised is almost too perfect. The zealot who learns compassion. It is the stuff of movies, a man in black and white who learns the meaning of life and wakes up in colour. Of course it isn't quite that simple, Traill didn't become the kind of humanitarian liberal we feel comfortable with today; he was still distinguishing between Protestant and Catholic deaths right at the end. But he did give his time, his money and ultimately his life in an attempt to save those less fortunate than himself. For Traill it was no sacrifice: he was high on the urgency of it all. Instead of hostile congregations, he had an indifferent government to harangue. The Archbishop of Dublin might ban him from delivering sermons, but the British Prime Minister read his letters from Skull. His weighty prose at last found a subject that fitted its doleful metre: '*half our population will ere long be blotted from the book of being*'.

He had prepared for calamity all his life and now he was living in the eye of the storm, *'where all is wretchedness – unutterable wretchedness, lamentation, mourning and woe'*.

His obituary in *Cork Constitution* stated that, *'there was no person in the country or even in the United Kingdom, who had done more work for the starving people than Traill. He had fortune, and he spent it liberally.'*

After his death a poet named A. Southern composed a long lament for Traill:

> *He saw his flock o'erwhelmed and crush'd – his heart bled at the sight,*
> *He saw a dark and angry cloud, foreshadowing stormy night;*
> *He saw the wasted forms of those who sighed and pined for food,*
> *Yet to his post of gloom and death the reverend warrior stood.*
> *His name and memory a place will still find on the earth.*
> *A grateful nation in their hearts will prize his matchless worth.*
> *Bless'd with the highest, noblest gifts, he gave them to the Lord*
> *Whom he had serv'd; and now he has his heavenly reward.*

Sadly, the *'grateful nation'* was not much in evidence after Traill's death. Even the Church of Ireland failed to *'prize his matchless worth'*. On 9 July a commission demanded £218 in dilapidations to the Rectory from Traill's executors. The dilapidations included the damage done to an outhouse by the setting up of a soup kitchen.

Daisy Goodwin

* * *

There is no Rector in Schull today. The parish has been amalgamated with the one next door where the souperist parson worked. The incumbent there now is a woman.

In a leaflet that I picked up in the church they built to replace the one that was destroyed after Traill's death, the Church of Ireland is described as being neither *'Protestant nor Catholic, but a church that has taken qualities from both'*. The writer of the pamphlet traces a lineage that stretches right back beyond the Reformation to St Patrick. The church is sprucer and better attended than its Anglican counterparts in England, but there are still three times as many people coming out of the Catholic church on Sunday morning. But the Catholic church is in a back street and the Church of Ireland, where a service of communion is only held on alternate Sundays, occupies a choice position above the town, overlooking the sea.

TEN

I have inherited much from my mother but not her talent for leaving. To walk away and not look back is a skill I have always wanted, but I have never been able to draw those nice clean lines. My mother is an expert in moving on, a virtual pioneer travelling further and further towards the frontier, towards that last vertiginous drop. Walking through the door into the next chapter is a family trait. The Traills liked to keep their narratives neat, with dramatically satisfying endings. Whatever their failures may have been, nothing was allowed to get in the way of the story. The Reverend Robert could have lived on through the Famine, but to die saving the people you once despised, is a much better ending. The Reverend's sons Robert and Edmund could have followed the careers that their mother had so thoughtfully picked out for them, but then the dramatic impetus would have been lost. Respectable lifetimes as doctors or civil engineers would have slowed down the story too much. It was time to move on, to walk away without turning back. This was their chapter and they were not going to surrender authorship to anyone, even their mother. Poor Anne, she didn't understand the plot at all.

Robert, my great-great-grandfather, and his brother Edmund were the youngest of the Rector's eight children. When Robert was born his father named him after himself and prayed that he too might become a minister. But his widow had other ideas. The Church of Ireland had never appreciated her husband and his '*superhuman*' efforts. It had behaved shabbily after his death. Besides, Robert's cousin Anthony was already earmarked for the Church and would be first in line for any family preferments.

Anne was sensible enough to see that her sons needed careers even though entering a profession involved some loss of caste in the hierarchical world of Ascendancy Ireland. Professions like medicine and engineering were dominated by Roman Catholics as these were the only careers that had not been prohibited to them by the Penal Laws. It was an imaginative mother indeed who put aside the prejudices of her class to choose such futures for her sons. Maybe Anne had come to consider medicine as a respectable career after living in Skull, where the Doctor was the only other person of similar social standing to the Rector. Civil engineering was an even more adventurous choice of career, but Ireland like the rest of Victorian Britain was in the grip of railway fever and any job connected with it must have seemed like one with prospects.

With both her sons at Trinity College and at least one of her daughters married, Anne must have felt enormously relieved. For the first time in years she could think of the future without fear. Her children at least would not have to endure the life of the poor relation. They would be settled members of society, not perhaps as wealthy as their Traill or Hayes relations but substantial nonetheless. They would live in Dublin, not in some benighted spot with no congenial souls for miles. Her children would be part of things, not forced into self-imposed exile by their own intransigence. She would have some status beyond that of the widow of a troublesome priest.

But Anne's carefully imagined future was never going to solidify into reality. Her sons were too young to remember the awful circumstances of their father's death and the dreadful period of insecurity that followed it. Anne's vision of a modest but rewarding future held little attraction for young men with grand ideas: they needed to kick-start their story.

The authorized version of how the Traills went to Argentina, I first heard from my aunt beside the swimming pool. The Traill brothers had rejected South Africa as too hot and Australia as too far. Someone – who? – had told them that Argentina meant land of silver, so that's where they decided to go. The brothers borrowed five hundred pounds from their family to buy land. A good way to start a story, but something was missing. Why had these two Anglo-Irish boys, brought up as Catholic-fearing Protestants, chosen Argentina, a Catholic Spanish-speaking country, when they could have settled in a colony like Canada which was made in their Protestant Anglo-Saxon image?

It was my mother who supplied the crucial detail. 'Didn't one of the brothers fall in love with someone unsuitable? They must have eloped.' At the time I rather discounted this theory as being just too good to be true, a romantic embellishment. My mother might leave everything behind for love, but those ancestors in stiff collars didn't act on impulse, or did they? Did my mother write her own story or was she operating under plot constraints laid down generations before?

I knew I had to go to Argentina again to find out how far back the story went, but for months I put it off. The silvery destination of my adolescence now seemed too far, too difficult. Before, half a lifetime ago, I had relished the idea of being away, of having no destination except to broaden my mind. 'Oh, Daddy,' I said as I begged my father to let me go, 'if I don't go how will I see the world?' Now I was full of excuses – my daughter was going to a new school, I had a new television series to make – but behind them all was the fear of saying goodbye, of leaving home and not looking back. Are the ties strong enough to resist the forward push, the urge to jump? Argentina held the answer to a lot of things.

My departure date kept shifting. My head swirled with conflicting desires. It was my childhood in microcosm: to strike out like my mother and find my own frontier, or stay at home like my father, safe in my family cocoon. I was not planning a particularly long journey, a month at most, but every day away seemed like a betrayal of my daughter, and every day I put it off a betrayal of myself. In the end it was my cousin Robin who settled things.

I had written to Robin and his brother Derek about six months before to tell them I was coming to Argentina to find out more about the Traills, but I had had no response, and I was beginning to wonder if they too had jumped. But then one day the phone call came. I picked up the phone and heard the static gurgles of a South American connection. 'Oh, Dyesi,' Robin's vowels were still peninsular, 'I was wondering whether you would like to come to the Oxford and Cambridge dinner on the nineteenth in BA. The ambassador is an Oxford man, of course,' Robin like me had been to Cambridge, 'but it's quite a decent show. It's black tie so you'll need to bring a frock of some sort.'

There was a pause. 'This book you're writing,' another pause, 'Eileen had a very highly coloured view of the Argentine, you know. Things are rather different now.' A warning. I mumbled something about being more interested in people than politics. We said goodbye. I picked up the phone and booked my flight. I had a date. A journey into the interior could be put off but an engagement had to be honoured.

The day I left I took my daughter to school. 'How many days will you be away, Mummy? Twenty-four is too many, I think ten is enough. Please come back after ten, please, Mummy, please, say you will.' I held her hand tightly and said I'd do my best. 'Oh, that means you won't do anything. Please come back after ten, Mummy, please.' I went through all the people who were there to look after her in my absence: Daddy, her nanny, her grandmothers, aunts, the friends she was having tea with, but I know I lacked conviction. How could I tell her that it would be all right without me, that this mother was coming back? We were at the school now, brisk goodbyes all around us, girls scampering off to their classrooms.

'Don't go yet, Mummy, please.' Ottilie gripped my hand, her face grey with misery.

I took a deep breath, kissed her and walked away. When I looked back – and of course I looked back – she had disappeared into a crowd of children. The tears were everywhere now and I had to go before one of the brisk mothers saw me.

I don't remember crying much as a child; my goodbyes to my mother were dry and jerky, holding myself stiff against fierce hugs. But looking at Ottilie's face that day

I felt all the tears I had put away at her age come flooding back. Part of me, a big part, wanted to cancel my trip – to be there when Ottilie came home, to supply the happy ending I had missed. But if I didn't go I would never know why my mother had to walk away. I felt angry with myself for putting that look on Ottilie's face and angrier still with my mother for ignoring that look on mine. There must have been something stronger than I could imagine to make her keep going, to stop her looking back.

Before I left, one of my cousins, Derek, who was something of a family historian, sent me a pamphlet he had written called 'The Traills of Argentina'. It was full of family trees, jerkily reproduced pictures of men on polo ponies holding trophies, and family documents. One of these was the marriage certificate of Robert Traill, son of the Rector, and Alice Pattison at St John's Church in Liverpool on 7 July 1866. Alice Pattison's residence at the time of marriage is listed as Dublin, Ireland and her father is described as a gentleman farmer. Her nationality is given as Irish, but Robert, although it is noted that he was born in Skull, is registered as British. She was twenty-two, Robert twenty-one. The only witnesses at the wedding were Edmund Traill and a Martha Parsonage.

Derek's pamphlet made no comment on the circumstances of the wedding, but everything about this marriage certificate confirmed my mother's half-remembered story. This was not an ordinary wedding. Alice must have been very unsuitable indeed. If she had been the right sort Robert would have married her in Dublin with due pomp and circumstance, instead of this hole-and-corner ceremony in Liverpool with only his brother present. From the marriage certificate it is clear that she wasn't under age, and she wasn't married already. One major disqualification remains:

could Alice have been a Catholic? I think that may have been the whiff of scandal that my mother scented three generations later.

At this point I have to stray into conjecture anchored by the scanty bones of evidence that still remain, but the colours I am using are from a family palette, the pigments all local. It is a story that works with the facts such as they are and matches the emotional colouring of the Traills. Of course, I come from a family where nothing should be allowed to get in the way of a good story, but for me this one fits. And, after all, this is what I'm doing – trying to find a story that fits.

As a member, however impoverished, of the Anglo-Irish elite Robert would not have mixed much with Catholics socially. But Robert was a brilliant horseman who lived to hunt. Perhaps Alice was the sister of one of his hunting friends who could well have been Catholic.

My feeling is that the atmosphere at the Pattison house would have been very different from that of the chilly evangelical parsonages Robert had grown up in. Alice was a year older than Robert, pretty and lively, the first girl he had really known apart from his older sisters. Alice flirted with him, the family were kind to him, he fell in love. He fell not just for her but for the atmosphere that surrounded her. They didn't have prayer meetings in Alice's house, nobody stayed up all night reading the Bible. Nobody cared that Robert was nothing like his late father. His cousin Tony, who was already a junior fellow at Trinity and very much the coming man, used to lecture Robert for spending too much time playing games and neglecting his studies; and his eldest sister, Katherine, who had married a rich landowner called Synge, was always trying to get him interested in some heiress or other; but Alice thought he was wonderful and she let him kiss her.

But Robert knew that Alice and the Pattisons would be unacceptable to the rest of his family. His younger brother Edmund, who had met them all, tried to warn him. It was not just the religion, although given the militant Protestantism of the Traills that was bad enough. (Did Robert remember the gun turrets built onto the Skull Rectory, or had he erased that from his memory along with the image of his father writing scratchily in his study?) The Pattisons were Irish, they did not think that one day they would go to England and life would really begin. Alice's father, although he was described as a gentleman farmer on the marriage certificate, was really a grain merchant who in common with many of his friends had done rather well out of the Famine. Demand had been high and supply had been short, and Mr Pattison had made a very fortunate purchase of Indian corn in 1848 which he sold to the British government for a very tidy price. The profits had paid for the nice little estate on the outskirts of Dublin and the house in Fitzwilliam Street. Alice's mother had started wearing silk instead of muslin, her daughters had the widest crinolines of all their friends. When they married, the Pattison daughters would have magnificient dowries of fifteen thousand pounds apiece. But though the Pattisons were much wealthier than the Traills or even than Anne Traill's brother, the baronet who lived in Drumboe Castle but whose rents were falling year on year, the Traills would always consider the Pattisons to be not so much inferior as alien; as interesting, as odd and ultimately as strange as performing dogs or fleas. Even Robert felt this a little. Much as he loved being at the

Pattisons' house for its own sake, there was always that little frisson of rebellion: if only insufferable cousin Tony could see him now, that would make it so much more enjoyable.

Sometimes Robert even thought of his father. He tried to picture his face and failed but he remembered the scratchy pen, the flickering candlelight and the rough beard that tickled when he kissed him goodnight. All his life he had hated being called Robert after his late father; it was the greatest relief of his life when his mother had not insisted on his becoming a minister but had sanctioned his desire to study medicine. She had called medicine a noble calling but Robert had found it rather a disappointment: too many old ladies with dropsy and Latin names to learn. His mother expected him to do well and become the most fashionable doctor in Dublin, but Robert found the studying tedious and the patients irritating. There was too little time for his real passions, hunting and cricket. Most of his friends at Trinity could afford to treat their work lightly because they were from landed families: getting a degree was just another rite of passage before they married an heiress and settled down on their estates. Robert envied them their self-confidence, their strings of hunters, their cellars.

He rode much better than anyone he knew, but when he went to stay with his rich friends in the vacations he had to borrow their mounts. He was always identifiable as the rider of somebody else's horse. '*I would hardly have known that bay mare of Fitzwilliam's. I didn't know she had so much spirit in her. I must ask him if he would consider selling.*' The sisters of his friends would practise flirting with him but they were careful not to cross that invisible boundary that separated a 'catch' from a penniless medical student. Robert Traill was a good-looking boy with a wonderful seat but he was not husband material: he had to make a fortune first. The sisters saved their biggest smiles and the chance to turn the pages of their piano music for the likes of Charlie Hayes, Robert's cousin, who was the heir to a baronetcy and a tidy estate of ten thousand acres.

No wonder Robert spent so much time at the Pattisons; at least there he was appreciated for who he was now, not tolerated on account of what he might become in fifteen years' time. Robert was tired of living in a world where he could look but not touch, he was tired of waiting. He knew that even if he qualified as a doctor it would take him years and years before he too could have a string of hunters and the chance to turn the piano music of the Honourable Araminta. Years of smiling at old ladies and scratchy pens. He sometimes wished he was studying civil engineering like his brother Edmund; at least you did not have to be civil to be a civil engineer. If only his father had not spent his fortune helping those poor wretches. As he got older Robert could hardly think of his father without feeling angry: with a bit of capital behind him Robert knew he could do anything. But without land in Ireland you were nothing. His cousin Tony was all right: he would inherit all the family estates in Antrim, whereas he Robert was condemned to dispensing laudanum to ladies with the vapours, unless he managed to snare an heiress, which given his prospects was not very likely. Alice did not qualify in Robert's mind as this kind of heiress. He could not live with Alice in Dublin, it would be altogether too complicated.

It never crossed Robert's mind that the Pattisons might not consider him a suitable husband for Alice.

The more Robert considered his situation the more

hopeless it seemed. After one particularly humiliating vacation in the winter of 1865 which he had spent staying with his friend Lord Frederick Fitzroy, Robert decided that he could not endure this life in waiting any longer. Robert had hardly known his father but he had inherited his inflamed touchiness, feeling every careless remark, every wandering glance, as a mortal insult. He was always challenging his friends to duels over some imagined slight, but luckily his friends were too confident to take him at his word. But Robert was sick of being held at arm's length – after one card game at which he had lost his temper and Freddie Fitzroy had told him to go outside and cool off like a dog, Robert took a horse from the stable, Freddie's favourite as it happened, and rode off at a vicious gallop. About half a mile out of the park gates, the road was blocked by a group of peasants making the most desolate noise, the women wailing and tearing their hair. Robert stopped, arrested by a misery equal to his own. Was it a wake? he asked one of the men. The man looked surprised. This was no wake, yer honour, this was something far worse; Bartley Geary the Gearys' eldest son and the finest lad in the whole village was emigrating to America.

On the way back the thought of leaving began to swirl in Robert's mind, filling all those bitter crevices left by his father's death and his own lack of fortune. He would go west like Bartley and make his fortune. Anything was better than a lifetime of smelling salts. It would be a decision, the first thing in his life he had made for himself. For a second or two he thought about his mother and her plans to keep house for him when he qualified. But that was after all her plan. Going west was the only, the obvious solution. When he got back to Freddie's house he was smiling. He apologized to Freddie for riding the hell out of his horse and made himself so agreeable to the ladies after dinner that they almost forgot that he was the penniless son of a clergyman who by all accounts had been most troublesome. Poor Anne Hayes, what an unfortunate match it had been.

Robert told no one of his plan except Edmund. His brother listened to him in silence. 'But where are we going to go?' Robert heard the 'we' with gratitude. Somewhere from the recesses of his memory Robert remembered a conversation from one of those country-house dinners. 'Finest land in the world for farming is on the 34th parallel. Fortunes to be made there by the right man.' Or was it the 33rd? He was sure it was one or the other.

Edmund fetched a chart of the southern hemisphere that a botanist friend had left in his rooms. Robert followed the 34th parallel on the chart and traced its line around the world with a cricket-callused finger. It splayed over South Africa but as far as Robert was concerned it was in the wrong direction: he had a fancy for sailing west. The next land mass he hit was Australia but it was full of convicts and Ribbonmen. The finger moved on across the Pacific leaving a shiny snail track behind it. At last it hit land on the crenellated triangle of South America in the middle of Argentina. The 34th parallel ran like a railway line through the empty map until it bisected a dot called Santa Fé that lay at the end of a river called the Río de la Plata. Robert and Edmund knew no Spanish but from the Latin they knew they translated this as the River of Silver. How could they fail to make their fortunes on the Silver River?

They were not the first to go west in search of a silvery reward. Three hundred years earlier Don Diego de Sevilla had heard of the Río de la Plata from the Jesuit missionaries who had come back laden with silver ornaments 'donated' by the native tribes. He assumed that the silver had been found in the river of the same name, an assumption that the Jesuits did nothing to check. They needed the support of a powerful grandee. Why should they tell him that the Río de la Plata had been named not after the precious metal it contained but because the silvery sheen of its waters stayed the same elemental grey no matter how blue the sky above it? If Robert and Edmund had had a newer map they might have found the Río de la Plata translated as the River Plate – a base metal tricked out to look like silver, a rich deceiver.

If Robert and Edmund had been systematic in their research they might have come across one of the many advertisements placed in *The Times* by companies such as Thomson Bonar and Co. appealing for able-bodied men to buy plots in a colony they were establishing at Fraile Muerto in the Santa Fé province. For a modest outlay settlers were promised land which would yield returns far beyond their expectations. In the prospectus, after pages extolling the richness of the land for crops and cattle-farming, the settlers were advised to bring a breech-loading rifle and revolver, *'not that these arms are necessary but to show the tame Indians that the colonists are armed, the moral effect being sufficient to protect the lives and properties of the latter'*. The prospectus glides over the significant numbers of British settlers who were massacred every year during raids on their fledgling colonies by Indians. Although the president of Argentina in the late 1860s, Domingo Sarmiento, did everything in his power to encourage European immigration – *'We can in three years introduce 300,000 new settlers and drown in the waves the creole rabble, inept uncivil and coarse, which stops our attempt to civilize the nation'* – not everyone agreed with him. Argentina in the 1860s was very much a frontier, tricked out as a shimmering silvery horizon.

But to Robert and Edmund, Argentina was still a land of shining possibilities. A place for them to make the kind of fortunes that should have been theirs by right. A chance to escape the dreary professional futures to which their father's death and their mother's prudence had condemned them. A country to return from, bronzed and fabulously wealthy, 'good matches' at last. Any hesitation came from Edmund, who as his mother's youngest child and the fussed-over pet of several older sisters was less unhappy with his lot than his brother. He had been born the year his father died so there were no memories of the scratchy pen for him to escape from. But the adoration of his mother was nothing compared to the hero-worship he felt for his brother.

He had always found Robert's impulsiveness, his passionate rages and his sudden smiles worrying but he knew by now how to coast through the peaks and troughs. Robert always went first and Edmund would follow; Robert never looked back but Edmund would. He always had more to leave behind. Edmund was enjoying his civil engineering studies; he dreamed of building railways, bridges, viaducts. In the vacations he stayed with his mother and sisters in Dublin. He found Robert's grand hunting friends exhausting. He hated the balls and parties which Robert used to complain about but still attended, always hopeful. Edmund found all those women with bare shoulders and feathers in their hair rather alarming. The older ones always reminded him of turkeys. He would rather stay at home with his calculus than feel all those heads poking towards him ready to gobble him up.

Left to himself Edmund had no reason to leave Dublin but how could he live without Robert? Or live with himself for letting Robert go alone? Everybody knew that he needed Robert but no one, not even Robert, knew how much his older brother relied on him. Robert had not asked Edmund to go with him, he had just assumed that his brother would at once follow his whim. Edmund knew that not to go would be a betrayal. It was worth giving up everything not to disappoint his brother.

Robert wanted to go at once. He was infuriated to find that February was the wrong time of year to sail to South America and that no boats would be leaving until June at the earliest. He had left already in his mind; he did not want to waste time saying goodbye. He thought of going to Liverpool and waiting there on the off chance that a boat might leave earlier than June but Edmund refused. Edmund was determined to borrow some money before they left, capital with which to buy land once they got to Argentina. Robert thought this was unnecessary – they would earn the money when they got there – but Edmund insisted. He knew that Robert simply couldn't bear the idea of asking any of the Traills for money and would rather the whole enterprise foundered for want of capital than go through the humiliation of approaching his uncles. There was always that unspoken thought that Robert was turning out as wilful and as wrong-headed as his father. But Edmund forced him to go and it was worse than anything Robert had imagined.

His father's brother Anthony lectured, remonstrated, even prayed with him in order to dissuade him from this voyage to a godforsaken heathen country. In the end, realizing that Robert and Edmund were adamant, Anthony gave them twenty-five pounds for their poor mother's sake.

Their mother's brother the baronet was more sympathetic to their plans: he knew the value of adventure and wished he could spare them more than fifty pounds but there it was, the rents were down that year.

Both brothers dreaded telling their mother. Anne knew, of course, long before they plucked up the courage to tell her. She had seen the gleam in Robert's eyes, the flushed red patches on his cheeks and the worry in Edmund's face, the columns of figures he was adding up in his head. Argentina was a shock, though. She had thought they might be planning to join the army, go to India perhaps, but to go to a place that she had to search for on her late husband's globe and a Catholic country too! It was almost as bad as the Rector telling her that it was his duty to go and live in that godforsaken parish in West Cork. And she had so hoped to have her sons settled around her here in Dublin. But she also knew that Robert was not happy at Trinity, and she suspected that he might run into trouble of some kind, if indeed he was not mixed up in something already. She had tried to find out from Edmund if there was a reason why Robert was so anxious to leave but Edmund of course always sided with his brother, it was impossible to get anything from him.

It seemed hard to lose them both at once but Anne knew that Edmund would not let Robert go alone: she hoped they would look after each other. The boys did not ask her for money – they had grown up too much in the shadow of her poor-relation status for that – but in fact she had managed to save a couple of hundred pounds, the remains of a legacy. She was going to keep it to buy trousseaus for her daughters but the boys needed it more. Robert did not want to take it but she had insisted, pressing the bank draft into his hands. 'It's a loan, not a gift. When

you make your fortunes you can pay me back with interest.'
Robert still did not want to take the money – the sense
of obligation was too strong – but Edmund had intervened. 'We will make you rich, Mama,' he said, kissing
her. And at that moment he believed it.

Two hundred and seventy-five pounds seemed like a
fortune to Robert, enough to buy everything he had ever
wanted. But Edmund still wanted more: the passage he
knew was only about twelve pounds but they had to buy
land when they arrived and then all the supplies and livestock they would need to live there. In the end the rest of
the money came from an unexpected source. Their eldest
sister, Kathleen, had recently been widowed and had been
left a sizeable fortune by her husband. Kathleen had a
romantic nature and being so much older than her brothers
she felt somehow responsible for them. Although most of
her estate was entailed on her son she could spare one
hundred and twenty-five pounds. Maybe the boys *would*
come back rich and famous: the Traills certainly needed
some good fortune. And like her mother she was worried
that Robert was on the verge of trouble. She well remembered the extremes of her father's moods, the all-night
prayer vigils, the long absences in Skull and the bitter
tempers he would bring back with him. Papa was always
fighting, and Robert her brother had the same violence in
him. Her mother never spoke about it but Kathleen knew
she felt the same way. And there was also a little part of
Kathleen that did not want to be tainted any more by her
family; she was so grateful to have escaped the Rectory
she did not want to be whispered about as the sister of
that Robert Traill. One hundred and twenty-five pounds
was a small price to pay for her peace of mind.

Now that they had the money, Robert was even more

impatient to be gone but Edmund had no intention of hanging around in Liverpool spending money waiting for a boat. They would book their passages on one of the steamers that left in July and wait in Dublin till then. Robert could even get his degree.

The last person Robert told of his plans was Alice. He had not been to see her since he had made his decision to go. He wondered whether she would wait for him, but there was no reason why she should: after all they could never marry. When he came back with his fortune made he would be able to choose the Honourable Edith or Araminta of his choice. To marry a Catholic girl, even if she was pretty with a dowry of fifteen thousand pounds, really wouldn't do. But Robert could not leave without telling Alice, without saying goodbye, not when there were so many months to wait until the boat sailed. If he could go tomorrow then he might walk away without looking back, but to spend another three months in Dublin without seeing Alice would be impossible.

But he left it as late as he could. Alice's brother Johnny kept asking him round complaining that he would get no peace at home until he produced his friend. In April Robert could stay away no longer. He found himself in the parlour of Fitzwilliam Street with Alice, her sisters and her mother. It was very hot in there and he could feel the colour rising in his cheeks as he told them about his plans to make his fortune on the silver river. Mrs Pattison and Alice's sisters were impressed, looking suitably alarmed when he said he did not think they would be in much danger from Indian raids, but Alice was silent. She sat on the window-seat apparently watching the passers-by but Robert could see that the back of her neck, the strip of flesh between the lace of her bodice and the heavy mound of her chignon, was going red. Alice was like him, she flushed easily.

Later, when the announcement was made and one of the girls was playing the piano, Robert went over to where Alice still sat in the window-seat looking out of the window. She was motionless, the usual whites and reds of her complexion quite reversed. A wave of tears was waiting to break on her lower lashes. Robert knew that he was about to say something irrevocable, to make a decision that, unlike the Argentine, he could never come back from. He had always carefully avoided this possibility even in his thoughts. It was the bigger jump, but the mottled flush on the nape of Alice's neck compelled him to speak.

'Alice, will you come?'

He saw the little knob of Alice's thoracic vertebra stick out as she nodded her head.

'But it's impossible,' she whispered. 'They will never let me marry you.'

Robert was falling further and further. 'I'll write to you,' he said. His cheeks were burning now, he had to leave. But as he walked down the street he did look back to see Alice still sitting in the window. The next day he wrote to her and asked her to elope with him.

In his letter he told her that the boat was leaving for Argentina on 10 July from Liverpool. Edmund and he were going to leave Dublin at the end of June so that they could equip themselves for the trip. If Alice would come she should meet him in Liverpool. It was impossible for them to marry secretly in Dublin; too many people knew them, and if the vicar was to find out that Alice was a Catholic . . . Better to marry in Liverpool: couples got married in a hurry there all the time. If he went there three weeks ahead he could get a special licence and they could get married the moment she arrived. He hated to leave her to make the journey from Dublin by herself but he could think of no other way. Also, could she please bring any money that she had and warm clothes for the journey. The voyage to Buenos Aires would take six weeks.

There were lots of things that Robert did not put in his letter. He did not write, for example, that he loved Alice, or that he would not go without her. But neither did he explain what lay in store on the other side of the world. Perhaps he did not know, or maybe he wanted to keep things neutral. This had to be Alice's choice, he did not want to push her too far in one way or the other. Part of him felt certain that she would come but not sure enough to put too much love in his letter. He hated the idea of it being passed around among the sisters with Alice laughing her fluttery laugh. And maybe he did not want to say too much because there was also a part of him that hoped she would think better of the whole idea. Taking a woman on this trip was not going to be easy. And he had the odd twinge of regret for the Honourable Ediths and Aramintas and his position at the piano. If Alice came, they could never come back to Dublin, they would have to take their fortune to England instead. This was not such an unpleasant thought. Robert had never been to England and the idea of going there with a fortune pleased him hugely. But behind all these thoughts was the fact of Edmund. He had not told his brother yet, he did not dare. He knew what Edmund would say, how his face would contract with worry and disapproval. But if he told Edmund now, he might decide not to come, and whilst he could go on without Alice he would be lost without Edmund.

Alice did not reply to his letter. Robert went on with

the goodbye visits. He played his last cricket match, and scored his first century. For a moment or two his resolve wavered, but then he ran into his cousin Tony while celebrating his victory and had to listen to a lecture on the dangers of drink. He sold his books and used the money to buy a ticket for Alice. He had done everything he could.

In Liverpool he and Edmund found a place to stay in Islington, a district near the port packed with lodging houses. Theirs was full of respectable Scotch–Irish farmers and their families on their way to Canada. These families were emigrating in earnest. The yard behind the house was piled high with heavy wooden dressers, wheel-backed chairs, hope chests covered in iron studs. In the morning these families would meet to pray together, each one with its own leather-covered Bible. Robert enjoyed walking through the house during these gatherings, calling for his breakfast as loudly as he could, the heels of his boots striking a heathen tattoo on the stone floor.

Robert and Edmund argued about what they should take with them. Edmund felt that they needed very little beyond money and weapons: everything else they could buy when they got to Buenos Aires. But Robert tried to persuade him that they should buy linen and crockery, even a rocking chair. Edmund was amazed. Why was his reckless brother suddenly so interested in comfort? Robert almost told him then but the thought that Alice might not come made him hold his tongue. As each day passed he changed his mind a hundred times about whether she would come or not, and he changed his mind a hundred times about whether he wanted her to come or not.

Robert had quite decided that it would be better if he never saw Alice again when, a week before they were due to sail, the lodging-house maid came into the room where they were having breakfast to tell them that two ladies were here to see Mr Robert Traill. Robert got up at once, walking furiously through the families at prayer. There in the parlour, a room so stuffed with furniture that there was hardly room to stand, stood Alice in her widest crinoline, accompanied by an older lady. He stepped towards Alice, tried to take her hand but she wouldn't look at him. Both of them were overcome with what they had done.

In the end it was Edmund who arranged everything. He even found the posy that Alice carried up the aisle of St Stephen's Church, the first Protestant church she had ever entered. After the ceremony they went back to the lodging house, passing through the farmers and their families, the farmers' wives looking closely at Alice's waist. Edmund was so busy he had no time to talk to Robert, and besides there was nothing to say. Robert had made his choice. But he wished, though, that he had tried a little harder when he saw how Alice flinched when she entered the church, how she minded when the lodging-house landlady asked about her trousseau. How could Robert think this was going to be easy? He wondered if Alice was pregnant, but since she had gone to so much trouble to preserve the niceties by bringing her nurse as chaperone, he rather thought not.

The facts suggest that Robert and Alice did not actually consummate their marriage for three years. Robert tried on the boat, in the bullock cart that took them and their belongings from Rosario to the land they had bought in the province of Santa Fé, even in the tent that they lived in before they finished building their house, but Alice closed herself against him. She would not even undress in front of him. Robert did not insist; he did not need Edmund's careful forbearance to tell him what he had done. It was only when the house was built and Alice was able to arrange her meagre collection of keepsakes on the shelves in their bedroom – a lock of her mother's hair, a shell from the beach at Howth, a picture of St Ursula – that she finally relented, her body no longer rigid with grief. In 1870 my great-grandfather was born: his parents named him Robert after his father and his grandfather, the unfortunate Rector of Skull.

The only photographs which survive of Robert, Edmund and Alice were taken much later when they were grandparents themselves, the brothers obscured by great bushy beards, Alice's still heart-shaped face muffled by a lace cap. The only youthful image of them is that marriage certificate and my mother's half-remembered story: surviving like the rings inside a tree trunk, every half-tone variation in the striation mute witness to a hard winter, a passionate decision. And as I walk west from my daughter's school trying not to cry, there will be a little flaw in the rings of my heart, a faint tracing of that bigger disturbance near the core.

ELEVEN

I landed in Argentina in November, in the middle of spring. On the plane I sat next to a woman professor, who was going to Buenos Aires to give a lecture on *Martín Fierro*, the gaucho classic. Her parents were Danish but she had grown up in the Argentine; she had gone to the same Buenos Aires boarding school as my grandmother.

I told her about my journey, about the Traills. 'Traill, you mean Tra-eel,' she gave it two Spanish syllables, 'yes, I have heard the name.' The Professor flicked through her mental index cards. 'The name is familiar although I have never met a Traill.' She paused. 'My best friend in Buenos Aires, in fact I'm going to her daughter, my goddaughter's wedding tonight . . . Juana's husband he left for a woman called Traill. I can't remember her first name . . . It was a terrible scandal at the time. Patrick and Juana had four children. People just didn't get divorced then like they do now. But Patrick was crazy for your Traill relation, there was no stopping him.'

I wasn't sure if I should apologize but settled for a disowning look. 'She will be there tonight at the wedding.

Nobody wanted her to come but Patrick insisted, and as he's paying . . . I don't suppose I'll be speaking to her but if I do I will tell her I met you. And now if you'll excuse me.'

With that remark she turned away from me, swallowed a pill, pulled down her eye mask and pushed yellow cylinders of foam into her ears. But I was not ready to sleep yet; I watched the movie without headphones and wondered why I felt so guilty about a woman I had never met. But there was also that little thrill of connection, of a piece fitting neatly into the pattern I had begun to make out in the reaches of the Traill past. Beneath all the stories, the neat grid map of the family tree, were these little humps of passion, hill forts of desire . . . contours of excitement. I did not need directions. This was familiar territory.

Robert, Edmund and Alice landed in Buenos Aires in November 1866, a hundred and thirty-two years before my aeroplane touched down in Ezeiza Airport. Their journey took four months, mine was only fourteen hours. When I arrived in Buenos Aires the jacaranda trees along the Avenida de Mayo were bursting with purple blossom. It was one of the first hot days of the summer and the streets were full of women teetering in new sandals. The small park behind the apartment where I was staying was full of football; men with proper strips playing five-a-side in courts surrounded by nets and pavilions for changing; outside the official enclosures teenagers in Nike trainers playing on the tarmac and at the edges of the park smaller boys kicking a slightly crumpled ball in the dust. Buenos Aires was a city both familiar and strange. The same brand names, but different scents, the people with their European features arranged in another order.

The first thing Robert noticed was the mud. It was raining as their boat dropped anchor twelve miles away from the shore – the River Plate in those days had no deep-water port. It was raining as they were transferred with all their belongings first to a barge and then to a rowing boat and when they finally found themselves on the quayside, the dirt roads that led to the centre of the city had turned to thick red rivers. Robert's legs were still shaky from the voyage. Within minutes of stepping onto dry land he stumbled and fell face down into the red clay. Alice and Edmund laughed so much that they too were in danger of slipping over. It was the first time that Alice and Edmund had laughed together. The first time almost since Edmund had given Alice her wedding posy that their eyes had met.

I think this is the moment when the story stops being a Trollopian romance and becomes something altogether tougher. The ambiguities of the relationship between Robert, Alice and Edmund are rather lost in the violence of their new surroundings. It was as if the infuriating Lady Glencora Palliser had suddenly been whisked away from the drawing room of Omnium Castle and dropped in an abattoir.

The second thing that Robert noticed was the smell. The road from the port to the city ran past the *saladero* or killing grounds where cattle, horses and sheep were brought from all over the country every day to be slaughtered. Some of the animals were killed to supply meat for the city, some of the meat was dried for *charque*, a kind of beef jerky, which was exported to Brazil where it was used to feed the slaves, but most of the animals, including all the horses, were killed for their hides and tallow. There was as yet no way of preserving meat for export in the 1860s.

Robert could not place the smell at first, but all those months on the ship had made him unusually sensitive to it. As they got closer to the south side of the city he began to feel quite overcome. The ground here was no longer red but black where the blood from the animals had mixed with the dust to make a crust six inches thick. The sky was full of *chimichangas*, the carrion birds of the pampas, waiting to pick clean the carcasses of the dead animals which stripped of their meat and hide were left just where they had been killed. There were bones and piles of offal everywhere, great yellow lumps of tallow being sniffed at by stray dogs. Robert wanted desperately to gallop away from this inferno but the bullock cart that was carrying Alice and all their belongings could go no faster. As they moved on for what seemed like an interminable distance, Robert noticed that the walls lining the road were not built from stones as he had first supposed but from layer upon layer of animal skulls. They were a grotesque version of the grey rocky boundaries that separated one potato field from another in the landscape of his childhood.

The smell never really went even after they passed the four square miles of the *saladero*. It just deepened and filled out to include the aromas of the approaching city. It was worse than the very worst part of Dublin, worse than the smell in the hold of the ship. They never really got used to it even after they had been in the city for weeks. Even in the late 1860s Buenos Aires, or Ayres as Robert would have spelt it, had no drainage and no supply of fresh water. Water had to be bought from water men who carried it around in buckets, each bucketful containing about half a pound of red clay in solution. If you poured it into a glass, before it had a chance to settle it was the same colour and texture as blood. Some of the better houses had *algibes* or cisterns where the rainwater from the flat roofs was deposited, but that water was full of scarlet wrigglers, the larvae of mosquitoes, which the inhabitants drank quite calmly, wrigglers and all. Not surprisingly, typhoid and typhus, the disease which had killed Robert's father in Ireland, were endemic in Buenos Aires. I wonder if Robert as a medical student knew enough to insist on boiling their drinking water. The Traill brothers, their immune systems weakened by months at sea, could so easily have travelled across the world only to die from the same bacteria as the Rector of Skull. But this generation of Traills' portion of bad luck had not started yet. They were at the stage where the river was still silver and there were happy endings in sight.

The British Consul in Buenos Aires was a Scotsman called MacDonnel. He greeted the Traill brothers coolly. He had seen too many young men like them set out with high hopes only to return ruined a year or so later. He had written to this effect to the Foreign Office only the previous week.

'*The River Plate*,' he had said, '*requires a class of immigrants willing to toil under the greatest inconveniences and privations, not gentlemen of education with scanty capital, insufficient to last them until the time when they can reasonably expect to reap the fruits of the labour of those they employ . . . In short, what is required by this country are labourers and not gentlemen of limited means.*'

The Traill brothers clearly had no idea of what lay in store for them in Santa Fé. It was unfortunate that they had been en route when he had issued his warning to all British immigrants that the River Plate Republics were presently unsafe for settlers.

In the last year no fewer than twenty-one British settlers had been murdered in the provinces but none of the people responsible had been brought to justice. In his communiqué to London he had written, '*For a gaucho who has murdered a gringo, there is especially in the camp, usually complete immunity, shelter on the part of his countrymen and complete inactivity on that of the authorities.*' The central government might actively want to encourage European immigration but the policy had little support from the mighty caudillos who ran the outlying provinces where most of the Europeans actually settled. Most of the murders that took place were conveniently attributed to Indians but MacDonnel knew from some of the eyewitness accounts he had received that culprits were as likely to be Argentine nationals who resented these foreign interlopers having title to land they regarded as their birthright.

> *The chief obstacles to the success of the British immigrant consist in the climate; the language, habits and customs of the natives; the tardy acquisition and hazardous tenure of land; the invasions of Indians; the unjust seizure of property both by rebel and government troops; the absence of a means of transit and communication, whether by roads, navigable rivers or railways, the defective administration of justice; and the jealousy with which he is regarded by the inhabitants of this country.*

MacDonnel made the Traill brothers sit in his office while he read them the official warning that they missed in their precipitate departure. He was distressed to learn that there was a Mrs Traill. There had been an appalling case recently in the Santa Fé province at Fraile Muerto where an English woman had been brutally raped and then murdered in true gaucho fashion. A man stood behind her and slit her throat from ear to ear with his *facón* or long-bladed knife. As British Consul he could only advise them to settle somewhere else.

Robert, Edmund and Alice were three of the 13,696 immigrants who arrived in the Argentine Republic in 1866. Although young men of education and limited means were troublesome to MacDonnel, the Traill brothers and those like them formed a tiny proportion of the immigrants to Argentina in the 1860s. Most of them were Spanish, from the desolate fishing villages of Galicia. The second biggest group was from Southern Italy. There was also a small but significant number of Catholic Irish, more prosperous probably than their compatriots who emigrated to North America but from a very different caste of Irish society from the Traills. These groups had in common their religion and the fact that the situation they found themselves in was materially better than the life they left behind. Even though life expectancy was much lower in the Argentine – at thirty-one it was twenty years less than an adult male might expect if he lived in Ireland – wages were much higher. Most of these peasant immigrants settled in and around Buenos Aires, having no wish to exchange one form of rural poverty for another. There was no homestead movement as there was in North America. The bulk of these rural immigrants did not share the Traill brothers' dream of making a fortune from the pampas. They were simply looking for an escape from poverty and privation. These immigrants generally assimilated rapidly into Argentine society. Even the Irish who did not have the linguistic advantage of the Spanish were generally completely integrated in one generation.

Catholicism was clearly a force behind the swiftness of the Irish absorption into Argentine society, but so was the absence of any reason *not* to belong. They had everything to gain from becoming part of their new country.

But Robert and Edmund had not travelled halfway across the world to become Argentines. What they wanted from this new country was the living they felt they had been cheated of by their father's misguided charity. They listened impatiently to MacDonnel's warnings about the dangers that awaited them: coping with a hostile indigenous population was, after all, something that they as the sons of an Anglo-Irish clergyman were quite familiar with. They had no intention of failing.

After the Traills left, MacDonnel went back to the report he was writing:

> *The most undesirable class of immigrant is the young gentleman of very slender, if any, means: who by education and antecedents is neither fit to tend a flock of sheep, sweep a store, nor make himself generally useful. These come in not insignificant numbers; useless and helpless they sink lower and lower in the social scale.*

Six months later the Foreign Office official reading this report pencilled next to this: 'A horrid nuisance the whole world over.'

The journey to Argentina took four months; the journey to their new home lasted six weeks. The first part of the journey was by boat, a tramp steamer that stopped at all the islands on the River Plate delta. In Rosario the brothers purchased twelve thousand *hectáreas* (about forty-five square miles) of land in the interior of the province on the 34th parallel. The price was one centavo per acre. To get to their land they went upriver to Coronda, the nearest small town to their new estate. Robert and Edmund knew that they needed to have their land marked out by the provincial surveyor in order to establish legal ownership, but the surveyor, when they eventually located him, showed absolutely no interest in leaving his new mistress to make the long muddy journey to mark out the Traills' territory. It took them a week and four hundred pesos to persuade him to come. In Coronda the Traills bought horses and a bullock cart and they engaged the services of a man and a boy. All this was accomplished despite the fact that they spoke not a word of Spanish and no one they encountered spoke English. How familiar did this hostile environment feel, I wonder, this flat unrelenting landscape, the muddy roads, the hostile peasantry?

The journey from Coronda to their land took four days. On the second night one of the bullocks pulling the cart escaped and they wasted half a morning trying to capture it again. Robert and Edmund could ride but they had no experience whatever of handling cattle. The man they had hired watched them for a while and, perhaps realizing that the gringos had all the food, he decided to show them how to lasso the animal as the gauchos did. Robert picked it up quickly – he was a cricketer, after all – but Edmund, who was short-sighted, found it next to impossible. That night the peon showed them how to secure their animals, in this country with no trees or fences, by tying their halters to a bone and then burying it deep in the ground. There was no shortage of bones. But despite this tip the brothers took it in turns to sleep that night. To lose any of their animals in this flat sea of land would have meant at best they would not be able to carry on; at worst they would not be able to go back.

On the fourth day of travelling north-west the surveyor announced that they had reached the edge of the territory the Traills had bought in Rosario. It took them the best part of two days to ride around the forty-five square miles. The marking out was a matter of gesture. The surveyor sat on his horse and waved his arm to the west: '*Aquí a agua.*' The Traills followed the direction of his arm but it was impossible to make out the boundaries in this ocean of landscape which rolled on and on, mile after mile. This land was virgin pampas, no buildings, no trees, not a patch of shade, only at the edge where the land met the sky there was a haze of silver that if you squinted your eyes could be a shining city.

It was a landscape that could drown you in its vast anonymity or suggest a future of unlimited possibility. I hope that to Robert and Edmund it was the latter, that their dreams reached as far as the silvery horizon.

And how did Alice feel: elated by the possibilities that lay ahead or tired, hungry and uncomfortable? How much did she regret the impulse that had led her to follow Robert to Liverpool? Had she discovered that the ache of worry would subside with alcohol, or did that come later? Later; I think that at twenty-two Alice would still have believed in happy endings.

The land the Traills had bought lies three hundred miles west of Rosario. It lies in the middle of some of the flattest and most fertile land in the world, but a river that runs through one side of it has made a miniature depression that floods when it rains, making the land virtually useless for four or five months of the year. The *alcalde de campaña* who sold them the land in Rosario might not have known that the plot they were buying had this kink but then he might also have enjoyed taking the gringos' money.

The Traills knew nothing of the depression; it would take them weeks to discover the river. The land they saw had clumps of pampas grass, anthills, vizcacha burrows, broken wagon wheels, the occasional scrubby bush in an endlessly repeating loop, but nothing so recognizable as a river. Their immediate task was to build themselves a shelter, but where in their forty-five square miles of land should they put it? In a land without character it was not a logical decision.

At last Robert came across an ombu tree, one of the rare indigenous trees of the pampas. To call it a tree was perhaps an exaggeration, but, as it was the only thing of any height for miles, in pampas terms it qualified. It was black and spiky and the shade it cast was negligible but it was something to tie the animals to, a point of reference in this featureless plain. It took them days to collect enough wood from the scattered thorn bushes to build a frame big enough for Robert who was six foot tall to stand upright in. They made a roof from *pajas bravas* or pampas grass (the kind that now grows freely in suburban front gardens), and plastered the walls with mud. When they had arrived, the mud had been everywhere but by the time they found enough wood to build the house the ground had dried. They had to wait another week for it to rain again.

They had some help with all this but not much. The man and the boy had their own notion of what was required of them and disappeared for three days halfway through the building of the hut. Robert and Edmund thought they had gone for ever but on the fourth day Robert caught sight of a lopsided letter H moving jerkily towards them. At a distance of about half a mile Robert could see that the H was in fact a tree trunk being carried by the peon and his boy. Robert was relieved to see them return but irritated by their obvious pride in their mission: he could not see the point of the post now that the hut was finished. The peon, unable to explain in words, dug a hole for the post and set it upright in the earth. It stood about nine foot tall, taller than Robert, taller than the ombu tree, taller than their hut. The peon firmed the earth around the base of the post and then began to rub himself against it, snorting and bellowing as he did so. The boy, catching on, began to do the same: running up to the post, throwing himself against it, scratching furiously and then running away.

Robert had no idea at all what they were doing – could it be some heathen papist ritual? A good-luck dance? He realized by their smiles that they meant well, but what did they mean? The post was certainly going to come in handy for tying the animals to, but this elaborate charade suggested that it was more important than that.

The post remained there mute and unexplained until weeks later when Robert and Edmund and the peon returned from their first cattle-buying trip. The animals were dirt cheap but in this land with no fences keeping them was a problem. The big estancieros had scores of gauchos to herd the cattle, but this was not an option for the Traills. Robert could hardly believe how expensive horses were here compared with cattle. But in this country with nowhere for cattle to scratch themselves the meaning of the post was revealed. The cattle might wander over the forty-five square miles looking for fresher grazing but the desire for friction always brought them back to the peon's *rascadero*. Later Robert hung a salt rock there too

and the land around the post became latticed with innu-
merable lines of desire as the animals came back again
and again to rub and lick.

At Christmas the heat began. Robert was amazed by
it. He had grown up in a country where it had rained
almost every day. It had been hot on the boat when they
crossed the equator, but there had always been a breeze.
Here at midday when there was no wind the plain was
as hot as a furnace. When the heat became unbearable,
Robert and Edmund would lie down in the paltry shade
of the *pajas bravas* and wait for the *pampero*, the cool
south-west wind that picked up as the afternoon wore
on. It was too far to go back to what Edmund liked to
call the house. They did not dare to ride their horses in
the middle of the day when the water supplies were so
patchy.

Alice had grown used to spending most of the day alone.
It was almost a relief after the relentless intimacy of the
nights when she, Robert and Edmund slept together in
their one-room hut. She had hung up a linen sheet to
divide her and Robert's side of the room from the straw
palliasse where Edmund slept, but there was no privacy
from sound. When the day was at its hottest Alice would
lie down on the floor and press her cheek to the cool
smooth surface and try not to think about anything.

In the afternoons she would put off lighting the fire for
as long as she could. If she lit it too soon it became unbearable in the hut but if she left it too late the fire would not
be hot enough to cook the meat when the men came back
from the fields. Alice hated cutting the meat, forcing a
knife through gristly sinew and yellow fat. She longed to
eat something else – a potato, a slice of bread – but beef
was the only food in plentiful supply. Once they killed a

steer they had to eat it as quickly as possible as there was no way of keeping the meat in this heat.

On New Year's Day Robert rode over to the nearest pueblo, a journey of about three days, and brought back a dairy cow. None of them knew how to milk it. The peon's boy had to show them. Milking the cow was the part of the day that Alice came to enjoy most. She liked to put her head against the cow's warm flank and feel its steady pulse.

Alice rarely thought of her family but she did miss her dog, Bubbles. She wondered who would be looking after him now.

In the evenings Robert and Edmund would fall asleep almost as soon as it got dark, exhausted by their labours. While they had candles Alice would spend the evening writing letters that were never sent, or reading. The first year she had only two books, the Bible and *Can You Forgive Her?* by Anthony Trollope. But most evenings she would sit in the dark listening to her husband and his brother muttering in their sleep.

Alice had been six months in her new home before she met another woman. Robert had taken the biggest, fattest cattle to Coronda so that they could be slaughtered for their hides, leaving Edmund to look after the livestock and his wife. Robert felt odd leaving Edmund in charge but his brother was such a bad rider that it would have been impossible for him to handle the livestock on his own, and somebody had to stay with Alice. He remembered what the British Consul had said about the Indian massacres in Fraile Muerto.

Before he left, Robert showed Alice how to fire a rifle. It was important that she knew how to protect herself against all comers. But he still felt strange leaving her alone with Edmund. He drove the cattle as fast as he could to Coronda for 'trooping' to the *saladero* in Rosario, where they would be killed and the hides tanned and sold. With the money he made from selling the steers he engaged another man and he made sure that this one had a wife. She would be able to help Alice, and though Robert preferred not to think about this, she could act as a chaperone.

The first day that Robert was away, Edmund and Alice hardly spoke. Edmund was out all day with the cattle, and Alice tried to clear the thistles that had sprung up around the house, so tall that they blocked all light into the *rancho*. As the thistle heads ripened they exploded with a little pop releasing showers of thistledown into the air. Alice hacked at the stems with her *facón*, the long-bladed knife the gauchos used, but they were tough, and she needed to swing her blade two or three times before the plant fell. When Edmund came back rather later than usual he found Alice asleep on the mattress, her face and hair covered with a white blanket of thistledown.

The next day Edmund was digging a ditch to mark the eastern boundary of their land when he felt a nip of cold at his neck. He looked up and saw a heavy black blanket of cloud moving towards him, the cold wind rushing ahead like a warning. The flash of lightning lit up the plain as he got on his horse. The usual heat haze fell away and he could see the house glowing like a purple bruise against the quicksilver sky. His horse, terrified, galloped faster than Edmund could handle. He dug his fingers into the horse's mane and clung on, unable to steer. He prayed that the horse was heading towards the house. Suddenly there was a clap of thunder, the loudest noise Edmund had ever heard, the horse reared and Edmund fell to the ground, his fall broken by a clump of thistles. The horse galloped off in ever-widening arcs of panic, so Edmund picked himself up and stumbled in what he hoped was the direction of home. The sky had gone dark again: he could hardly tell where it ended and the land began. He opened his mouth to shout for Alice but no sound emerged. He realized that he must have been screaming all along.

The wind snaked around his neck. As he found his way onto an old animal trail he was hit by eddies of dust and thistledown. He almost choked before he found his way back to the house. Just as he made out its squat outline in the geysers of debris, the clouds broke and hailstones the size of hens' eggs came pelting out of the sky. One hit him in the eye just as he reached the doorway. Blinded by the warm trickle of blood he groped his way inside, reaching out for Alice. He felt her hand grip him tightly and then start back as if stung. He was feeling for her when another hailstone pierced the fragile grass roof and hit him on the shoulder. Alice, her hand sticky now, dragged him down to the floor and pulled their rickety wooden table, their only piece of furniture, over their heads. They crouched there together for a time they could not measure, listening to the thuds of the hailstones on the table above them. When the icy chips from the sky had softened into rain they went outside, and there on the edge of the sky underneath the veil of black was a streak of silver; the storm was passing.

Edmund was too exhausted by the storm to begin to repair the roof of the hut. One corner had survived the hail and the ground beneath was still fairly dry. Edmund lay down thankfully on the hard ground and passed out.

In the morning, the light struck him strangely, assaulting him from unfamiliar angles through the lace-like tatters of the roof. Alice stood framed by the doorway. I needn't have bothered, she said, waving at the thistles which lay flattened as if felled by a giant scythe. Edmund wondered for a moment what she meant. Outside, the landscape had been scourged by the storm; the *pajas bravas*, the cardoon-like thistles, the termite mounds all gone. The *pampero* had reclaimed its territory.

Only the scratching post remained; already the cows were hitching their rumps against it, moving into position for the day ahead.

It took Edmund a few hours to find the body of his horse; the flies were already clustering around the charred black-and-red hole in its side where the lightning had pierced it. Edmund could hear his mother's voice telling him that this was a sign from God, that he had been saved because he was one of the elect. But the feeling of belonging to a Secret Society of the Saved had gone. The certainties of the faith he had grown up with were fading in this empty arena, thousands of miles from the prayers, the services, the conversations where each member of the family tried to cap another's quotation from the Bible. In his present world ruled by the capriciousness of Nature, the feeling of divine superiority that had kept his family buoyant through the humiliations of his childhood was in as many tatters as the roof of the *rancho*. Here there was only luck.

As he pulled the halter off the horse's corpse and hoisted the sheepskin he used in place of a saddle onto his back he noticed something white and gleaming in the grass beyond. He was going to ignore it but something about its roundness in this sea of jagged stumps attracted him. He put down his burdens and picked up what he realized was an egg. It was bigger than any egg he had ever seen before, the shell creamy and thick like parchment. There was no sign of any nest: it was as if the same wind that had annihilated the vegetation all around had carefully picked up this egg and gently set it down here without a crack.

When he got back to the house Alice was vainly trying to get the water out of the hollows of the floor using an improvised broom made of thistles. It was activity for its own sake; the sun was already beginning to climb in the sky and the water was disappearing under its hot stare. Edmund showed her his find. Ostrich, she said, a fleeting memory of a fan her mother once had clouding her face. Breakfast, said Edmund, as he realized how hungry he was.

It took them ages to coax a fire out of the sodden thistles but they agreed that the scrambled ostrich egg was the finest thing they had ever eaten. Even the brackish water from the waterhole tasted better when sipped from the half-ovals of the shell.

When Robert returned that night with the new hired hand and his wife, he rode through miles of flattened countryside, picking out the sad mounds of dead cows. The storm had missed him and his party; he wondered what force could have changed the landscape overnight. As the evidence of devastation got worse, he kicked his horse into a gallop until he could make out the shape of his house, but it was only when he saw the thin ribbon of black smoke curling out against the spreading bruise of the sky that he let the horse's pace slow. As he finally got to the *rancho* he saw it clearly as if for the first time. He looked into the faces of his wife and his brother and saw something he had not seen before. He ran his hand so hard over the dents in the kitchen table where the hailstones had fallen that it came out laced with brown splinters.

That night he and Edmund finished the bottle of brandy they had brought with them from Dublin, whilst Alice and the hired woman cooked great ribs of beef on the smoky fire.

TWELVE

Two years later the brothers were prosperous enough to build a proper house, a wood-and-brick estancia with a verandah down one side. The lombardy poplars that they had planted when they arrived were already nearly twenty feet tall and protected the house from the worst of the wind and lent some blessed shade.

The Traills could hardly believe how quickly things grew: a plant or a tree that would take a lifetime to establish at home grew here like a weed. Already, the empty plain that had confronted them when they arrived was dotted with clumps of trees, each one a sign of hope and habitation.

The first few years were the hardest. Things could so easily have gone the way of the British Consul's direst predictions. A British settler, Richard Seymour, who had been in Argentina since 1849, wrote a letter to *The Times* in 1870 complaining about the large number of younger sons who, '*under the pretence of becoming farmers, simply pass their time going from one estancia to another, merely amusing themselves and staying as long as their entertainers would keep them.*' But the Traills, surprisingly in view of what came later, worked hard and made a success of the estancia. If they had bought their land in 1868, just two years later, they would have paid over ten times as much for it, as the British had begun to build a railway line connecting Rosario with Santa Fé. The Traills, whose land lay midway between the two, could not have been more fortunately placed. And five years after they bought their land they were able to fence it off with the new American invention of barbed wire.

Barbed wire put an end to the wild nomadic life of the pampas. The marauding bands of Indians and gauchos that caused such terror to settlers in the 1860s and early 1870s had disappeared by the end of the decade, as the frontier was pushed further and further back. To begin with it was a fairly equal battle; small farms like the Traills' could easily be picked off in a raid. The older, more established estancias with their armed ranch hands who could defend themselves were further away from the frontier. The Argentine army instead of protecting its own frontiers was engaged in a war with Paraguay which lasted until 1870. It was a lawless time. The murder rate was one for every 900 inhabitants, compared to the figure in England at the time which was one murder per 178,000 inhabitants.

On New Year's Day in 1872 a band of Indians and gauchos descended on the settlement of Tandil south of Buenos Aires and massacred thirty-six of its inhabitants, all of them European. The culprits were never apprehended. This act was reported as an atrocity as far away as England where the government, egged on by public opinion, made a formal protest to the Argentine authorities.

The Argentine press responded with outrage. An editorial in *La Nación* protested that:

In Ireland, agrarian crime is unchecked by the authorities, property is destroyed and people are killed; nobody will testify, and the culprits go free. If that happened in Argentina what would be said? . . . Foreign residents already have more rights than the natives; simply by being a foreigner you can have your case tried before the Supreme Court. Foreigners have more guarantees than the natives, but they want even more; they are trying to create a nation within a nation, a city within a city. They are not satisfied unless they bring the diplomatic corps into everything.

The relationship between Britain and Argentina was touchy even then, but the point the editorial makes about the foreigners trying to create a nation within a nation could have been written about the Traills.

They had settled in Argentina, true, but it was the land they engaged with, not the nation. Their sense of identity, their economic sustenance, came through the umbilical cord of the railway which connected them directly with Britain. The railways were a symbol of this nation within a nation. Financed by British capital and built by British engineers, they connected the agricultural areas to the great port of Buenos Aires, imitating the river systems in the way they drained towards the harbour, carrying beef and grain directly to the markets of Europe. Argentine nationalists would later complain that these railways were built to service the British and European economies, not to develop the Argentine one. There were no branch lines connecting one Argentine city to another, the traffic was all one-way. When the first refrigerated ship was invented in 1876, this process accelerated as Argentine beef, formerly only a by-product of the tanning industry, became the country's major export.

The Traills were part of the Fray Bentos gravy train.

The Traill estancia came to be known as Las Limpias. *Limpio* in Spanish means 'clean, pure, innocent'. Las Limpias translated literally means 'the clean women'. Most estancias were named after physical landmarks – as with Los Olivos. A name with no topographical origin like Limpias was an oddity. Did the Traills choose this name to emphasize their white Anglo-Saxon purity in this land of rank smells and swarthy skins, but because of their sketchy knowledge of Spanish they got the gender wrong? Or was the name coined by the locals, an ironic nickname for the gringos, made all the more insulting by the feminine ending, which the Traills adopted not really understanding its real import? Maybe Limpias refers to the whiteness and quantity of Alice's laundry. In a land of single men and rough mud huts, Alice's lace-trimmed chemises and bloomers fluttering in the wind must have been something of a landmark.

Or could Limpias mean 'the shining ones', a way of signalling that the Traills were part of the elect, 'in the world but not of the world'? Robert and Edmund were a long way from the evangelical certainties of their childhood, physically and mentally removed from the clannish circle of right-minded thinkers they had grown up in. The brothers' formal religious beliefs may have faded in the heat of the 34th parallel but not their sense of being part of an elite. The Traills had been born and brought up in Ireland but they described themselves as British. They took their nationality with them to Argentina, there was no reason to relinquish it. They were in the nation but not of the nation, living the life of Protestant landowners in a Catholic country. And each piece of good fortune must have reinforced that belief. They had been chosen.

THIRTEEN

The house that Robert and Edmund built still stands – but only just. When it was built it must have been visible for miles, the only interruption to the endless connection between land and sky. Now the shell of the house is hidden behind a thicket of lombardy poplars which tower over the lush green plain.

I could see the trees from the garden of my cousin Derek's house Las Limpias Two. I had driven here with him from Buenos Aires, a straight black line of five hundred miles. Two hours into the journey we started to drive through pueblos called Murphy, Armstrong, Kavanagh and Driscoll. The Irish may have been assimilated in one generation but they left their mark on the landscape. Every so often we would pass the wooden H shape of an estancia gate with a wooden sign saying 'Media Luna' or 'Escobar' at the end of a long avenue of trees. Derek would gesture at these amulets of civilization.

'That's the Gibson place. Old man Gibson shot himself last year. I think it's up for sale now,' or 'The MacMahons live there. James still runs the estancia and Eric is the

President of Coca-Cola.' Every twenty miles or so there was another gate, another scrap of the empire that never was, legacies of hundred-year-old hopes.

About five hours out of the city, Derek pulled the pickup off the main highway onto a dirt road. Having been silent for a while, he turned to me with a little snort of irritation.

'The Traill lands would have started about here. There was a time when they had two hundred square miles. Two hundred miles of the best farming country in the world. If only they'd held onto it . . .' He banged the wheel of his Brazilian-made pickup.

'If they'd had the sense to keep hold of it then I might be driving a decent car.'

Derek's vehicle did not have air-conditioning or even four-wheel drive, a lack that was becoming apparent as we drove through the heat of the day, slipping about on the road which recent rains had turned into a river of mud.

Derek was my first cousin once removed, the son of my grandmother's sister Daphne, the bull breeder. Derek had been born in the Argentine but emigrated to Canada in his twenties. Like the Traills a century before, Derek had been brought up by a widowed mother. Like the Traills Derek had grown up landless in a society where land ownership was paramount. Brought up British in the Argentina of the thirties, Derek had two choices: to manage another British estancia or emigrate. The possibility of following a career in Buenos Aires was simply not an option.

Despite having spent all his life in the Argentine, Derek's Spanish wasn't good enough to get him into an Argentine university even if he had considered the possibility. Derek went to university in England and then, displaying the family fondness for frontiers, he moved to the westernmost edge of British Columbia. He married, had three children, divorced and then when his mother died, he came back to the Argentine to work the land which he had inherited from her.

Las Limpias Two is basically a prefab. Daphne built it after the war as a temporary measure and had never got round to moving out. It has small windows and a flat roof, not unlike the *rancho* that Robert and Edmund built when they first arrived in Argentina. The first time I went there, as a teenager, it was midwinter and the wind blew hard through the gaps in the polystyrene walls. Now it was summer and the low ceilings made the rooms dark and oppressive. The recent storms had blown down the power lines so that after the sudden pampas sunset, the house would lie in darkness until Derek managed to find the kerosene lamps.

In other ways too Derek's life had come full circle from the Traills' first years in the Argentine. The plot of land he farmed was only three and a half thousand *hectáreas*, a tiny fraction of the original Traill stake, but like them he had never farmed before and he was doing nearly all the work himself. He did employ one man but was considered eccentric by his Argentine neighbours for giving him the whole weekend off. The man had a wife, who in the normal Argentine course of things would have cooked and cleaned, but Derek, after years of living in Canada, felt uncomfortable about having a maid. Despite the discomforts of his situation and the constant reminder of a lost family fortune, Derek did not seem to be a disappointed man. I think he left his disappointments behind in Canada; the life of a pioneer farmer suited him very well. Like all farmers he moaned about the prices he got for his crops; it had been a very bad year for sorghum but his real complaint was that the scrap of Traill land he was left with was the very worst bit, the low-lying strip of river plain that flooded every winter. I felt sorry for him until I asked him what the land he farmed was worth. At today's prices about a million dollars, he said. But can you imagine what value all the land the Traills owned would have . . . Now that's something to think about.

I tried to work it out but the number had so many noughts on it that I gave up. I began to see why Derek minded so much that the Traills had failed to hold onto their land: with so many noughts involved a few of them might even have trickled down to me.

I slept that night in the same bed I had slept in nineteen years ago. Behind the brown polystyrene walls I could hear scuttling. My great-aunt Daphne had always slept with an axe under her bed; in the event of a fire she could use it to hack her way out of the house. I lay as still as I could. I did not want to puncture the walls by a careless movement and let out the rats. I felt alone again that night: not eighteen and starting out, but six years old, trying not to mind the dark and the sounds of murderers. I wanted to call home to tell Ottilie I was coming back, to hear the sound of my husband's voice, to remind myself that home was still there. But the lines were down, felled by the storm. I tried hard to remember why I had come; in the dark I could just feel the familiar smooth-sided edges of despair. I had gone too far to get back, I was going to fall, I wanted to fall.

In the morning I woke up with my hands crossed over my chest like a corpse, the bedclothes hardly creased. It was the way I used to wake up every morning when I was a child.

At breakfast Derek asked me if I wanted to see the old

Limpias. It was a slow day for sorghum, evidently. To get there we would have to ride: the roads were impenetrably muddy. I once heard the biographer Richard Holmes say that the only way to experience a landscape in the same way as a nineteenth-century subject was to get out of the car and walk, or in this case ride, as I am sure the Traills never walked anywhere.

Derek found me an old polo pony, with a mouth so sensitive that you only had to brush the reins and the mare would turn instantly. Compared to the tough old nags I had learnt to ride on in the New Forest it was like driving a Lamborghini. I tried to adopt the same pose as Derek: back straight, reins held casually in one hand. In his jeans and white hat, Derek looked like one of the characters from *The Virginian*, a TV series of my childhood, but then I could only see his back as Derek liked to ride at a fast trot, his body never leaving the saddle.

He gestured to a clump of poplars on the horizon, the tallest ones for miles. That's the old Traill place, he said. It did not look that far away but in this *Alice-through-the-Looking-Glass* country distances were never what they seemed. The vast expanse of pampas that the Traills had once owned was now trellised by barbed-wire fences enclosing bright green crops or black-and-white cattle. Every inch of this soil, which had been so casually acquired by the Traills, was now scrutinized, cultivated and owned by other people. In Argentina the law of inheritance is based on the Napoleonic code and all children receive equal portions of their parents' estate. The good Catholic Argentines who had bought tracts of land from the Traills would probably have had nine or ten children and then thirty or forty grandchildren: the scraps of land that reached the third generation were very small indeed. The once smooth surface of the pampas was now crazed like the glaze on my grandmother's Chinese horse.

The fields around the Limpias were being grazed by dairy cattle, tended by a man in a beret. He was delighted, *encantado*, he said for us to look at the house. When I told him that I had come from England, he said that he was from Corrientes himself and he wished he could go back there. His master worked him too hard at the *tambo* (dairy): one of these days he would just leave.

The patch of ground where the ruins of the house stood was surrounded by barbed wire. When we got to the fence my horse reared – something about the place frightened her, and she refused to move. The cowherd offered to hold the horses as we climbed through the barbed wire. The grass around the house was high, a reminder of a former lushness before the cows turned everything to mud. Rising out of the long grass was a charrupon tree. One of the few indigenous trees of the pampas, they were a very rare sight now as their famously hard wood had been used by the British for railway sleepers. The tree was gnarled and black, its frilly spring foliage slightly absurd, an old lady in her granddaughter's dress. The sun was high in the sky by that time, but the air inside the house was cool, protected by the remains of the wooden shutters that still hung at the windows.

The house was single storey, a series of five rooms which opened into one another. Originally there would, I suppose, have been a verandah which meant that you could enter each room separately. The ceilings were high, about twice the height of Daphne's prefab, the windows tall and narrow with deep stone sills. It was a house built for darkness, a refuge from the glare of the plain. The air was dusty now with falling plaster and ancient cobwebs but it must once have been as cold and sweet as water. As I pushed the door open into the second room, a bedroom perhaps, I saw the walls had been stencilled all over in blue. Had Alice spent hours stippling the blue pigment onto the white distemper walls, wanting to turn this house into a home? I thought of my mother stencilling the walls of her poky house in Swanage. An ameliorative instinct passed from one generation to the next.

Derek was impatient with my interest in paint finishes. He wanted to show me the kitchen, identifiable by the stone sink under the window. Look, he said, no running water or electricity. That's the trouble with the Traills, they really had no idea how to make themselves comfortable.

I thought of Las Limpias Two, where he now lived, and agreed.

See that? – he pointed to a corner of the kitchen ceiling – that's a trapdoor up to the roof. If the women were alone in the house and they heard Indians they had to get up on that roof pretty bloody quick and haul up the flag to let the men know they were in danger.

The trapdoor had long since fallen down, but bizarrely there was still a ladder lying on the floor. I picked it up and set it against the wall. The rungs were still solid, made no doubt from charrupon wood. I climbed up and pushed my way rather gingerly through the remains of the hatch. Half in, half out, I clambered onto the roof, hoping that the plaster would not give way beneath my feet. My eye had become so used to the flat plains of the pampas, to a life lived at ground level, that I felt almost dizzy with the change in perspective. At this height I could see how endless the landscape still was, how the distinct mosaic of ownership and inheritance was blurred by the relentless sweep of the land to the horizon. Although I was only about twenty-five feet above the ground the flatness made it feel much higher. My terrors of the night before lifted, swept away by a rush of elation that pushed me to the edge of the parapet. The ground below looked soft, welcoming.

I wanted quite badly to jump, but somewhere I was still worrying that the roof would cave in. Both my parents were there at that moment, my mother pushing me forward, my father worrying that the structure was not sound. I took a step forward and my foot met with no resistance. I could hear Derek's voice calling up. 'Are you all right up there?'

The balance had shifted. I scrambled back down the ladder into Alice's kitchen.

'Alice's gravestone is meant to be here somewhere,' said Derek.

I thought I'd found it when I stumbled over a small white tablet sticking out of the ground about five yards from the house. There were some letters carved in the stone, but not many, not enough surely for the mother of eight. I tried to make them out with my finger. I could feel the right angle of an L, the straight channel of an I: the word inscribed on the stone was not Alice but Lightning. Underneath was a date: 1896. Not a beloved wife but a beloved pet. Derek came over.

'Lightning was Bob Traill's best polo pony,' he said. 'When the animal died he insisted on burying it standing up with its saddle on. It must have taken them bloody ages to dig a big enough pit.'

The house had been lived in by an Argentine family after it had been sold by the Traills. They had demolished the verandah and some of the bedrooms to build a spacious garage from breeze-blocks. But the floor plan of the original house was still visible; from the block that was still standing another wing extended like the bottom of an L. Each room of this ghostly annexe was built on slightly different foundations, as if this part of the house had been extended several times: a house that had grown as children were born, married, had children of their own, or perhaps a house that had had no choice but to contain each generation.

This is where my grandmother Eileen had lived until adolescence. A house with no running water, no electricity and no neighbours within an hour's ride. Not like Surrey at all.

We never found my great-great-grandmother Alice's grave. Derek told me later that she drank herself to death. The only thing anyone remembered about her, he said, was how strong her Irish accent was. My grandmother had been named Alice Eileen, but for some reason had rejected Alice, preferring to be known as Eileen. Poor Alice, a woman who nobody wanted to remember.

Except for me. I wanted to know why a woman who had deserted everything she knew for what she thought was love, had left in this family of legends almost nothing behind her, except a chance remark of my mother's and an unmarked grave. I tried to fill in the ruins of Las Limpias, to recreate the space that my great-great-grandmother had lived in.

The house took two months to build. All the stone had to be brought to the site by mule. One mule train bringing the stone from Rosario had followed the wrong track and had to double back adding another two or three hundred miles to the journey, delaying the build by three weeks. Robert had decided on the sort of house he wanted after a visit to their nearest English neighbours, the Dobbses, who lived only a hundred and fifty miles away in the Rosario direction. He had spent a night there on his way back from Rosario and had been amazed at how civilized the place had been: tiled floors instead of adobe, a verandah to keep the rooms shady, a parlour with a piano and a bookcase. Edith Dobbs had even planted a rose bush. Of course, thought Robert, Dobbs isn't likely to go home, but he was impressed even so. He looked at Edith's neat pile of hair and the white pinafore she wore to protect her dress and thought of Alice as she looked when he came in from the fields, her face shiny from the fire, her hair slipping down her neck, her dress spattered with fat. After dinner Edith played the piano while Robert and her husband discussed the rumour Robert had heard in Rosario about the Great Southern Railway company building a line from Rosario to Santa Fé.

Robert was fired up by the thought of the railway. On the ride from Rosario his head had been churning with the possibilities, but Dobbs, who had settled his land ten years ago, was cynical. That railway's been coming for years, he said. I've stopped believing what I hear in this country. Not everybody wants a railway as much as we do. Those big cattle barons up in Santa Fé don't want anyone touching their land. And no one's going to build a railway when there are Indians about. Did you hear about Edward Gibson – had his throat slit by one of his own men. The murderer's disappeared, everyone knows who he is, where he is, but no one's making a blind bit of effort to catch him. What a country.

Robert agreed that this was a country that didn't know the meaning of fair play.

Dobbs must have been ten or fifteen years older than Robert and yet with their long beards they could both have been any age between twenty and fifty. Robert had let his beard grow on the boat. It had passed the awkward stage and had turned into something really quite luxuriant by the time he disembarked in Buenos Aires. In this country beards such as his were a rarity. Native-born Argentines preferred to be clean-shaven or to wear neatly trimmed goatees. Robert thought these barbershop creations were rather effeminate. He felt rather proud when people on the streets of Rosario stared at his beard and whispered, 'El Inglés.' He had tried to persuade Edmund to grow one, but his brother had so far refused to see the benefits of hiding his chin.

The house was finished at the end of the summer of 1870. It was exactly like the Dobbses' except for an extra room for Edmund. The following year they had to build an extra room for little Bob. Alice had discovered she was pregnant with excitement tempered with a portion of regret and fear. Regret for something she didn't quite understand and fear at having to give birth with no one to help her besides Concepción, the peon's wife. She would have so liked her mother or one of her sisters to be there. Now, in the evenings, instead of staring into the darkness she made baby clothes, decorating each seam with precise rows of faggoting, using stitches her mother had shown her in the drawing room of Fitzwilliam Street. Sometimes she woke up in the night disturbed by the baby's kicking and as she stumbled to the outhouse she wondered whether she would ever see her family again. She knew that Robert would never agree to let her bring up the child as a Catholic. He liked to pretend that her Catholicism did not exist, and she was careful not to remind him of it. But she knew that he was ashamed of her, that he did not want to introduce her to the Dobbses, even though Edith Dobbs had sent her a note offering help at her confinement. Robert had insisted that as a medical student he had delivered scores of babies and needed no assistance. Concepción, who did not speak Robert's language, had sent word to her cousin Inés who attended all the births in the pueblo of San Jorge.

When the pains began the men were in the fields. By the time they returned Alice was bearing down, screaming with agony. Robert ran into the bedroom and came out instantly, looking sick. The babies he had delivered in Dublin had all come to him neatly wrapped in white napkins from the midwives: he did not remember all this noise and blood. He sat on the verandah with Edmund, pulling at his beard every time he heard Alice scream. In the morning when he was a father he caught sight of his reflection in Edmund's shaving mirror and noticed with satisfaction that his beard had at last achieved the volume and shape that he had so admired on the cricketer Grace.

The baby had blond hair and very pale blue eyes that never darkened. He was called Robert after his father and grandfather but was always known as Bob.

Alice felt so tired after he was born. She would lie on her bed trying to feed the baby without falling asleep. Before the birth she had found it difficult to sleep. Now she could hardly stay awake. The baby was sweet but he never wanted to sleep when she did. Alice knew that her sleepiness was beginning to irritate Robert. After a long day working in the fields he did not want to come home to find his wife with hair coming down, the baby screaming and the dinner not ready, but Alice saw his angry face and found herself yawning. Sometimes Edmund would come back early and play with the baby while Alice tried to push her hair into the neat chignon she had worn in Dublin. But two years in the sun had left her hair coarse and frizzy and there was no maid to coax it into shape.

Six months after Bob was born Alice realized she was pregnant again. The fatigue got worse. Sometimes she spent the whole day staring at a patch of sky through the window, Bob crawling about the floor at her feet. She was sitting like this when Concepción, who had been doing the laundry, appeared in the doorway. '*Los indios, señora, los indios.*' She mimed a man firing a gun. Alice looked at the woman as if she was underwater, a message coming from a long way off. But then Bob, startled by the urgency in Concepción's voice, began to cry and Alice suddenly surfaced. She could feel the hot salty taste of fear pricking in her mouth.

She picked up the baby, who was screaming now. She went to the door and saw the cloud of dust from the Indians' horses strung out along the horizon like beads. Concepción had found the ladder and was holding it against the kitchen wall. Alice knew she had to find something: what? The gun, where was the gun? She tore round the house, moving faster than she had for months, trying to find her weapon, the baby still screaming on her hip. At last she found it on the shelf in Edmund's room. Was it loaded? She wasn't sure. At the foot of the ladder she hesitated. Should she give the baby to Concepción, who was reaching down to help her, or the gun? The baby, of course it had to be the baby, the baby had to be safe.

Somehow she got up the ladder onto the roof. She could see the Indians' faces now. Reaching down she kicked the ladder away with her foot. Where was Robert? Concepción had tied her skirt to the flagpole, Alice had never quite got round to making a flag. The women shouted, their voices lost in supplication in the wind. Alice picked up her gun and fired. The charge made her reel back in shock, but

Concepción's shout told her that she had seen something move on the other side. The men had heard, they were coming back.

Alice could just see them on the other side: they were moving but not fast enough. The Indians were full size now, minutes away from the wooden corrals to the north of the house. Concepción started to say a Hail Mary, and without thinking Alice found herself joining in, the familiar words smoothing down the jagged edges of her fear. The next time she opened her eyes she saw that the Indians were in the corral trying to herd the cattle. If it was the cattle the Indians were after then there was a chance that Robert would get to the house first.

She peered at the Indians again, her lips still knitting Hail Marys, blessed art thou amongst women. One of them was close enough for her to see his face, which was thin and brown: Alice had never seen anyone with such dark skin. The man looked up at her, laughed and turned his horse's head in the direction of the house, but a sudden stampede of bullocks cut him off and he was swept away in the turbulent stream of men and animals. The laugh was the worst thing. Alice suddenly felt cold, Hail Mary full of grace forming on her numbed lips. She had once overheard Robert and Edmund talking about what the Indians had done at Fraile Muerto, but they would never openly discuss such things in front of her. The words 'a fate worse than death' had sounded strange when Robert said it but she knew what he meant. She raised the gun to her shoulder and aimed at the laughing Indian. The shot went wide but the noise wiped out the echo in her head. She found herself turning to reach for the baby.

She was still lying curled up on the roof, Bob clutched in the bend of her curved body, her fingers telling an imaginary rosary, when Edmund found her. Robert had gone straight to the corral to save the cattle.

The story of the Indian raid became Bob's favourite bedtime story but only the way his father told it. His mother hesitated too much and did not put the bangs in the right places. He liked to sit on his father's knee when he was describing galloping after the Indians. He liked the way his father's legs pumped up and down in pursuit. His mother never did exciting things with her knees. When she got to the Indian bit she would hug him really tightly and sometimes she would cry. Once Uncle Edmund heard her crying, he came in and picked him up. 'Why does mother always cry when she talks about the Indians?' Bob asked his uncle.

'Because she thought you were all going to be killed.'

'But Father would have killed them first.'

'Very possibly, but your mother was all alone at the time. If she hadn't been so brave those Indians might have murdered all of you.'

Bob did not know what murdered meant but he knew what Indians did – his father always showed him by drawing his finger very sharply across his throat, making a hoowitt noise as he did so. When he had fights with his younger sister May he liked to pull her back by the ears and draw his finger across her fat little throat and make the same hoowitt noise. This always made Father laugh. Mother didn't like it though.

Exactly eighteen months after May was born, Alice had another son. As she lay back after the final push Alice saw Inés, the midwife, crossing herself. When Alice looked at the baby she saw that it had been assembled carelessly: the arms were too short, the legs stuck out at funny angles, it did not look as though it had much chance of surviving.

Robert whistled when he saw the infant and decided to name his new son Basil after his elder brother who had died in Cairo having failed to make his fortune in India. It would have been an unfortunate name to give a normal child. But despite all these handicaps Basil survived, and every time that Alice looked at him she knew he was her punishment for not bringing her children up in the True Faith. The next child, another son, was born only a year later. He was named Edmund after his paternal uncle but was always called Ned which, although he never knew it, was also the name of his mother's brother. Ned had the Traill colouring: blond hair, pale blue eyes,

Alice saw nothing of herself in him at all. She had been hoping for another daughter. After years spent with no female company at all she was hoping to have a flock of girls to soften the hard plains of the pampas. She remembered the hours she had spent whispering with her sisters, the apple peels they had thrown over their shoulders hoping to catch the initials of their future husbands on All Hallow's Eve. The nights when she and her sister Bridget would plan their futures right down to the ages and sexes of their children. Then her family had gone boy girl boy girl girl girl: Patrick, Deirdre, Francis, Catherine, Theresa, Clare. They all had dark hair and dark blue eyes like her: the boys were strong and handsome, the girls had calm expressions and white skin. The youngest, Clare, was so good that she was going to become a nun.

Alice kept her fictional family with the rest of her Dublin memories, folded away tightly at the back of her mind – too precious, too painful to unravel. Sometimes she would try and superimpose those imagined children on her real offspring, but the fit was too loose, the real children too fair and too noisy. The family of her dreams had been quiet and loving; her real children were only quiet in front of their father. Sometimes she would try and gather them round her to tell them a story but within minutes Bob or May would fidget and Basil would cry because Ned was sitting on her lap. In those days Robert treated his children precisely as he himself had been treated as a child. His childhood had been full of serious talks punctuated by beatings. 'Spare the rod and spoil the child' had been one of his mother's favourite expressions. With no man to administer punishments his mother had had to whip her children herself, an act she hated but she did not want her boys to grow up wild because their father was dead.

Robert, too, was trying to make up for something when he punished his children. He did not want *his* children to run wild in this country with no fences. Robert had had to beat little Bob twice for talking Spanish. He did not want his children to grow up like natives. It was Alice's job to make sure they grew up the right way, but Alice was too fond of them. The softness that he had loved in Fitzwilliam Street was irritating now. It was not the Honourable Aramintas he regretted not marrying now, but the capable women like his mother and his sister Kathleen, or even Edith Dobbs, who were always aware of their duties, who knew what to do without having to be told.

Alice could not help her upbringing, of course, but all that (Robert had almost erased the memory of Alice's Catholicism from his mind) must not be allowed to infect the children. After all, one day they would be going home: not to Ireland of course, but to England. He did not want to take back a pack of heathen savages. The sooner the boys went to a decent boarding school the better. The only advantage of living here was that they could all ride like the devil. Even Basil, whose arms were too short to hold the reins, had learnt to grip with his knees and steer with his feet. Robert had bought a special side-saddle for May in Rosario. She had started off with a sheepskin like the boys but now she was six it was time she learnt to ride like a lady. When they got to England he would buy her a proper riding habit like the one his sister wore and he would beat her if he found her riding astride again.

The beatings became more frequent as Robert and Edmund got richer and richer and the return home got correspondingly closer. The herd of cattle had trebled in the last year. They had made so much money on the last sale that they had been able to buy another fifty thousand *hectáreas* of land. In another couple of years they would be able to quadruple the size of their holdings. The railway was still to reach them but when it did . . . Robert thought of the Traill estate in Co. Antrim with satisfaction, a mere backyard compared to the amount of land he and Edmund owned.

He probably had more land than the Duke of Leinster. He wanted to go back and show off his fortune but Edmund wanted to wait, to buy even more land. Unlike Robert, Edmund did not think their present good luck could last for ever. The year before, there had been a plague of locusts which had devastated the estancias to the south, but the black cloud had not passed over Las Limpias. Every morning he had expected to find the land flattened by a giant scythe, but every morning it stretched out in front of him green and unblemished to the silver horizon. Edmund knew that Robert saw their luck as a sign of divine grace, a part of their birthright, but he could not forget the hailstorm that had killed his horse. His eyes were encased in a cobweb of lines etched by his habit of scanning the horizon for trouble. Where Robert gazed on a shining vista of unlimited possibility, Edmund peered at the four horsemen on the other side of the horizon.

*   *   *

So far Robert and Edmund had paid from their savings for all the new land they had bought, but as the rumours of the railway grew louder every day they realized that this was their last chance to expand cheaply. Against Edmund's instincts they decided to borrow money in order to buy up the land that lay between the Limpias estate and the rumoured route of the railway. But even though he winced as he signed the mortgage papers, he knew that buying this new land would give him the opportunity to build his own house. It was time for him to leave Las Limpias behind.

 When Edmund announced that he was going to build a house on the new land, Robert laughed and asked him when he was going to get married, but Alice said nothing. Edmund rode over to the new land the next day looking for a place to build his new home. Jorge, the gaucho, who rode with him took him to a spot where a well had been dug, presumably by Indians. Jorge called this spot Chirù, an Indian word that Edmund was unable to translate. After a lot of miming Edmund gathered that a famous chief was buried nearby. There was certainly a huge boulder not far from the well which looked as though it might be a memorial of some sort.

 Edmund started building his house the next day. The design was similar to Las Limpias with a verandah and a trapdoor in the kitchen roof for protection against raids from Indians or the bands of soldiers who roamed the country looking for recruits. Edmund, as a gringo, was exempt from military service but his men were not. Like Las Limpias this house had iron bars over all the windows. Edmund could barely remember the Rectory at Skull except

for the funny slitted windows that Robert told him were
there to make it easier to shoot the Catholics. As he stood
on the roof of his house putting up his flag, a Union Jack
that Alice had sewn together, he wondered what his father
would have thought of this fortified house standing isolated
in a Catholic country. He thought of his mother and now
Alice, living in houses with bars on the windows. He sometimes thought of marrying himself but the memory of Alice
lying on the roof of Las Limpias after the Indian raid had
always deterred him. It was easier to put it off till he went
home.

The day after the house was finished Robert brought
Alice and the children over in a bullock cart. Jorge had set
up an *asado*, a little way from the house and was cooking
one of the new season's lambs. The children were busy
throwing stones down the well, waiting to hear the faraway
splash. Alice sat on the verandah with Ned, her eyes blank.
Robert had admired the house extravagantly but Alice had
said very little except to offer Edmund their old kitchen
table, the one they had sheltered under during the hailstorm. Of course we've got a new one now, she said, with
so many mouths to feed. That old table would do very
nicely here. Something to remind you of Las Limpias.

Robert laughed. Eddie will be needing a bigger table
himself soon. He's not going to sit here in this fine house
all on his own for long. I expect he's got a girl in mind.
One of the Gibsons perhaps, Edith Gibson is a fine-looking
woman and an heiress too. I can see the two of you setting
up in fine style. No battered kitchen tables and bullock
carts for you. You'll have to go about in a nice new
barouche.

Edmund had never met the Gibson girl, as Robert knew,
but Alice, who had not left Las Limpias for seven years,

who had not met another English woman in that time, had no way of knowing whether her husband was serious or not. The thought of Edmund marrying made her feel tired. Everything, she thought, is happening so quickly, Edmund leaving Las Limpias, this new house, and now maybe Edmund married. She had lived with Edmund all her married life and now he was gone. Eight miles might as well be eight hundred miles. She watched numbly as Bob tried to push Basil down the well until their father, roused by Basil's screams, pushed Bob away and boxed him on the ears. Basil sniffled up to her. Apart from Ned, who was too small to have any choice, Basil was the only one who ever looked for her. She stroked his hot curly head and his stubby arms.

She could see Robert making towards them and could hear his words before he opened his mouth. 'Come on, Basil, don't be such a baby. You've got to stand up to your brother, isn't that right, Eddie?'

Edmund mumbled something about it not being a fair fight.

'All the more reason that the boy learns to defend himself. There's no excuse for cowardice. What's going to happen when he goes to school? He can't hide behind his mother's skirts then.'

Basil, who was four years old, started to cry again. Alice pulled the child onto her lap and whispered into his ear, 'Don't worry, darling, no one's going to hurt you, not while I'm around.' Robert walked away from the house in disgust, snapping the foot-high thistles with his stick as he went.

They spent the night at what Edmund called Chirù (he tried to make this foreign-sounding word as English as possible by pronouncing it to rhyme with 'yahoo'). The next day Robert, Alice and the children went back to Las

Limpias. That night Robert slept in Edmund's old room and Basil slept in his place next to Alice. Robert continued to sleep there except on the occasions when Edmund was too tired or too drunk to ride home.

The following spring was the first that Alice had not been pregnant or nursing a baby. Robert began to feel more strongly than ever that it was time to go home. He had had a letter from his sister Kathleen asking him to take on her son Anthony Synge as a farm manager. Some of his neighbours employed Argentine major-domos but Robert could not imagine leaving Las Limpias in the hands of a native. He wrote back and told her to send the boy out at once. It was too late now to worry about what his family would think of Alice. He rode over to Chirù to tell Edmund what he had done, half-hoping that Edmund would offer to stay behind to look after things. But he found to his surprise that Edmund was determined to go too.

Since leaving Las Limpias he had become friendly with the English brothers, the Dobbses, who lived at Las Lomas. Their sister Gertrude had been staying with them for the last three months and now she was going back to England. Gertrude was quiet, with a small face that seemed to droop under the weight of her mass of dark hair. She had found the heat of the Argentine summer under her brothers' corrugated-iron roof too much. The only time she dared to go out was at dawn when the ground was misty and the sky was pink. She was out one morning trying to pick some flowers for her scrapbook without much success – all the flowers were too big and fleshy – when she first saw Edmund riding to Rosario with her brothers. Edmund looked at her for a long time before he remembered to get off his horse and shake her hand. The hand was small and surprisingly cool. But it was a touch that he remembered.

He had only met her two or three times since then but he liked her aloofness, the way she looked away when she spoke, the sense that she understood more than she said. He did not want to protect her in the way that he wanted to with Alice. He just wanted to stand next to her, to be part of her stillness.

When Joshua Dobbs announced that Gertrude was going back to England, Edmund gasped, an audible snatch of air. He felt as if something was being taken from him. The next day he rode over to Las Lomas, but found the house silent and shuttered. He did not know that Gertrude was lying down in her room, he was too shy to call out. He rode away again.

Robert's plan suddenly made everything possible. He would sail to England on the same boat as Gertrude, there would be time then. Robert and Alice would come later when Kathleen's boy was settled. All Edmund's misgivings about leaving were gulped down in his euphoric relief. Hailstorms, locusts, marauding *montañeros* no longer loomed on the horizon. In his imagination he was already standing on the deck with Gertrude. It did not occur to him that she might not want to stand there with him. He had made his leap, that was enough.

Edmund proposed to Gertrude in Rio, but she waited until the boat reached Lisbon, some three weeks later, before she accepted him.

Nine months later, in the spring of 1880, Robert and Alice were ready to leave Las Limpias. Robert had been impatient to go from the moment Edmund had left, so impatient that he had hardly noticed his nephew Anthony, who had arrived a month before. He had left himself no time to worry about the boy's competence. He had managed when he was the same age, twenty-one, why shouldn't

Anthony? Things were a lot better now than they were ten years ago. The railway was a hundred miles nearer, the Indians had been driven out, there were even a few English estancias within a day's ride. All Anthony had to do was to keep the stock alive and stay out of trouble.

The boy had been surprised to meet Alice. Robert had mentioned in his letters that he was married but Anthony had been taken aback to meet a woman with a strong Dublin accent, one very different from his mother's. In fact, Aunt Alice as he felt he ought to call her was not at all like the women in his family, his mother or his grand-mother. Anthony did not know quite what made her different, but he had never seen a woman spend so long doing nothing. Even when the house was in a frenzy of preparation for the forthcoming trip home, Aunt Alice would spend hours on the verandah looking at the horizon without even a piece of embroidery to occupy her. Once Anthony had thought she was asleep, but as he crept past her to his bedroom he noticed that despite her stillness her eyes were wide open. Anthony could not remember his mother or his grandmother ever being still: 'The devil makes work for idle hands' was one of his grandmother's favourite sayings. He wondered what she would make of Aunt Alice. For his own part he quite liked her: she was the only woman in his life who did not tell him what to do.

Alice watched the bullock carts being loaded. They were leaving Las Limpias with less luggage than they had arrived with. She had packed a trunk full of her and the children's clothes, but Robert had told her to put it all back: they would buy everything new when they got to England. They could hardly walk through Piccadilly dressed like peons, he had said. Alice said nothing. She was trying to remember a time when she had not been able to see the horizon in every direction. As a child she had watched the Queen ride through Temple Bar in Dublin. She wondered whether she would see her riding through the streets of London: the sounds of that day, the cheers, the bands, her nurses muttering came back to her. She realized that the only music her children had ever heard were the lullabies she sang them at night and the *habaneras* that Concepción sang when she hung out the washing. She would need to teach them 'God Save the Queen'. She would have to explain to them about hills.

On the boat the children stood for hours on deck, hanging onto the rails and looking down at the sea. They found the sensation of being up quite intoxicating. Bob had never been so high in the air before and he was sure that he could fly if only he could slip off those railings; he knew the air would catch him and blow him away. But the Scottish nursemaid that Robert had hired in Buenos Aires tied ropes to the belts of the four children so that they went about the deck leashed like a pack of dogs. All Bob's dreams of flight ended in sharp tugs on the rope.

'Honestly, Mrs Traill, if I didn't have those children tied up they'd all be feeding the fishes by now. You'd think that Master Bob at eight would be a bit more sensible, but I've only got to turn my head for a second and he's up on those rails ready to jump off. I believe the child really thinks he can fly.'

Alice tried to summon the indignation that the nurse clearly felt was owing at this point but secretly she sympathized with her son. There were times when she stood at the ship's rails and felt how easy, how desirable it would be to commit herself to the air. She looked over the edge and the drop seemed like an embrace. She thought that she too should perhaps have a rope tied round her waist. Only the sound of her children's voices cut through the fumes of temptation which filled her head. It was the weather that saved her. After leaving Rio the ship ran into storm after storm, which made it impossible for anyone to go on deck. Being swept overboard by a forty-foot wave was not the surrender for which Alice was yearning.

And in England, on dry land, there was nowhere to fall. Edmund had taken a house for them in Norfolk in the middle of a broad plain as flat as the pampas they had left behind. As she walked through the rose garden Alice could still see the horizon in every direction. She walked in the garden every day after breakfast and found the scent of roses irresistible after so many years of flies and heat. Robert was in London on the day when Edmund came to announce his engagement. Alice stared at the horizon as Edmund told her about the plans for the wedding. Later she asked him the colour of Gertrude's eyes. She smiled as he fumbled for the answer. Looking at Alice he found it impossible to keep Gertrude's face clear in his head. He knew what should be there but it was as if the clear outlines in his head were being melted by the heat that came from his sister-in-law. He could see angry red marks forming like blisters on her neck. He took her hand and it was hot and dry as if she had a fever. But the weight of Alice's hot square hand reminded him of Gertrude's cool white one in the pampas dawn.

'Gertrude's eyes are blue,' he said, letting Alice's hand drop. 'They are blue and she has a very fair complexion with no freckles or other marks at all. I believe she has very small feet.'

Alice said nothing and Edmund did not know how to continue. He could not bear to look at the furious weals on her neck that he knew were spreading under her dress across her chest.

'Gertrude is very fond of sketching. She's done some really fine drawings of Las Lomas. Pity she didn't do Las Limpias and Chirù, it would be nice to have something to show Mother.'

At last Alice looked at him. 'Your mother is coming for the wedding?'

'Well, if she doesn't come over for the ceremony, Gertrude and I will be paying her a bridal visit.'

Alice was silent again. He watched as her fingers plucked at the *passementerie* on the front of her dress. She was twisting the bobble so viciously that it was bound to snap, but when it came off in her hand she looked at it with surprise and annoyance. She took a breath as if fighting for air. 'It must be very nice to have everything arranged so suitably.'

Edmund chose not to hear the bitterness in her voice. He really had to leave: it was a long ride back to the house where Gertrude's parents lived. He had thought he would spend the night but he realized that he could not bear to be here alone with Alice. She was standing in the rose garden gazing out at nothing as he rode away. She did not look round.

He did not see Alice for a year following that encounter. She did not come to his wedding to Gerti. Robert had said that Basil, the unfortunate one, had been ill. 'High time he went to school if you ask me. Can't have his mother fussing over him all the time. I tried to persuade her to leave him but nothing would convince her.'

Gerti was appropriately concerned about the little boy but Edmund could only think of Alice. As he stood next to Robert in St George's, Hanover Square, waiting for Gerti to reach him at the altar, he remembered the hurried little ceremony in Liverpool. The maid – what was she called?

Martha – had cried noisily all the way through, but Alice and Robert had been quite oblivious to everything. He remembered taking Robert's arm to give him the ring and finding it rigid with tension. Now, he could scarcely believe that Alice had been so determined. It was as if that terrific demonstration of will had been her last decisive act. He wondered if Robert had ever regretted marrying Alice – had he been waiting for her in Liverpool or had he been hoping to get away? They had never talked about it. He wanted to ask Robert how he had felt but just then he heard the gasp of the organ and the expectant scrape of wood against stone as the congregation turned to look at the bride.

The next time Edmund saw Alice, a year or so after his wedding, she had just been delivered of a second daughter. The blankness in her face alarmed him. He remarked on it to Robert who pointed at the laudanum bottle on the dressing table. 'The doctor gave it to her after she had the baby to settle her nerves, but now we need something to wake her up again.'

Edmund was left with a bruise of Alice's hollow eyes in his head, but the bruise faded when Gerti had their first son, Ralph. There was no room for Alice now.

FOURTEEN

We did not gallop home. Our visit to Las Limpias had exhausted Derek. He could not bear the idea of so many missed opportunities.

'The Traills could have been running Argentina if they'd wanted to, but they just didn't have a clue. They owned two hundred square miles, two hundred square miles . . . If they'd held onto it, it would now be worth fifty, sixty million dollars. But they had to lose it all. Damn shame really, when you think about what might have been.'

Back in the gloom of Las Limpias Derek showed me a large book full of photos of old estancias. Flicking through the pages of graceful verandahs and tiled courtyards made me realize just how modest the original Las Limpias had been. Other immigrants had built themselves Moorish palaces, half-timbered baronial halls, Disney-like chateaux; the Traills could have afforded to build a house to rival anything they had seen in Ireland, they could have had the country house they always wanted here in Santa Fé. Instead they settled for a dwelling. They did not even plant an avenue of trees to line their drive. In this landscape, where even the smallest shack has its avenue of tipa trees, nothing could be a clearer symbol of the fact that the Traills did not want to put down roots. Only the stencilling in the bedroom suggested any desire to settle.

Derek was right, it was infuriating. If only the Traills had not been so obsessed with going home I might now be sitting under one of those shady verandahs looking onto a vista of fountains and pergolas, instead of in a polystyrene shack overlooking a rusting water tower.

I shared the irritation that Derek felt but I also understood his preoccupation with what might have been. He had, after all, come back to live here. The glamour of the lost fortune lay like a mist over the landscape, disguising its imperfections. The memory of money was a lure as well as an annoyance. I could understand his ambiguity, I knew – know – that remembered wealth is a seductive thing.

When I was eight years old my father married for the second time and my brother and I came to live with him and my stepmother in London. The house we moved to was in Knightsbridge, the sort of house that only bankers can afford now. It was tall and thin with ninety-seven steps between the basement and the top floor. At the back of the house, instead of a garden, there was a glass-roofed conservatory with geraniums in pots. We kept terrapins there and at the end there was a room where the piano and the television were. This room had a private entrance from a side street. The house had once belonged to Lillie Langtry and this room was where she entertained Edward VII. It was always called by us the Salon d'Edouard. I had only the haziest idea of who Lillie Langtry was or what she did with the King in the Salon, but I knew that the house had once been a great deal more exciting than it was now. It was a house of layers. If you picked enough cream paint off the spindles of the banisters when you were trying to eavesdrop on adult conversations you eventually came across a layer of gold. The whole staircase had once shimmered with gold leaf. There was a little semicircular room off the stairs where my brother and I held the meetings of our various secret societies – here the folding doors had been painted shut but when you picked at the layers of magnolia paint that held them together there was smooth fascinating mirror underneath.

I showed my father and he laughed. I expect that's where Lillie Langtry and Edward VII did ooh la las, he said. This remark was baffling but I continued scraping away till my nails and fingers were raw. I could not understand how anyone could paint over a wall of mirrors: what could be more entrancing than to watch your reflection repeated over and over? I used to lie awake at night imagining the house in its original splendour. The gold stairs, the red carpets, the shiny mirrored walls. The only room in the house that came close to the house's original sumptuousness was my own bedroom, which my stepmother, in a conciliatory opening gambit, had done up in a rich red plush. The rest of the house was creamy magnolia, but my room looked and felt like the inside of a box of chocolates. I would bury my face in the velvety pile of the bedspread and feel the redness seeping through my body. The rough smooth feeling of the pile as I rubbed my cheek this way and that against the nap of the fabric was a dependable sensation in a time when emotions were constantly shifting.

We left that house when I was fourteen for a warehouse on the Thames. My stepmother, who is among many things a socialist, hated living in such a plutocratic part of town. She believed that the postcode was exerting a baleful influence on my values. I heard her asking my father whether he wanted his children to grow up thinking of Harrods as the local shop.

The new house in Rotherhithe was presented as a wonderful opportunity – I would have my own bedsitting room with private bathroom – but I knew better. My father's tone was too placatory to be convincing. I could tell that this move was not designed with my interests in mind. It was bad enough having divorced parents, but to have to live somewhere 'interesting' as well – I suspected that this was the end of the normal part of my life. My fears were confirmed when my father got rid of his Volvo estate and bought a bright blue Mercedes bus which he fitted out with aeroplane seats. Car makes were not something I had ever given much thought to, but no one else I knew came to school in a delivery van, even if it was a Mercedes.

I never got a chance to say goodbye to the Knightsbridge house. We went to stay with my mother in the summer holidays and when we came back we went straight to Rotherhithe. Sometimes I walk past it on my way to the dentist, the same dentist I saw when I lived in that house – teeth are very conservative things – and remember my red bedroom. I pointed it out to my daughter, who looked it over with an eight-year-old's acute eye for property values. 'You must have been very rich then, Mummy, to live in such a big house. Why don't we live in a house like that?'

It is no use telling her that we are much happier in our Edwardian terrace in Shepherd's Bush, that she has things I didn't have – a mother to take her to school, for example. All these lines merely disguise the fact that I don't have an answer to why we don't live in a house like that now.

A series of choices were made that meant I would never live in SW1 again, choices that are too close to see clearly. It is much easier to look back and see where the Traills went wrong, to sigh over their wilfulness. But every time I walk past the house in Knightsbridge, and look up at the windows where my red plush curtains hung, I know for that moment what it is like to be dispossesed.

My mother has never cared for money. She has her own currency. But the part of the family story that she always lingers on is the period when they became rich – not just rich but fabulously rich.

'They were called the Argentine millionaires, darling, they went everywhere. They were friends of the Prince of Wales. There were cartoons about them in *Punch*.'

I suppose she must have heard this from her mother. The money was largely gone by the time my grandmother was born but she had grown up in its aura. Living in Las Limpias under a corrugated-iron roof must have kindled my grandmother's appetite for stories of a golden past. Did her parents tell her about what had been lost or did she weave a story for herself from the fragments of adult conversation, the faded daguerreotypes of shooting parties that hung on the walls, the ostrich-feather fan that lived in the trunk under her grandmother's bed? As the flow of money from one generation to another dwindled to a trickle, so the volume of riches left behind grew with each generation. As the pain of losing the money lessened, so the amount that was lost increased.

When I first heard the story from my aunt, the fortune had accrued so much emotional interest that it had reached Getty-like proportions. The larger the amount, the more thorough the ruin, the better the story. But visiting Las

Limpias brought this fortune into perspective for me: clearly, for my grandmother any existence was richer than living in this house without roots. So the modest manor house that the Traills bought in Long Stratton in Norfolk must have seemed palatial in retrospect, in the same way that my red plush bedroom in Knightsbridge now seems like an unattainable haven of luxury.

It is hard to know exactly how much money the Traills had. I think the Argentine millionaire tag was a later addition, an embellishment added by my grandmother on a rainy night. There were Argentine millionaires in the 1880s and 1890s who became a byword for a certain kind of conspicuous consumption, rather in the same way that oil-rich Arabs were stigmatized in the 1980s. But these millionaires were more Latin than Anglo-Saxon and gravitated to Paris not London. They lived in *hôtels particuliers* not manor houses in Norfolk.

Robert no doubt would have been mortified to hear himself described as an *Argentine* millionaire, when he had clearly been at pains to set himself up as an English country gentleman. He bought Alice a brand-new brougham to go about in. He sent Bob and Ned to Eton. He made no attempt to do any work, but instead he developed a gentleman's interest in the sport of kings and began breeding racehorses.

I can only imagine that racing was the connection between Robert and the Prince of Wales. The Traills were not aristocratic enough to be part of the Prince's set by right, nor rich enough to qualify like the Rothschilds or the Cassels through sheer munificence. I think Robert must have become a sporting crony – a man who sold horses to the Prince of Wales. But he did not try to capitalize on this connection, if it was a connection, by taking a house in London. Perhaps he felt that Alice would not 'do' in London. Robert, who had smart enough friends to put him up for White's, would stay at his club when he was in town.

By coming back to Britain in the 1880s the Traills were going against the huge tide of money that was flowing westwards at the end of the nineteenth century. When they arrived in Argentina there was about £5.3 million of British capital invested in Argentina; by 1875 that figure had increased exponentially to £23 million. The surge of railway-building in the seventies and eighties was almost entirely financed with British money. But instead of using the influx of capital to increase their holdings in Argentina, the Traills borrowed money against their land to finance their retirement in England. Their land would be worth about US $60 million according to today's land values. It was an optimistic move based on a belief that prices would continue to go up and that natural disasters would continue to pass them by. But Robert could be forgiven for thinking that the future was set fair. After the difficulties of the first few years he and Edmund had made money without really trying. The opportunities, like the railways and the introduction of refrigeration, had come to them. A steer that in 1870 was worth one peso sold for twenty-seven pesos ten years later. Why should they anticipate disaster? What was the point of being rich in the pampas? It was time to go home.

They had no intention of spending their money in the country where they found it. When the Traill brothers arrived in Argentina they had five hundred pounds. By the time they went to England they were in the top 2 per cent of Argentine landowners. They could easily have relieved the boredom of life on the pampas by building a mansion on the Avenida Veinte Cinco de Mayo, a huge boulevard in Buenos Aires lined with jacaranda trees that was conceived on as grand a scale as the Mall or the Champs-Elysées. They could have joined the Jockey Club, whose only entry requirement was ownership of five thousand hectares, and become part of the Argentine establishment. They could have joined the Sociedad Rural de Argentina, an organization of the most powerful estancieros. They could have attended the opera at the Teatro Colón. They could have bought their furniture at the Buenos Aires branch of Maples, the most exclusive furniture shop in the world, whose only other establishments were in London and Paris. They could have been contenders in one of the fastest-growing economies in the world.

By the 1880s Buenos Aires was no longer a city of *saladeros* and sewers but a boom town full of millionaires looking to spend their new-found wealth. The population had increased from 1.74 million to 2.5 million between 1869 and 1880 – an increase of 44 per cent. Argentina was becoming the richest and most populous country in Latin America.

But the Traills never even considered diverting themselves in Buenos Aires, let alone learning enough Spanish to become part of the ruling clique. They simply got on the British-built railway and travelled (like the thousands of tons of grain and beef which Argentina exported every year) straight to England without touching the country which produced their wealth. It was as if the Argentina of Buenos Aires and opera houses was in a parallel universe, a Catholic, corrupt, complicated, foreign universe that had no relation to the windswept world of cattle, cricket and corrugated iron which the Traills inhabited. Buenos Aires, the so-called Paris of the Southern Hemisphere, might as well not have existed. The delights of the Retiro district were as nothing compared to the lure of a manor house in Norfolk.

The thing that is puzzling is why after years of living in the pampas Robert should have chosen a house in country as flat and featureless as the one he had left behind. Was he perhaps now more Argentine than he realized, feeling trapped unless he could see the horizon in every direction?

By no means all the British in Argentina were as insular as the Traills. The pages of Borges are full of Eduardo Gormans and Jaime Wilsons. Borges himself had a Scottish grandmother. It was clearly possible for Anglo-Saxons to blend into Argentine society, but assimilation was more likely to take place in the cosmopolitan capital not in the isolated country. The huge growth in Argentina in the late nineteenth century was largely taking place in the capital; the adjoining provinces remained almost wholly rural and undeveloped, dominated by great landowners. The Traills' isolation stemmed from cultural differences but they were not the only landowners to feel no sympathy with the *porteños* or inhabitants of Buenos Aires. As the capital grew, its centripetal pull was resented by the quasi-feudal caudillos of the provinces who were accustomed to running their own affairs. In their isolation from the blandishments of the capital the Traills were, albeit unwittingly, conforming to a long-standing division between the city and the country. They were as indifferent to the long-term welfare of the nation as the most reactionary landowner in Mendoza or Jujuy. All their aspirations were a thousand miles away.

Missed opportunity was a recurring theme during my stay with Derek in Las Limpias Two. Late at night he would bang the formica table with his fist protesting at his ancestors' lack of imagination. Why couldn't they have seen that Argentina not England was the future? Derek would make this point as he flicked from channel to channel on his satellite TV trying to find an English-language station. Derek thought the Argentine news was propaganda. During my stay in Argentina, President Menem was paying a state visit to England. Every news bulletin began with a new rumour about the future of the Malvinas. Derek would watch these reports shaking his head. 'Poor bloody Falklanders, the last thing they need is some jumped-up Argy governor running the show trying to feather his nest.'

The only thing that exercised Derek more than his lost inheritance was the scale of corruption in Argentine public life. 'Nobody pays taxes in this country, they just pay bribes.'

Derek blamed the Traills for not seeing beyond their prejudices, but it did not occur to him to examine his own.

Every day Derek would snort over some new example of the institutionalized corruption which he believed was endemic in Argentina. He had chosen to live in a country whose morals he despised, but he blamed the Traills for not going native.

The Traills did not enjoy their good fortune for long. For the sake of the story I wish it had been longer. But in 1887 the Trollopian neatness of life in the Manor House, Long Stratton, was spoiled by a disaster that was more Hardyesque in its bleakness. A freak south wind blew up from the Antarctic and brought snow to the pampas for the first time in a hundred years. Two-thirds of the Traill herds froze to death. Anthony Synge, Robert's nephew, who had been left in charge of Las Limpias, was in Rosario visiting a brothel when the snows fell. When the girl with whom he had not yet managed to agree a price saw the white flakes falling she rushed to the window and started crossing herself.

Anthony could not understand her reaction – all he could see out of the window was that it was snowing. He wanted the girl to come back so they could start: it had taken the best part of a week to get here, he was becoming impatient. But the girl was transfixed by the falling snow, and kept reaching out trying to catch a flake as it fell. It was the first time she had seen snow – she was only four-teen. Anthony felt his desire ebb away: somehow his mother had come into his head. The girl hardly turned her head as he left; she was giving herself to the snow.

Anthony spent his brothel money on two bottles of brandy. He drank one straight off and sipped the other as he started the ride back to Las Limpias. His horse could always find his way back even when Anthony was so drunk that he had to be tied to the saddle. But the cold kept him awake and more sober than he would have liked. As the snow began to fall more heavily he could hear the cattle bellowing in distress. The warm fug of the brandy was being torn apart by the icy fingers of panic.

He spurred his horse on, hoping by some miracle that the snow would not have reached the Traill lands. But as he crossed the stream that separated the Traill property from the Dobbses' place, he saw that Las Limpias had not been spared. The ground had become a flat white sheet interrupted by the hummocks made by the cows as they lay down and froze to death. As he got closer to Las Limpias he found Santiago, one of the peons, trying to round up the remaining animals into the corral nearest the house. There was no shelter for the animals: the only way to keep them alive was to herd them together so that their combined heat kept the cold away. But the cattle were too scattered. Santiago had managed to round up only a few hundred and though he and Anthony worked all night, in the morning nearly two-thirds of the Traill herds were dead.

Anthony finished the rest of the brandy on the ride to the telegraph office in San Jorge, words like 'calamity' tolling in his head. He sent a telegram which read, 'MOST CATTLE KILLED BY SNOWSTORM PLEASE ADVISE SINCERELY A SYNGE.' He went straight from the telegraph office to a *pulpería* (a wine shop/bar) run by an Irishwoman from Co. Cork and stayed there till she threw him out the next day.

The sun was shining in Norfolk when the telegram arrived. It was 14 August and Robert was making preparations to go grouse-shooting in Scotland. He had just had a pair of twelve bores delivered from Purdey and was in the gunroom when the butler found him with the telegram.

He read it, put it down and then put the guns carefully back in their case.

Three months later, Robert was riding north from Rosario. As he approached the furthest limit of his lands he began to get hints of a foul stench upwind of him. It became stronger and stronger as he got closer to his own territory – a terrible smell which reminded him of that first day in Buenos Aires riding the skull-walled lanes of the *saladeros*. He was now able to make out the fences that marked the edge of his land on the horizon; they seemed strangely solid. As he got closer, he saw that the barbed wire in every direction was covered by the hides of cattle which were being left to cure in the sun. The fence hummed with the flies that were feasting on the rotting flesh.

Robert, who had been travelling night and day since he landed in Buenos Aires two weeks before, felt the salty bile rising in his throat and was sick. He had spent the whole journey south with a knot at the bottom of his stomach wondering how bad the damage would be. He had left before Anthony's letter arrived, breaking the news that at least five thousand of the cattle were gone. Now he could see for himself how bad it was: the fences were full and the fields were empty. He kicked his horse into a gallop towards Las Limpias.

He found Anthony asleep on the verandah, a half-empty bottle of brandy in his hand. He kicked the boy in the ribs harder than he had kicked his horse, but his nephew did not even quiver. Robert noted with disgust that Anthony was wearing *bombachas* (baggy trousers) and the strange kind of loincloth which all the gauchos wore. The boy had gone native. He picked up the bottle of brandy and finished it off: there was nothing else to do.

His letter to Alice was full of directions. She was to shut up the manor at Long Stratton and come back to the Argentine with both the English children, by which he meant the youngest ones, Johnny and Blanche. The older boys and May were to be left at their schools for the time being. *I am most anxious that Bob should be prepared for Cambridge*. He asked Alice to bring him his guns and his favourite stallion Forrester. *I am minded to see what we can make of him and the* criollo *ponies that abound here.* Robert may have been forced to abandon his grouse-shoot but he was not about to give up the trappings of a country gentleman even if he was in the southern hemisphere.

By the time Alice reached Las Limpias Robert was optimistic again about the future. He had mortgaged a large tract of land which had given him enough money to buy new livestock. He had written to Edmund telling him not to hurry back, reassuring him that he was quite happy to run Chirù in his absence, '*although we shall have to find ourselves a new major-domo. Anthony I'm afraid has gone to the bad, drink, gambling and worse. I have sent him over to stay with the Gibsons in the hope that some female company will have a good effect on him. I hesitate to write to Kathleen, I hear that Johnny* [Anthony's younger brother] *is proving most troublesome. I sincerely hope that she does not imagine that she might find the end to her troubles here. I do not think I have the patience to deal with two of her sons.'*

Bob and the other 'Argentine' children did not see their parents again for five years. In the holidays they went to stay with their grandmother in Dublin. Anne Traill was under the impression that Alice was a girl whom Robert had met in the Argentine, in the way that Edmund had met Gertrude. As the two women had never met, Anne had no idea that his son's wife was an Irish Catholic. Alice's past was never acknowledged by Robert's family – later, when Robert's great-great-nephew came to write a book about his uncle the playwright J. M. Synge (the troublesome Johnny of Robert's letter), he described Robert and Edmund as leaving Ireland single and fancy free. *'When they were established in the Argentine, they found suitable wives among the English families that lived around them.'*

When Anne asked the children about their mother's family, they looked at her blankly. 'I would imagine, ma'am, that she is an orphan,' said Bob. They were not even able to supply her with their mother's maiden name. Anne was puzzled by her daughter-in-law's lack of family but not concerned: the few notes she had received from Alice had seemed everything they should be. It did not occur to her – how could it? – that her son would have broken all the rules of his class, his caste, his religion in marrying Alice. It was something that these days Robert could hardly believe himself.

Bob hated staying at his grandmother's house in Orwell Park, Dublin. He had always lived in houses in open country. He found the narrow Georgian terraced house that his grandmother lived in gloomy and claustrophobic. No one had thought to explain to him why it had been necessary for them all to leave Long Stratton so suddenly. He knew it had something to do with the Argentine, but in the eight years he had spent in England he had forgotten quite what the Argentine was, or why it should need his father's urgent attention.

He could remember his pony Thunder and the trap-door in the kitchen and the ladder you were never allowed to climb if Mother was around, and sometimes when the sun shone in England he remembered playing under the verandah at Las Limpias waiting for it to be cool enough to go outside. But Bob thought of the Manor House as his home; it was certainly a place where he remembered being happy. And now it was gone because of something in the Argentine. Nobody could tell him if he would live there again, or whether his parents were ever coming back.

After one holiday in Dublin with his grandmother Bob wrote to his father and asked if he could spend the rest of his vacations at school. He never got an answer, and the next vacation he found himself with his brothers and sister on the boat train to Holyhead. This vacation was even worse than usual because Aunt Kathleen had moved into the house next door and insisted on holding family prayers morning and evening. Bob knew how to distract his grandmother – he would ask her about the water-colours which hung in the drawing room of her childhood home. How she loved to talk about the deer park and the long gallery where she used to play the piano after dinner.

But his aunt was not so easy to distract. Her favourite pastime at meals was quoting from the Bible and then looking around at the children demanding they give her chapter and verse. The Synge children, even Johnny, were prompt with their replies (years of practice had made them familiar with Kathleen's favourites) but the Traills were not. Kathleen would cluck and mutter, 'Robert's children are practically heathens.' She wrote a letter to her brother expressing her concern at his children's lack of readiness to enter the kingdom of God. '*I cannot help but feel that their spiritual welfare is quite in jeopardy. I think they would greatly benefit from a prolonged period here in Dublin. I fear that the schools they attend are not at all particular about the type of religious instruction their pupils receive. The children are lamentably ignorant of the Bible. Even Johnny is more advanced in his knowledge of the scriptures.*'

As Robert was still dealing with the problems caused by Kathleen's older son Anthony, he was not best pleased with this criticism of his parental abilities. '*I am very satisfied with the schools . . . the children attend. I am sure that their knowledge of the Bible is quite adequate. Acquaintance with the scriptures is no guarantee of later success.*'

Robert did not write that a rigorous religious education had failed to inoculate Anthony against drunkenness and lechery. Perhaps he wanted to spare his sister's feelings, but he also knew that he could not afford to antagonize her. Prices had fallen for the first time in ten years, and it was increasingly difficult to get credit. A sister with money in government bonds was a useful asset.

Bob did not go back to Dublin. He spent the next holidays with a friend in Norfolk before going up to Cambridge in the autumn. Kathleen had suggested that he go to Trinity College, Dublin, like her own sons, where Tony Traill was now the Provost. But Robert intended to return to England and he wanted his son to know the right people. Trinity College Dublin was hardly an entrée into society. And while he was not the most affectionate of fathers he saw no reason why Bob should have to suffer 'terrible Tony'.

So Bob went to Trinity College, Cambridge in 1890 to read Classics, as his father felt there was no better training for a gentleman.

Basil and Ned remained at school. Basil, who was bullied because he didn't look right, wrote to his mother begging her to take him away from this *'unfeeling place'*. But it was no use. Robert, who had never been to a boarding school, was a great believer in them. Even when Basil was found foaming at the mouth having some kind of fit, Robert assured the housemaster that it was much the best thing for him to remain in a *'healthy wholesome atmosphere with plenty of companions of his own age. He must have no excuse to become isolated and shun his contemporaries.'* Robert could see first-hand the effects of isolation on a fragile character.

Bob had rooms on Great Court in his first year. His allowance was generous enough for him to live comfortably but he liked to live splendidly, and was consequently always in debt. He rowed for his college and played cricket for the Varsity. He hunted whenever possible. He did the minimum amount of work. He was religious in his avoidance of the more spiritually minded undergraduates. He made no secret of the fact that his parents were living in the Argentine but he did not advertise it. The Argentine was synonymous in the late 1880s with the most dodgy of speculations.

Bob had been to see *An Ideal Husband* by Oscar Wilde, in which the plot hinges around a fraudulent Argentine canal scheme, and had heard the knowing snickers in the audience. It was a place to have a flutter with, not a place to come from. Bob felt as little connection with the country of his birth as he did with his grandmother's gloomy house in Orwell Park.

If he had a home, it was here in Great Court where the wildness of the skies had been tamed by the precise geometry of the college. Bob liked the rectangles, the paths that led you in definite directions. As yet he had no idea what he would do when he left – the Bar possibly. He had no intention of going back to the Argentine and becoming a major-domo on an estancia like his cousins. His vision of his future was altogether more glorious. He wanted his father to come back and open up Long Stratton before the hunting season started. A few men in his college were thinking of starting a polo team but he would need a string of ponies to join.

He wrote to his father in the Michaelmas term of 1891, asking him to send him some ponies. '*I think those criollo ponies would do very well here for hunting and polo. I think that there would be many horsemen here who would appreciate the turn of speed that these animals possess . . . Although you would have to bear the shipping costs, I feel confident that I should be able to sell them at the end of the season at a handsome profit.*' Bob liked the phrase '*handsome profit*': it had the swagger he aspired to. He hoped that his father would be impressed by his commercial acumen. He also hoped, although this was a thought that he hardly expressed, that his father would come with the ponies.

He never thought of himself as missing his parents. Basil and Ned had cried at first when Robert and Alice went back to the Argentine, but Bob at fourteen had felt that crying was for babies. He had tried to avoid thinking of his parents at all. Now it was hard for him to remember their faces. It was their feel and smell he remembered: the roughness of his father's beard, his mother's warm cheek. Sometimes at school he had watched his friends with their parents and wondered what it must be like to have your family around you in that way. Would his mother wear a hat like that, would his father give him a gold sovereign? He found it impossible to imagine. He wanted to place his parents beyond vague memories of beards and rocking chairs on verandahs. He wanted his father to be strong and brave and his mother to be good and beautiful. He wanted to know who his people were.

Bob hoped that his father would reply to his letter at once. Mails to and from the Argentine took at least a month each way, so if his father wrote back at once he would get an answer by Christmas. Bob thought it was likely that his father would write back immediately. It was true that sometimes Bob would not get a letter from the Argentine for six or even nine months but the business of the ponies was such a good idea and just the sort of thing that the father he remembered would love.

By Christmas Bob had still heard nothing. He went to stay with his friend Johnny Felstead, whose father was an MP. The house was full of Cyril Felstead's Tory friends. The talk was mainly about Ireland, which Bob found tedious: he could see no reason why anyone should care what happened to Ireland. But on the second day that he was there, one of the guests who was one of Lord Salisbury's Private Secretaries received a telegram from

Whitehall summoning him back to London at once.

That night the dinner conversation swirled with speculation as to the reasons for the Private Secretary's sudden departure. One man, who Johnny had pointed out to Bob as 'stinking rich', looked up from his soup and said, 'The Baring affair is pretty serious. Salisbury will either have to support the bank or intervene in the Argentine. There's too much British capital in the place to let it go. Very glad I sold short in '89, wouldn't like to be holding Argentine railway bonds now.'

Johnny's father snorted at this. 'You can't seriously imagine that the government would be foolish enough to involve itself in this affair? If banks are credulous enough to risk their capital in fraudulent schemes it is surely for them to take the consequences. The government can't go to the rescue of all the greedy speculators in the country.'

There were murmurs of assent from Cyril Felstead's Tory friends, but the banker was unabashed. 'If Baring's fails on account of the Buenos Aires waterworks scheme, then the whole City will face ruin. Debts would be called in, prices would rise, there would be a run on the banks. No one,' here the banker paused for dramatic effect, 'no one in this country would be unaffected. Even around this table anyone who had a mortgage on their land would find that the banks would be pressing for repayment in full. I only hope that Salisbury acts quickly enough.' The table fell silent at this. The last few years had been bad for farmers, and Cyril Felstead was not alone in borrowing money against land. The banker knew this: Cyril was not the only person present who had come to him in financial difficulties.

Bob only half-listened to this conversation. He could see that old man Felstead was rattled by what the banker chap had said, but he couldn't quite see why the Buenos Aires waterworks were causing such a commotion. How could anything that happened in the Argentine possibly affect anyone here? He thought that the banker chap was just trying to make an impression. He was surprised, having said as much to Johnny whilst playing billiards after dinner, when his friend looked rather serious. 'I should think father is very worried, if Mayne [the banker] thinks it's serious. He is not an excitable man.' He paused to take a shot. 'I'm sorry, Traill, I'd forgotten your people are out in the Argentine, aren't they? From what Mayne was saying it sounds as if the whole country is just one big swindle. Hope your family don't get mixed up in it.'

Bob thought of the last letter he had had from his father, which had spent four pages describing how he had at last managed to cross his stallion Forrester with one of the *criollo* mares. 'Oh, I don't think my father has much to do with financial things. He's more interested in horses.'

Bob realized as he said this, that he had only assumed his father was rich. But then he remembered Father telling them that his estates in the Argentine were bigger than the county of Norfolk. 'If that land was here in England I'd have a handle to my name and the village church would be full of ancestral tombs going back hundreds of years. It would take generations to acquire the kind of estate we have in the Argentine. And it only took us ten years.'

Nothing surely could happen to an estate that large. Bob hoped that the Argentine problems would not interfere with his horse-breeding plans. The New Year came without any more mention of the Baring crisis, although the Private Secretary who had left in such a hurry never returned.

There was a blizzard blowing up when Bob went back

to Cambridge. Bob gasped as he walked through the gate at Trinity and saw the familiar contours of Great Court obliterated by snow. When he was a child in Las Limpias his mother had tried to explain snow to her children: 'It's like white sand. It crunches when you walk on it. After a while it melts.' But to children who had never seen ice (or, for that matter, sand) her explanation made little sense. Alice had struggled to find some frame of reference that her children would understand. 'Imagine that the pampas were covered in white thistledown, so thick that you could walk on it.' Bob had succeeded in picturing the plain as a downy white pillow; he imagined sleeping outside on its cool white softness. He had been surprised the first time it snowed in Norfolk to find that it was so hard and so cold. He thought not for the first time that his mother was not reliable.

But today, seeing the sharp lines of that familiar rectangle softened and swollen, its surface only broken by the solitary tracks of footprints, he understood what his mother had meant – that there was something inviting about the drifts of whiteness; he could imagine pulling the snow over him like a blanket and falling asleep for ever.

In his room he found a letter from his Uncle Edmund asking him to come to Dublin at Easter. '*Mother is very frail now and in your father's absence I think it is fitting that you should see her before the end. I have written to Robert but I think it is most unlikely that he will be able to leave the Argentine at the present.*'

There was another letter from the college bursar asking him to pay his battens (college bar bills) and a letter from Ned asking to borrow some money because he had spent all his allowance, and complaining that the boys in his form were teasing him because of Basil's fits. '*I wonder*

191

that Mama and Papa did not take him back to the Argentine. I do not think they can understand how badly suited he is to school life.' But there was no letter from his father. Even if his father had not written back at once, he should have received something by now. He was surprised that his mother had not sent him a Christmas present. They had never made very much of Christmas in the Argentine but in England there had been a tree in the hall at Long Stratton and goose and plum pudding. Could it be that his mother had forgotten?

Bob looked around for his flask and found it empty. He would have to go and sweet-talk the steward into extending his credit until the next instalment of his allowance was due. He wondered if Hardcastle, the Boat Club secretary, was back: he would certainly have something to drink. He looked out of his window to see if Hardcastle's lights were on, and as he did so he noticed one of the porters walking across the court towards his staircase, trying to keep to the paths, as only fellows were allowed to walk across the grass. No amount of snow could cover the boundaries of that privilege. The porter walked bent forward, clutching his bowler hat. Bob wondered what had brought him out of the warmth of the porters' lodge.

As the porter turned, still following his path of deference, Bob thought with a rush of excitement that it might be the letter. In the minute before the knock came at the door he had captained the winning team and held the winner's trophy in his hands. He was smiling as he opened the door. 'Telegram for you, sir.'

Reaching in his pocket, the smallest coin Bob could find was a shilling, but still flushed with victory he pressed it in the porter's hand.

'Thank you very much, sir, happy New Year, sir. Would you like me to wait for a reply?'

Bob took the telegram out of the envelope and read it. The porter had to repeat his question twice.

'Not bad news I hope, sir,' said the porter with anticipation. He always enjoyed an undergraduate tragedy.

Bob shook his head stiffly. 'No reply will be necessary, thank you.'

The porter lingered, hoping for something to tell the others back at the lodge, but the young man in front of him said nothing, just stood there holding the telegram in his hands, smoothing the paper out with his fingers as if trying to wipe away the words.

Afterwards Bob would remember that minute between the porter turning towards his staircase and the knock on the door as the last time in his life when he looked forward to the future. The telegram read, 'MONEY GONE STOP RETURN HOME NECESSARY STOP PASSAGE BOOKED LIVERPOOL 16TH FATHER.'

The pillow of credit that had kept the Argentine economy buoyant for so long had been snatched away by the Baring crisis, and families like the Traills who had financed their foreign excursions by borrowing against their landholdings were suddenly faced with implacable creditors. The paper money they possessed was now worthless. The Traills were forced to sell all but a tenth of their land to pay off their outstanding debts. Robert had to borrow money from his sisters in Ireland to avoid bankruptcy. He had put off sending the telegram to Bob for as long as he could, but as bank after bank closed their doors he realized that he could no longer support his children in England. He had held onto the idea that this was a reversible situation for as long as he could, but as the financial crisis in the Argentine worsened he could no longer see his way home. He wrote to Edmund asking him to come but Edmund was determined to stay in Dublin while his mother was still alive. As Robert could not afford to send Edmund the money that was rightfully his and keep his children in England, he had no choice but to send for his children. Robert knew that his brother had every right to the money but still he resented him for it. For the first time in his life he felt completely alone, a feeling which persisted even when Edmund did eventually return. In the month after he sent the telegram to his son he noticed that his beard, which had always been the colour of gold, was now faded to a dirty silver.

The Argentine economy eventually recovered, exports picked up. Foreign investors forgot that the Argentine was not a safe place to put their money. But the Traills never regained their dukedom in the pampas. It was no longer enough to be in the right place at the right time. It was not enough to be English any more. The families who survived the Baring crisis were the ones who took Argentina seriously, who saw that profits and politics could no longer be kept separate. But just as Robert had seen no limits to their good fortune ten years earlier, now he could see no end to their descent. He had foreclosed on his own future.

Bob had left Cambridge that night, slipping out of the gates just before the porters' rounds. He had nothing with him except a small Gladstone bag with his razor and a couple of shirts. He hoped that the college authorities would follow his instructions and send the rest of his stuff after him, particularly his oar, but it was more likely that they would sell everything to pay his bills. To take any more with him now would make the porters suspicious.

He had left without saying goodbye to his friends: he could not bear the thought of their pity. He would rather that people thought he had done away with himself than to admit the truth: that he was an Argentine bankrupt.

He had given the porter who brought him the telegram his last shilling, and all he had left were a few pennies – enough he hoped to buy him a third-class ticket to London. He could easily have borrowed some money from Johnny Felstead and travelled to Liverpool in style but he would rather freeze on Cambridge station than lose face in front of his best friend.

In London he pawned his hunter watch and the silver flask his father had sent him when he went up to Cambridge. It was only right that these gentlemen's possessions should finance his flight.

The boat back to the Argentine was a steamer which had spent years crossing the Atlantic to North America, but was now so old and decrepit that it was considered only fit for the South American route. Bob's berth was in steerage. He shared a cabin with three shepherds from the west coast of Scotland who had been given a free passage to Patagonia by the Southern Land Company. The shepherds were about the same age as Bob, and even though the dialect they spoke was almost impossible for him to understand, he knew that they were excited about their new life; that their long incomprehensible conversations were full of hope and fortunes made.

The boat ran into a series of storms as they passed the Bay of Biscay, but still the shepherds muttered happily. After they had crossed the equator the weather improved and Bob slung his hammock on deck. But still he could not sleep: the shock that had numbed his journey had been replaced by anger. How could his father have been so careless as to have lost everything? His father was the one who was adamant that Bob should go to Cambridge, and yet he was the cause of Bob's shameful flight. Why hadn't his father given him some warning, why had he allowed him to go on thinking he was rich?

Bob felt hot with embarrassment as he thought of all the conversations he had had with his friends about the ponies that his father would be bringing over. He sensed at the time that some of his friends were sceptical about his plans. How they would be laughing now. Bob felt the humiliation wrench at his stomach. Sometimes he would stand at the rail and consider throwing himself into the water as a way of escaping the wretchedness of his thoughts, but the fact that he could not swim always acted as a deterrent. He wanted to surrender himself to the elements but it should be a fair fight.

One morning off the coast of Brazil one of the shepherds was found dead in his bunk, his arm stiff where he had thrown it out in the night. The ship's doctor could give no reason why the young man had been extinguished so suddenly. Bob watched the shepherd's body being brought up on deck in its cardboard coffin (wooden coffins were kept for the parlour-deck passengers). He stood at the stern as the Norwegian captain muttered the words for those who die at sea. He could not look away as the coffin was pushed into the sea. The coffin was filled with rocks to commit the body to the deep, but as it hit the water the cardboard sides split open, the rocks sank and the shepherd's body floated free, the waves soon stripping it of its winding sheet so that it floated white and naked in the ship's creamy wake. For the first time since the telegram had arrived Bob felt himself filled with the desire to laugh. The sight of the buoyant corpse filled him with great bubbles of merriment. He felt a great knot of mirth bursting from him in an explosive snort. That night he got blind drunk with the two remaining shepherds and wept with them for their loss of hope.

Two days later the blue waters of the South Atlantic began to turn grey with the mud from the River Plate. Bob could just make out a long low strip of land on the horizon. This was the Argentine then, no skyline rising to greet the visitor, just grey water and a distant smudge of land. Bob wondered whether he would ever learn to think of it as home.

The evening after we visited the original Las Limpias, I remembered to ask Derek where the name had come from. 'I've always thought it had something to do with clean white women,' he said with a slight leer. 'Can't have been many of those around here in the 1860s.' Derek's Spanish, though not fluent, was much better than mine, so I had no reason not to accept his translation. It fitted the picture of the Traills as white Anglo-Saxon Protestants with an invincible sense of their own superiority. The clean white women made me think of Picasso's *Demoiselles d'Avignon*, great sculptural nudes rising out of the plain.

Later in London I was talking to a friend who grew up in Venezuela about the oddness of this image. He listened to my extrapolations upon the meaning of Las Limpias for a while, and then he said, 'But you know what Limpias really means, don't you?' Clearly I didn't. 'It means "cleaned out, broke". At least that's what it means in Venezuela. Does that fit?'

It fitted all right. But why had Derek not known this? Was Limpias the Traills' own rueful name for their changed circumstances or a semi-contemptuous name invented by the locals? It would be typical of the Traill talent for the dramatic detail if they had indeed called the place after clean white women, only to find twenty years later that this other shade of meaning chimed exactly with their new condition. How economical of them to find a name for all circumstances: or did they know that the fall was bound to come?

I still could not understand why Derek, who was so involved with the Traills working their land, sighing over their mistakes, should not have known the real meaning of Limpias. He must have been aware of it and yet had chosen to ignore it. It was perhaps his way of reversing the Traills' infuriating acceptance of their fate.

FIFTEEN

'The turnout is really very good this year. Last year was a bit disappointing – no more than about thirty. Thought I might give it a miss myself, but then I thought you might find it amusing.'

My cousin Robin came to the Oxford and Cambridge dinner every year, but this was the first time he had come with a female companion. Ray, his wife, had not gone to university and his children had refused to go to England to be educated. Only graduates from Oxford or Cambridge were allowed to attend. I knew when he phoned from England to invite me that he was concerned that I might not know the form.

'It's black tie for men,' he said, pronouncing it 'blyeck tie', 'and whatever that means for the women. It's at the Embassy this year, Ambassador's a Balliol man, but quite a decent chap.' 'Chap' was pronounced 'chyep'. 'So I'll tell them you're coming. What college were you at and what years were you there?' I told him, realizing as I did so that the last time I had seen Robin had been just before I had gone to Trinity, half a lifetime ago.

Robin was finding his dinner jacket snug. He shifted uncomfortably in the back seat of the taxi, trying to ease the pressure on his stomach. 'I've put on a few pounds since I last wore this. That's the problem with this damn [dyem] leg, can't seem to keep the weight off any more.'

Robin had fallen off his pony in a polo match last year and had torn the cartilage in his knee. The fall had changed his life profoundly. It meant that he could no longer play polo or even ride. The only game he could safely play was golf and even then he had to ride around the course in an electric cart. Robin liked to play hard: pootling around a golf course on what he called a 'motorized hostess trolley' was not his style at all. From the look he gave me as I got into the taxi, I imagined that the buggered knee had kept him off games of a different sort as well.

The old Robin would have run a cool eye over my attempt to dress suitably for an Oxford and Cambridge dinner in the southern hemisphere (bluestocking respectability or Latin glamour – I had tried to compromise by wearing long with a revealing split). But the new lame Robin looked approving and rather relieved as I got into the taxi. I realized later that he had been anticipating the sort of outfit my mother would have worn: she had famously married my father wearing a mini-dress made of white crochet. Robin did not know that I had worn a white meringue which could barely fit through the doors of the church to my own wedding twenty-five years later. My statement had been of a different kind.

I could not decide whether to get out of the car or wait for Robin to hobble round and open the door. In the end I waited, pretending to reapply my lipstick so as not to appear impatient.

The Ambassador's Residence was a statuesque mansion

on the Avenida de Mayo built at the turn of the century. Inside, it was as if the architect had taken the biggest house in London or Paris and then doubled or tripled all the proportions. We walked up a white marble staircase that opened into a vast reception room. On a table at the head of the stairs was a signed silver-framed photograph of a smiling Tony Blair with a bunch of gardenias artlessly arranged in front like church flowers.

'Oxford man, I suppose,' said Robin as we walked past.

The butler announced our names. 'Mr Robin Willans and Mrs Daisy Goodwin de Wilford.' In Spanish, married women keep these portmanteau names. Every kind of formality was being kept tonight.

Robin made straight for a group of red-faced men of about his age who all had names like Tommy or Dick. Most of the men in the room were over fifty and like Robin talked in an Edwardian drawl. None of them had even a hint of a Spanish cadence in his voice. Robin was greeted by one of them as '*Señor Willans el grande estanciero*', the Spanish words pronounced with the same resolutely English accent as my old headmistress had advised when pronouncing the word Majorca. 'Always use a hard j, girls. You don't say Paree do you, you say Paris. Pronounce it the way it's written, that's what we do in England.'

Robin introduced me as his cousin who was writing a book about the English in Argentina. One of the Tommies leant towards me. 'My theory is that the British put the Spanish in Argentina. Sir Francis Drake was so good at attacking the Spanish fleet off the coast here that they decided to settle rather than go to sea again. That's why the Argentines always call us *piratas*. We tweaked their nose once too often.'

The other Tommies ignored this remark and moved onto a discussion about beef prices, but I saw a man on the edge of the group, who was too young to be a Tommy and looked as if he might be a diplomat, wince and walk away.

Most of the people in the room were men of Robin's generation, plus a few younger ones, like the man who had winced, who were attached to the Embassy. There was a sprinkling of women, all in their twenties or thirties, who looked rather surprised to find themselves in this company. One woman (Sidney Sussex 1985–8) was the South American Sales Director of British Gas. 'I never know whether to call people Argentines or Argentinians,' she said. 'People can be very touchy.'

One man (St John's 1984–7) was wearing a Pitt Club tie with cricket trousers. He had driven up with his father (St John's 1948–51) from their home in Patagonia, a journey of about fifteen hundred miles. He had red hair and pale skin blotched with freckles. When he told me his name I remembered that I had seen a photograph of his house in Derek's book of Great Estancias. It was a huge wooden affair, half stockbroker Tudor, half Swiss chalet, the sort of house the Traills could have built but didn't. This man, Alistair, was fourth-generation Argentine. His great-grandfather had been an Orcadian shepherd who had emigrated to the Falkland Islands in the 1890s. Fifteen years later he had two million sheep and an estate in Patagonia twice the size of his native Orkney.

Alistair had gone to school in Scotland and then to Cambridge. 'When my father was at Cambridge there were forty or fifty Anglo-Argentines up at the same time. When I went, I was the only one.'

I asked what it had been like to be at a British boarding school during the War in the South Atlantic (this I had realized was the only neutral way of referring to the events of 1982: Falkland and Malvinas were such loaded words). Alistair drained his gin and tonic. ' Everybody knew which side I was on,' he said.

Robin told me later that Alistair and his father were some of the richest men in the Argentine. 'Only sons of only sons, managed to pass it all on intact without splitting it up between lots of children. Only way to keep those great estates together.'

At dinner I sat next to a genial Tommy (Christchurch, 1946–9) who had been at school with Robin.

'You've got a look of the Traills about you,' he said. 'Wonderful sportsmen the Traills. Always hitting things. I remember we used to play a marvellous game called Hoc Ten Po – bit of hockey, bit of tennis, bit of polo, lots of cut lips and heads, terrific fun. Hard drinkers too. I remember we used to drive the cattle down to the rail head, get blind drunk and tie ourselves to our horses so that we didn't fall off on the way home. The animals knew where to go even if we didn't.'

This Tommy had grown up in camp like Robin, but when he came back to the Argentine after leaving Oxford he had decided to leave farming and go into industry. He now owned several factories which made agricultural equipment. I felt that it was safe to ask him if he felt English or Argentine.

'My heart is Argentine, it's such a beautiful country, but my head is English. My values, morals, those sorts of things are all English.'

At that point the Secretary of the Oxford and Cambridge Society stood up to give the loyal toast. This was followed by speeches in which graduates of Oxford and Cambridge damned with faint praise the other university. One woman, who had been appointed Toast Master, read out amusing cuttings from the *Daily Mail*.

On my other side sat the oldest member, who was ninety-seven. Unlike most of the others he had not been born in the Argentine. He had been a barrister in Manchester in the twenties and had won a case for the River Plate Shipping Company which had given him a first-class ticket to Buenos Aires in gratitude. The oldest member said that Buenos Aires was full of the most beautiful girls he had ever seen. He fell in love at once and got married three weeks after landing. But his wife did not like Manchester. She hated the cold and the damp. The oldest member gave up the Bar and made arrangements to become a wool merchant in Buenos Aires. But just before they were due to set out for the Argentine, his wife caught pneumonia and died. The oldest member brought her ashes back to Buenos Aires where he had lived ever since. 'I used to look for girls who looked like my late wife,' he said, 'but now that I am almost blind I wonder if it is time to go home.' At least he knew where home was. Robin and his contemporaries, most of them of the third or fourth generation of their family to be born in the Argentine, could not point to home with the same certainty. They lived in the Argentine, carried Argentine passports, they might call themselves Argentines, but their heads were still English. They played by different rules. All of these men regarded Argentine political life as irredeemably corrupt but none of them would dream of changing things by getting involved themselves.

They were not excluded from the political system by their foreign ancestry. Argentina's current president, Carlos Menem, was a first-generation immigrant from the Lebanon. They had ruled themselves out by their ambivalence about the country of their birth. These men were not fortune-hunters like the Traills, they were not planning to escape to England, they might even have learnt to speak decent Spanish, but their feelings about the country they lived in were rooted in the late nineteenth century.

Their children, though, who had grown up at the time of the War in the South Atlantic, had no doubt which side they were on. Robin's children had refused to speak to him during the war. 'Six months of silence, it was damned difficult.' In ten, maybe fifteen years there would be no more dinners of the Oxford and Cambridge Society. Robin's children thought of Oxford and Cambridge as enemy institutions. And maybe they were right.

After dinner I talked to a man who, though his English was as fluent and idiomatic as the Ambassador's, was clearly Argentine. His name was Felipe and he had been to Balliol in the late eighties where he had read PPE. He can only have been in his early thirties, but had more poise than anyone in the room. He had the assurance of knowing exactly who he was and where he belonged. In a room where nearly everybody appeared to be in some way dislocated, awkward, he seemed to be happy in his skin.

I heard him talking to the Ambassador about the British government's plans to sell off the Embassy in favour of something more modest. Felipe struck just the right note between regret for the passing of an era and acknowledgement that the new Britain did not require anything so ostentatious. The Ambassador was listening to him with more than professional politeness: Felipe's opinions were clearly to be respected.

The conversation moved on to the forthcoming election for the Mayor of Buenos Aires, a crucial road test for the presidential election in the year 2000. Felipe was a political consultant who was running the campaign of the only independent candidate, a woman who had been tortured at the time of the generals and was now fighting a campaign calling for an end to corruption in public life. I asked him if he thought she had any chance of winning. The Ambassador laughed rather undiplomatically but Felipe considered. 'Argentina is still a young democracy. Only one hundred and fifty years ago in England you had rotten boroughs. You still have the House of Lords, though not of course for much longer. Politically, we are still evolving. Of course I would like to think that my candidate will win but as a realist I know that it is unlikely, but I feel that by participating we raise the expectations that the people have of the political process, so that maybe next time or even the time after they will feel able to vote for us.'

It was the most optimistic speech I had heard anyone make in Argentina.

I wondered why Felipe had chosen to go to Oxford and not to a university in Argentina. 'My mother is English, but it was my father who wanted me to go. Argentina is full of Anglophiles, except of course when it comes to football.'

Felipe was sending his children to St George's, the public school which, according to its founders, had been set up 'to educate boys in sound Christian virtues in a country whose moral standards were of the lowest order'. Robin had gone there in the forties and described it as 'a miserable bloody place, worse than any English public school – caning, fagging, the lot'. The school was now bilingual and co-educational but the teachers were all English, and cricket was compulsory. Felipe had recently raised a million pesos so that the school could build a new theatre. The money had mostly been donated by Argentine parents: 'I had terrible problems getting money out of the old Georgians. No respect for the old school tie. I thought the English liked to preserve their traditions.'

St George's is now the most expensive and sought-after school in the country. Argentine parents with no English connections put their children's names down at birth.

Later, when I was staying with Robin, I found an Old Georgian newsletter with a list of all the senior prefects since the school began in 1897. For the first ninety years the names are solidly Anglo-Saxon – Smyth, Dobbs, Gibson, Graham, Mannering – but by the late 1980s the hard Germanic consonants have been broken up by liquid Latin vowels – Anchorena, Martinez, Esposito, Sarmiento.

The legacies of British exclusivity like the public schools, the clubs were being preserved by precisely the people they had been devised to exclude. To aspirational Argentines there was nothing smarter than sending their children to St George's, or eating grey roast beef and Yorkshire pudding at the Hurlingham Club for Sunday lunch.

My cousin Patrick, who had grown up speaking English at home, and had gone to St George's and then to Cirencester, spoke English badly and reluctantly, his face contorted with the effort of speaking the wrong language; but his wife, who was a Catholic Argentine from BA, spoke English without an accent and would talk to her children only in that language, whilst their father would use only Spanish.

All the men of Robin's age at the dinner would have joined the English club in Buenos Aires, with its framed portraits of Queen Mary and its library full of books by Sapper and Alistair MacLean, as a matter of course, but their sons thought the place was ridiculous and refused to go near it. Despite its dwindling membership the club did a brisk trade at lunchtime supplying Argentine businessmen with steak-and-kidney pudding, Irish stew and spotted dick. In a country with the best beef in the world, a reservation was essential to secure a table at the English club on a Tuesday, when shepherd's pie and treacle tart were on the menu.

Felipe talked about London, where he had spent a year working in the House of Commons. 'I think you can tell a great deal about a city from its statues. In Hyde Park you have a statue of Peter Pan, the boy who never grew up. Here in Buenos Aires in the Palermo Gardens we have a statue of Red Riding Hood on her way to meet the wolf. You have a figure from a story celebrating innocence, we a character from a story which teaches children not to take things at face value. And of course in the Argentine version of the story, the wolf eats the grandmother all up. Both sides lose.' He smiled, baring his perfect white teeth. 'We Argentines can be a very violent people.'

At the end of the evening, the Secretary (Sidney Sussex, 1948–51) produced a book where we were all invited to sign our names and the names of our colleges. As I wrote my name and my college, Trinity, I wondered if Bob, my great-grandfather, the man who had left Cambridge so abruptly, had ever come to one of these dinners. My great-grandfather had died in 1939 and the dinners had started in the twenties, so it was possible, but as I turned back the pages looking through the lists of Gibsons and Grahams, Hudsons and Cunninghams I could not find a Traill. I asked the Secretary if he knew anything about a Bob Traill who had been to Trinity, Cambridge but who had not taken his degree.

The Secretary, who was drinking his third glass of port, looked at me glassily. 'No point in looking if the fellow didn't get his degree. Society very strict about that sort of thing. Had a few impostors in the early days, men straight off the boat pretending to be Oxford men so that they could get in with the right people. These days we're a bit more relaxed. I mean, I only have your word for it that you've been to Trinity, you could be an impostor yourself.'

There was a touch at my elbow. The young man who had winced earlier at the politically incorrect talk of the Tommies was saying my name with astonishment. 'Are you really Daisy Goodwin? I thought I remembered you when I saw your name on the guest list. I'm the Third Secretary here. We were at school together. You had quite a following in those days. I remember we used to have a list of all the girls and you were in the top three. I liked Emily myself but—'

At this point the Third Secretary's wife appeared. 'Darling, this is Daisy Goodwin, all my friends had crushes on her at school. How extraordinary to find you here. You must tell me what you are doing.'

But his wife had other plans. 'Remember the babysitter, darling.' As they moved away I heard her say to him, 'But she must be much older than that. I'm sure she went to university ages and ages before we did.' It felt odd to find oneself placed so accurately three thousand miles from home.

But my great-grandfather had not been eligible to attend these dinners. I wondered whether he had heard about the Oxford and Cambridge Society when he was living in Las Limpias, and had tried to join, only to be turned away, or had himself turned away from something that would remind him of what he might have had. The fact that he sent three of his children to Cambridge when he could hardly afford to do so suggests that the abrupt termination of his education had affected him profoundly. He wanted his children to belong even if he could not. He wanted to protect his children from the pain that had been inflicted on him, he wanted to give them the thing that he had most wanted. It was an instinct I could completely understand.

From the moment my first daughter was born, I was determined that nothing would ever come between us; there would be no anxious train journeys or divided holidays in her childhood. I would always be there. I wanted her to grow up taking me for granted. I didn't mind if she thought of me as boring but I needed her to think of me as a place of safety, a part of her life which would always be ordered and loving. I remember once trying to explain to Ottilie about divorce when one of her friends' parents were splitting up. I told her that when I was little my parents had got divorced and my mother had gone away to live with another man.

Ottilie said, 'But why didn't you hold onto her and stop her leaving?'

'I tried to but she had to go.'

'I don't think she was very nice to do that. Why didn't she stay and look after you?'

'I don't know,' I said, hit as I always was by that sudden rush of childish bewilderment. But it was also a triumphant moment. My daughter did not understand how a mother could leave her children. In her world mothers were always there.

I realize that in my efforts to redress the balance of my own childhood I may have swung too far the other way.

Just as my Argentine cousins were deliberately forgetting their English in order to prove their *argentinidad*, I have identified with my daughter more than is right in order to show that I am a mother who would never leave. And as I get closer to the Traills I begin to understand how my mother, even in her leaving, was trying to paint the landscape of my childhood with the colours she had always longed for in her own.

By midnight, most of my contemporaries had left, but Robin and his friends were still drinking. Every so often I could hear the word Pinochet ring out, the hard ch richoteting like a rifle shot round these diplomatic walls. I decided to walk around the Embassy gardens to bury myself in the thicket of cape jasmine that I could smell from the balcony. The gardens were lush and mysterious, a voluptuous oasis after the arid glare of the pampas. I remembered Derek saying, 'The trouble with the Traills was that they never knew how to make themselves comfortable.'

They could have had a garden of delights like this and a belle-époque mansion with marble floors; instead their houses were plain and Protestant, the verandah with the corrugated-iron roof the only concession to the languor of the climate.

I heard a step on the path behind me.

'I never wanted to come back, you know.' Robin sat down heavily on a sinuous white marble bench. 'I was going to join the Colonial Service. I heard that you spent the first two years in the Caribbean which sounded like a jolly good idea. I was accepted straight away, had a first-class degree. Thought I was all set. Might even have married Judy. But when my Ma found out she put her foot down. She said, "You've got to come back here and run the farm."'

Argentina was a man's world then. Still is. It was terribly hard for my mother after my father was killed, running a business she knew nothing about. It was unheard of for a woman to be in that position. She told me that she went to an auction once to buy bulls, she went round the pens carefully marking down the beasts she wanted to buy. But then it rained and the paper she was using got soaked and when she came to make a bid she discovered she couldn't read the numbers. The auctioneer shouted at her in Spanish, "Bloody woman who doesn't know her arse from her elbow." She was livid. I had to go back.'

Robin paused. 'Ma was so happy when Ray and I got married. She knew I wouldn't have to struggle the way she did. She wanted me to buy Los Olivos and become a grande estanciero.' Robin took a slug of his whisky. 'I wanted my children to go to England but they thought everything English was somehow stuffy. Should have been firmer with them I suppose, but wanted them to be happy.'

He stood up, confidences at an end. 'Time to go, eh?'

I followed him out of the expensive quiet of the garden into the neon-tinted glare of the Buenos Aires night.

There were no taxis. We walked down the hill towards the Torre de los Ingleses. When it was built in the 1890s it was the tallest building in Buenos Aires. With its height and its four round clock faces it was a deliberate echo of that other clock tower on the Thames. It was built as a gift to the city of Buenos Aires from the British community, as 'a symbol of the warm regard that exists between our two nations. The tower will have four elevations, with the arms of the British government on two sides and the arms of the Argentine nation on the others.'

The subscribers paid for a stonemason to come out from England to carve the lion and the unicorn and *Honi Soit*

Qui Mal Y Pense. The job took him four months to complete. The Argentine emblems, which were being carved by local masons, were not ready for another year.

The tower was intended as something of a peace offering to an Argentine government still smarting from the credit restrictions imposed on them by British banks after the Baring crisis. But it was situated directly opposite the Retiro station where goods from British-owned estancias were brought on British-owned railways to be loaded on to British ships at the adjacent docks; consciously or not it was a reminder to the Argentines that all this activity kept British time. In a country of low flat buildings that had inherited the *mañana* culture of its former Spanish rulers, to build a vertical monument to punctuality was an imperial act. What clearer way could there be to assert that British values were paramount? Even today, to keep *hora inglesa* in Argentina is to arrive exactly on time; it is also used as a term to describe someone who is rigid, obsessive, uptight.

That night the tower was lit by the glittering windows of the thirty-nine-storey Sheraton hotel which now towers over it. The square it stood in used to be called the Plaza Británica but was renamed the Plaza de la Fuerza Aérea in 1982. The tower itself was shrouded in scaffolding, the four round clock faces, the lions and the unicorns covered by tattered green tarpaulins. Someone had spray-painted *Las Malvinas Nuestras* on the doors at the bottom. There was a couple kissing with leisurely thoroughness on the marble steps; on the other side a tramp was sleeping stretched out, a plaster statuette of the Virgin Mary at his head. The clocks had long since stopped.

Robin said, 'They've been repairing it for years. I don't know why they don't just knock the bloody thing down.'

But I could understand the temptation to leave it standing, to leave the stopped clocks and the crumbling unicorns as a monument to *la hora inglesa,* to the futility of foreign timetables.

SIXTEEN

Robin took me to a polo match the day after the dinner at the Embassy. There was a traffic jam on the way to the ground. A demonstration by teachers – the government had reneged on its pre-election promise of a 10 per cent pay increase. Robin was not sympathetic.

'If they don't get a bloody move on we are going to miss the start of the game.' He glanced at his watch again and looked around for a way out. But we were wedged into an eight-lane block of traffic that stretched right across the Avenida 9 de Julio. The teachers shuffled past. As the procession trailed out into stragglers the cars began to inch forward so that the road ahead became a mortal tangle of people and cars. A middle-aged teacher in a head-scarf hit the bonnet of our taxi with her fist as the driver tried to nudge past her. But eventually we cleared the traffic. Robin looked tense. This delay meant that we would be at least fifteen minutes late.

But at the grounds – a huge expanse of velvety green turf almost in the middle of Buenos Aires – there were knots of people still standing round the gates. The game had not started yet: clearly only Robin had expected *la hora inglesa*. We sat in Robin's usual seats, halfway up, bang in the middle on the shady afternoon side: the seats of a professional. The match we were going to see was one of the semi-finals of the Argentine Open, the most important championship in Argentina, and by extension (because Argentine polo is the best), the most important polo championship in the world.

In polo every player is given a rating which becomes his handicap. A novice starts at minus two. The best is plus ten. The handicaps are apportioned based on the number of goals or passes the player has made in the previous season. In professional polo the combined handicaps of the four players in a team have to equal thirty-two. In England it can be a problem to find four players with high enough handicaps to make up a team. This is not an issue in Argentina: one of the teams playing that day, Chapalafeu, had a combined handicap of thirty-nine. The four Heguy brothers who made up Chapalafeu had originally had a goal handicap of forty, but Oracio the oldest had had his handicap reduced to nine after a careless swipe in a practice match had left him blind in one eye. Robin told me that the handicap committee which he sat on had argued for some time about whether the loss of an eye was the equivalent of losing a point, but in the end they had decided that form must be affected by partial blindness even in a player of the calibre of Oracio Heguy.

The other team, La Cañada, had the three Astrada brothers, who had two tens and a nine, and a fourth player who was an eight.

'Old man Astrada had four sons, thought he had a team.' Robin paused to wave at one of his friends. 'But one of the brothers turned out to be a homosexual and he couldn't hit the ball properly so they had to get an outsider to be their back. Polo's not a poofter's game.'

As we waited for the game to begin, men selling water, soft drinks, praline and ice creams threaded their way through the seats. I was becoming thirsty that hot afternoon but Robin ignored them all. At last sensing my interest, he turned to me and said, 'You don't want anything, do you?'

'No, I'm fine,' I lied. Polo clearly was not about refreshment. I didn't want to appear soft.

A bell rang, the game was about to begin. Chapalafeu came out first, their shirts Marlboro Red. La Cañada wore Veuve Cliquot yellow. The ponies' tails and manes were braided in their teams' colours. The players and their horses looked like miniature jewelled bugs against the great expanse of velvety green.

A signal was given and the game began. The teams clustered around the ball so closely that it was impossible to see what was happening. Players were wheeling and circling, drawing their horses round in tight circles trying to get a clear shot. Suddenly one of Chapalafeu got away and hit the ball hard down the field. All the players galloped after it, the tight knot of men and ponies unravelling as they picked up speed. The player who had hit the ball was so fast that he reached the ball first. I could feel Robin tensing. 'Don't just look at the ball, hit the damn thing and score,' he muttered, but the player stopped his horse in an instant and passed the ball back to one of his brothers. Another tight red knot formed around the goal, the Heguy brothers passing the ball back and forth to each other, trying to get a shot at the goal. But just as it seemed that they must score the bell rang announcing the end of the first chukka and all the players immediately galloped off to the ends of the field.

Robin sighed in exasperation. 'I hate all this damn passing, slows the game down terribly. I like a nice open field. All this passing back and forth is very dull, why can't someone just give the ball a good hard thwack? When I played with the Media Luna team we weren't in the first league, but we played a really hard game. By golly, we were tough. Chapalafeu are probably the best team in the world, but they're too worried about tactics, they should get in there, hit the ball and gallop down the field like hell. It's just not the game it used to be.'

Robin was an eight. 'Would have been a top-flight player in England but eights are two a penny here. Still, I always played with lots of spunk.' Robin's eldest son Patrick was a six and his younger son Andrew was a seven. Patrick had only played professionally for a couple of seasons, giving it up when he got married, but Andrew was still playing for a living. When the Argentine season was over he went to England to play on a rich man's team, his seven compensating for the millionaire's handicap of two or three. He would play all through the English summer, living in a cottage in the Cotswolds with some other Argentine players. At the end of the season, depending on the tournaments and the generosity of the sponsor, he would make forty or fifty thousand pounds. 'Andrew can make enough in an English season to live very comfortably here for the rest of the year, especially as he lives in our apartment here in BA. But otherwise he's bone idle, polo has spoilt him for anything else. He tried to get a job as a male model once, thought he had the looks for it. Agency took him on like a shot: he did some commercial for whisky or something and made a very reasonable amount of money. Agency kept ringing him up and asking him back, but Andrew wouldn't go back, said he didn't like all the hanging around. He plays here in the winter a bit, but he's not really good enough to play in the big league. But sometimes a player will drop out or a team will want to bring down their handicap and then they'll call Andrew in. I can't bear to watch him play, makes me too angry. He's got a real feeling for the ball, great natural ability but he's all over the place, wants to do everything. No idea what it takes to be a team player.'

The bell rang for the next chukka. All the players had fresh ponies. As each game has five to eight chukkas and the ponies are changed after each one, every team needs a string of at least twenty-four to thirty-two ponies with a few extra in case an animal goes lame or is injured. The teams also have to provide mounts for the referee. The cost of maintaining a polo team to match standard for a season is in millions. The teams that were playing that day were both sponsored by huge tobacco firms. Only multi-millionaires like Kerry Packer could afford to have their own private teams. The game started again, the red team scored immediately, there was a round of polite applause. Then a yellow player got the ball away, hitting it so hard that I could hear the thwack three hundred yards away. The Number 3s from both teams were urging their horses down the long green oval, but yellow got there first and scored; this time the applause was warmer. Robin relaxed a little. 'That's more like it,' he said. 'Time those ponies got a bit of a sweat on them.' At the side of the pitch two grooms were galloping the next chukka's ponies up and down to warm them up before they went into play. 'Never play a cold pony,' said Robin.

As the chukka ended a man of about Robin's age came over to shake his hand. '*Buenas tardes, Don Robin, qué tal?*' Robin replied in Spanish but did not attempt to introduce me to his friend. To introduce me as his English cousin, though true, might produce a knowing smile. I looked around at the other spectators. They were mostly male and middle-aged, but they did not have the paunches or the sweaty pallor of the equivalent crowd at Lord's. Despite the strength of the late-afternoon sun, no one wore a hat. The only women I saw were in the hospitality tent wearing tight white jodphurs and polo shirts with *Hennessy* embroidered on the back. This was a professional weekday audience: the match which had been meant to take place at the weekend had been postponed because of rain. 'Can't play polo in the mud, the ponies slip and it all gets very messy,' Robin explained. But though the stands were only three-quarters full, it was being televised and the next day an account of the match took up two pages in *La Nación*. Unlike in England where it is a kind of posh caprice – the preserve of princes and romantic novelists – polo has a real following in Argentina. Buenos Aires does not come to a standstill for the final of the Argentine Open as it did the Sunday that Boca Juniors played Inter, but everybody knows who is playing and has an opinion on who will win. No Argentine can ignore a sport in which Argentina is the world leader. And though most of the population live in the cities, Argentines still like to think of themselves as a gaucho nation. Even if polo is a rich man's sport, the players are considered national heroes, supreme examples of *argentinidad*. The love lives of the top players make cover stories for the Argentine version of *¡Hola!* Every convent schoolgirl dreams of being swept off her feet by a ten at Buenos Aires's famous Hurlingham Club.

By the end of the game the red team was in the lead by ten goals to six. Robin was disappointed by the score.

'In a decent game, a good team can score ten, fifteen goals a chukka.'

If the red team, Chapaleufu, was successful in the finals, it would be the sixth time they had won the Argentine Open, a record which would put them closer to the standard set by the North Santa Fé team who had won the championship eight times between 1904 and 1917. There was no match in 1914 because of the First World War.

This was where polo became personal as the North Santa Fé team was made up of Bob, my great-grandfather, his brothers Ned and Johnny and their cousin Joe Traill, Edmund's son. Ned had a seven handicap, Bob was an eight, Joe was a nine and Johnny, the youngest, had a ten-goal handicap. 'Best polo player in the world,' said Robin, 'until he went blind. Poor fella. Ended up falling out of a window and breaking his neck. Tragic accident they said, but it was pretty clear he'd done it on purpose. Couldn't play any more.'

Polo. Robin said 'pohloh', making the word sound sharp, explosive, dangerous. A pistol shot instead of the posh mint-with-a-hole sound I made. I tried unsuccessfully to change my pronunciation. I found my how-now-brown-cow vowels embarrassing, inappropriate to this vital, terrifying game. I have no feeling for sport myself and yet I could feel the pull of this game like a taut string. No other sport had such acceleration, when the players opened out into a long arc hurtling towards the goal, their desperate speed whipped through the ground. This was a game I felt was as much about not dying as it was about winning. I could imagine how the shots of speed and terror in polo must have been addictive to a family living in near exile in the flattest country in the world.

I found it odd, though, that my competitive grandmother – the one who played bridge and even snap to the death – should never have mentioned this Traill achievement, should never in a lifetime spent accumulating trophies have mentioned the cup her father won eight times. He had won it for the third time in 1908, the year my grandmother was born. I wondered why this spur of victory had not been included in the story of the decline and fall of the Traills. The only details I had heard before I came to Argentina about Johnny Traill, at one time the greatest polo player in the world, were the circumstances of his death. My family's unreliable narrators had chosen to record the manner of his fall, not the achievements of his life.

A few days after the polo match I was introduced to Veronica, Johnny Traill's granddaughter, who lived on a remnant of the Traill estates in a house called La Esterlina. She was married to a *porteño*, who hated camp and spent most of his time in Buenos Aires. In her late forties, she was tall and wiry, a lean English beauty: she could have ridden with the Quorn. She still wore her auburn hair long and her faded blue eyes had the faraway look of someone used to looking ahead at the horizon. Like Robin, she walked with a limp. Her stride started so gracefully but ended in an awkward hiccup as she dragged the injured leg along. Like Robin, she had hurt her leg falling from a horse.

She breeds polo ponies at La Esterlina and was schooling a pony in the *potrero* (paddock) when she fell. 'One moment of distraction, years of regrets,' she said as she took me round the *galpón* (stable), exchanging a caress with each of the ponies as she went. 'I don't know if I will ever ride again.' For Veronica as for Robin it was a life sentence.

We walked past the tack room with its rows of bamboo

polo sticks. Veronica's daughters, Maddalena and Inés, both play polo in the new Argentine Women's League. Veronica showed me the colours of her daughters' team and pictures of them playing an exhibition match. 'Maddalena is technically the better rider but Inés has real fire. If she wanted to she could be a champion.'

Veronica had never had the chance to play herself. 'My father would never let me play polo. He thought it was a man's game.' Veronica's two sons, Pablo and Agustín, do not want to play polo. 'They only want to go to parties and have a good time.' Veronica did not need to add that her sons took after their Argentine father, who, according to Derek, had not done a day's work in years. After her accident, Rafael (the husband) wanted to sell up and move to BA, but Veronica refused. She told me with enough sadness in her voice to make me think that her resistance was not limitless, 'My life is horses. I need to be here in the camp.'

Veronica was ten or fifteen years younger than Robin and Derek and though both her parents were Anglo-Argentines who would have spoken English at home, she spoke English haltingly and with an accent. But after an hour or two in her company the Spanish notes in her voice began to fall away and every so often I heard the vowels she had been born with. Her husband spoke no English or pretended not to. I felt that Veronica had been forced to choose between the two cultures. Selling La Esterlina would be severing the final link between her current life and her Traill past.

The house was cool and airy. It had the verandah, the high ceilings and the long green shutters of the traditional estancia. The rooms opened off a long central corridor whose walls were covered in photos of polo teams past and present: the classic after-match shot – mounted, helmets off, sticks held up in the right hand, smiles to the camera – interspersed with swooping moments of drama captured by the telephoto lens, in which a player would be grimly holding onto the reins with one hand, raising the other arm as if to wield a terrible blow.

At the end of the corridor I found a picture of the North Santa Fé team after their victory in the 1908 Argentine Open. The three brothers and their cousin Joe look almost identical in their striped shirts and white jodphurs, their high foreheads revealed by stringent short-back-and-side haircuts, each with a tuft of forelock in the centre like a pony's. They all sport (and 'sport' is the only verb possible) luxuriant Kitchener-like moustaches. My great-grandfather Bob is in the centre of the picture, his body straight to the camera, feet well down in the stirrups. His face is inscrutable, almost grave, not a flicker of triumph except perhaps in the strong vertical thrust of his stick. His brother Johnny is on the left, his body rather more relaxed; unlike his brother he has nothing to prove.

Veronica saw me peering at the photograph. 'That's my grandfather Johnny Traill. You know, when my daughter Maddalena went to play polo in England they wrote about her in the newspaper as Johnny Traill's great-grand-daughter. They still remembered.'

I asked if she had known him well. Her face clouded. 'No, I never met him. He died when I was a little girl. I think maybe he and my father were not so close . . .' Then she brightened. 'But we have all his trophies. Come, I'll show you.'

She led me out of the colonial cool of the old estancia into a modern extension, probably built around the fifties judging by the huge Flintstone-type fireplace in the middle of the room. Veronica surprised me by laughing. 'I know, it's hideous, isn't it. My father built it, he was going to pull down the whole house and rebuild it but then he died . . .' She paused. 'I think I'm the only one in the family to like old things.'

Johnny's cups were on the top shelf. Unlike the shiny plate trophies of his great-granddaughters, his memorials were dark with tarnish. I took one down, heavily dented as if someone had thrown something at it. Through the stain of years of neglect I could make out the following inscription:

> *ARGENTINE CHAMPIONSHIP POLO*
> *TORNAMENT* [sic]
> *1904*
> *WON BY*
> *NORTH SANTA FÉ*

On the other side were the names of the winning team, all with the same surname, only the initials varying: J.E., E., J.A.E., R.W., the same letters repeated and reworked in an endless loop of kinship. Veronica saw me feeling the dent with my thumb. 'I think my father used that cup for target practice.'

The way her voice trailed off made me reluctant to enquire further. Fathers and sons. Perhaps Johnny Traill had been kinder to his horses than to his children.

'If you're really interested,' Veronica sounded doubtful, 'my grandfather wrote a memoir. I have it here somewhere. Would you like to have a look?' I did, very much. She disappeared for a moment and came back with a ledger-sized book bound in red leather. 'My grandfather had this printed privately. He wrote it in his seventies, not long before he died.' I opened the book. The title page read, '*The Long Chukker*, by John Traill'.

'It's quite an old-fashioned book,' said Veronica, 'even the title. No one spells "chukka" like that any more.'

I read *The Long Chukker* that night in one gulp, trying to ignore the scuttlings in the roof of Las Limpias Two. The title, though clumsily metaphorical in intent, was actually quite literal. This was the story of a life lived through polo. A memoir in which horses figured more prominently than people. The first line reads: '*I have often wondered what my mother must have thought when, as a bride of eighteen, my father took her away from Ireland to the unknown vastness of South America. Why did he go? What prompted him at the age of twenty-four to begin such a completely new life?*'

But it is not a question Johnny Traill attempts to answer. His narrative was very different from the stories handed down by my maternal relatives. He wasn't interested in the questions of love and marriage that still fascinate me a century on. No, Johnny Traill's preoccupations were entirely equestrian. After that opening paragraph, his mother Alice is completely ignored. As a non-rider she really has no part in his story. Other members of his family get a little more space but only in the saddle His sister Edith gets a line, described as a '*superb horsewoman riding side-saddle even in the* potero' but his other sisters are only mentioned if they marry a decent player. His brother Basil is written out of the story very early: '*my victories of the early nineties were when we started our four Traill team – three brothers and a cousin Joe Traill. My other brother Basil was never good enough. He had, unfortunately, been dropped as a baby by a nurse, so that although he did play, he never became good enough to compete in*

tournaments.' Being dropped by the nurse must have been
the family's euphemism for Basil's disability. Much more
convenient to blame his problems on a careless nurse than
to admit that there was some kind of congenital disorder.

After pages describing a famous victory at the
Hurlingham Club, he lets slip that, *'In 1913 I was married.
She was not only the best wife a man could ever wish for,
but she was an excellent horsewoman too! She had beautifully light hands and was wonderful at schooling the
young ponies. She shared my passion for polo.'* That is
the only mention of his wife, whose name I discovered
later was Rita, although her brother 'Bunty' Roberts rates
a line or two on account of being a *'promising player
whose handicap went from five to eight in two years . . .'*

The most telling thing about the book is not what it
includes but what it omits. Johnny's take on the family's
financial ruin is typical. *'Perhaps Father had a hankering
for a squire's life, I don't know, but we settled in at the
Manor House and he bought a smart new brougham. I
was entered for Eton and except for the catastrophe which
struck our estancia, I would no doubt have spent my
young life wearing a wing collar and top hat and being a
scholar. As it turned out I never in my life wore one and
was much more at home in a polo helmet.'*

Johnny, unlike his older brother Bob, my great-grandfather, does not resent returning to the Argentine. After
describing the journey to the estancia, during which as
there were no passenger trains on the last leg, the family
was forced to travel in a wheat truck – *'I don't know
what the rest of the family thought about it, but I was
much in favour of the adventure and thought it decidedly
more amusing than travelling in an ordinary carriage'* –
Johnny then calls his first day at the estancia the most

important one of his young life. His father, who Johnny calls '*always impetuous*' decides it is time that his youngest son learns to ride and puts him on a little red *criollo* pony. '*I was put astride it and soon I was screaming with fright. I was positive the pony was bucking viciously, and no one could convince me that it was kicking to scare away the flies.*'

Read at this distance it seems more cruel than impetuous for a father to put his terrified seven-year-old son on a horse on the first day in his new home and insist that he learns to ride. It feels symbolic, a rite of passage to enter a new world, a world which only made sense on horse-back. It must have been extraordinary for a child brought up in England, where the only horses he knew were the ones that pulled the brougham that took him to parties. Here in the Argentine, horses easily outnumbered people. '*You can imagine that we had enough horses to ride when I tell you that the day before my eighth birthday, our wild mares were rounded up from open camp and corralled, and with foals at foot they numbered over two thousand.*' The horses were being corralled so that Johnny could choose one for his birthday.

In a memoir that does not include so much as an adjective to describe a person or a place, there is a remarkably detailed passage describing the colours of the wild horses.

My father's favourite was gatiado, *yellow with a dark brown strip down the back from mane to tail and brown stripes round the hocks. They were very* guapa *– good stayers – and he had twelve of them as his riding horses. Besides the* gatiado *there were* overo, *spotted;* ruano, *resembling a palomino being light chestnut with a white mane and tail;* picaso, *black*

*with white stockings and white face; rosillo, roan;
tordillo, grey; moro, iron grey; bayo, cream; blanco,
white with often a wall eye; as well as all the usual
colours such as alasan, light chestnut; zaino, dark
bay; colorado, light bay; and tostado, dark chestnut.
In the later years all the different colours were to die
out and after breeding with the thoroughbreds we
brought out, they mostly became the colour of English
thoroughbreds.*

Most of the Spanish words in *The Long Chukker* are
misspelt or simply wrong; another person, Veronica maybe,
had gone through the book correcting all the errors in
pencil, but there are no correction marks over this passage.
The colours of the wild horses and the precise detail of
their Spanish names had been etched into Johnny Traill's
memory. Perhaps this was the only part of his childhood
he could bear to remember so closely. He goes on to write
of his bewilderment at being asked to choose one pony
from so many: '*After wandering round the corral for nearly
an hour, I shouted, "Dad, come in and help me choose
one!" But he only shook his head. "Certainly not! Choose
one for yourself – that's the whole point!"*'

Choosing a pony was clearly another test of character.
There is a revealing little sentence at the end of this story:
'*Because he was the first pony I had really owned and
when he died suddenly, years before he should, I was so
heartbroken that I made up my mind never to get really
fond of another one.*' It is the only time that Johnny
mentions feeling love of any kind.

There is nothing tender about Johnny's other memories
of his childhood which are a string of anecdotes called
'Wild Cows', 'Wild Horse' and 'Narrow Escapes', which

have that lip-smacking delight in the macabre that I remember from my grandmother and her story of the dead donkey. His sister is tossed by a vicious cow with two-foot horns, a peon boy is kicked to death by a new stallion ('*we were all very careful how we approached the horse after that*'); Johnny is always breaking in horses that try to kill him: '*I narrowly missed cracking my skull open like an egg.*' The Traills had a taste for the Grand Guignol: the more disgusting the story the more clearly it is remembered and vividly described. Reading those stories of Johnny's I can remember the relish with which my grandmother told her story of the donkey, pausing with shining eyes to take in our reaction as she elaborated on the precise feel of decomposing flesh. It was gallows humour, a way of dealing with the unacceptable. The trick was to ride hard and not look back.

When Johnny is about fourteen he goes over to the Dickinson estancia Las Lomas with his brothers for a polo match. But the drains are so bad that Johnny catches typhoid fever and nearly dies. The doctor diagnoses an internal haemorrhage and prescribes ice as the only remedy. '*The ice had to come from Rosario, wrapped in a blanket and sawdust, a journey of five hours on the train. Someone went down with a trap and pair to meet it at Carlos Pellegrini and by the time it arrived at my bedside it had melted down to about one icebag full. The temperature was 104 degrees in the shade. I managed to pull through somehow, but I was never to be really fit again.*'

Elsewhere he talks about the gastric trouble that plagued him since childhood, a preoccupation with health which sits oddly with a lifetime playing professional polo. Perhaps illness was the only possible way for him to express his emotions, the recurrent gastric trouble the result of a childhood spent trying not to be scared. '*Recurrent attacks of colitis*' is the reason he gives for coming back to live in England to '*get out of the hot Argentine sun*'. Perhaps his recurrent stomach trouble had more to do with living with his family than it had to do with the climate. His periods of ill-health seem to coincide with long stretches of time at Las Limpias.

Tucked into the back of the book Veronica gave me was a collection of newspaper clippings. They were mostly reviews of Johnny's matches but there were also the hatch, match, dispatch notices of a lifetime. One clipping in particular added a sad coda to a passage from Johnny's memoirs in the chapter called 'Two Strokes I'll Never Forget'.

> *But rejoicing was short for no sooner had we brought the cup [Westchester] home than the First World War started and there was no more polo for four years . . . I was anxious to join up and asked the doctor if I was fit enough. He said rather briskly that if I wasn't fit enough to play polo, something I'd been doing all my life, I certainly wouldn't stand the strain of war for more than a month or so. I was very depressed and thought rather than be another mouth to feed, we'd better go back to the Argentine.*

The reason for his depression that Johnny does not mention I found in this pair of clippings, both from *The Times* of September 1914:

BIRTH

Traill – on Sep 29th, the wife of J.A.E. Traill of The Manor House, Newbury, Bucks, of a daughter.

DEATH

*On Sep 30th, Yvonne Alice, infant daughter
of Mr and Mrs J.A.E. Traill, of The Manor
House, Newbury, Bucks.*

I am haunted by the image of Johnny in his seventies living in Roehampton; nearly blind, writing *The Long Chukker* and remembering in his crepuscular present the endless shades and variations of the wild horses he had known as a child. At the end of the memoir he writes that he should have written this twenty years ago, as all the friends who would have enjoyed reading it are dead. Three months after finishing *The Long Chukker* Johnny walked out of his bedroom window and broke his neck.

Right at the end of the book there are two photographs, one of Johnny and one of his wife Rita. Both are on horseback captured in profile, both have the same erect posture and taut jawline. Johnny in his forties looks obdurate, Rita who is riding side-saddle looks as if she has been carved from granite. I remembered the dent in the cup and Johnny's vow never to have his heart broken again after his pony died. Did his two sons enjoy their childhood swinging polo sticks on bicycles? Could their handicaps ever be high enough to please their father?

The eldest son Jim became a pilot in the RAF during the war and was shot down by his own station after failing to give the right signal. His younger brother Jack, Veronica's father, survived the war and afterwards went to the Argentine to manage Johnny's portion of the Traill estates, the estancia at La Esterlina. He may have gone to the Argentine willingly, but it is quite likely that his father gave him no choice. Who else was going to manage the land while he Johnny lived in England?

I sensed from the way that Veronica picked her words carefully when talking about her father, that he was the most fragile of subjects for her. When she spoke about him it was as if she was picking her way past a sheer drop.

I was going to meet Veronica again the next day. Before I went I asked Derek what had happened to her father.

'Jack Traill, alcoholic of course. Funny, when Johnny never touched a drop. Shot himself in the mouth, very messy. Did it behind the house in the *galpón*. Foreman found him. Went to tell my Ma, not Jack's wife, so my Ma had to do all the tidying up and break the news. Poor bugger, not a happy home life, wife was an awful nagger. Better not ask too many questions if I were you.'

I was not surprised by Jack Traill's fate. Somehow I wasn't expecting a happy ending.

SEVENTEEN

I had been staying with Derek at Las Limpias Two for about a week when it started to rain. Not polite English drops but violent Argentine torrents which battered at the roof. In the morning the roads which had been like dry river beds had turned into muddy chutes. Derek looked out of the window. 'I was going to go into San Jorge today to pick up the new seed, but I don't think I'll even get as far as Traill in this bloody weather.'

I could hardly believe what I was hearing. 'You mean there's a town called Traill?'

'Oh, there's a town called Traill all right, why I don't know but there it is. It's even got its own bloody mayor.'

As a child I would sometimes say the word Traill to myself like a mantra. I loved the sound of possibility that lingered in the word, the road to somewhere soft and inviting ending on those two last velvety l's. It was a name that had romantic potential in the way that my own solidly constructed surname did not. It was like everything tinged by my mother: glamorous and somehow unattainable. Even here in Argentina I had not met any real Traills: the name had been lost in all the early deaths and daughters. I felt an almost physical sense of shock. I hadn't expected a town.

I wanted to go there at once, but Derek was reluctant; the roads were too bad, he said, but I suspected that the phantom limb of the Traill inheritance was hurting him that day. In the end, sad Veronica took me in her four-wheel drive; it was not the distant past that troubled her. It took about half an hour to drive there, across land that once would have all belonged to the Traills. At the end of the nineteenth century when the town was founded it would have been as quick to ride there across the open pampas as it was today to drive. Now that endless sweep of land had been divided and subdivided, the generous horizon broken up by barbed wire and spindly rows of poplars fighting an uneven battle with the prevailing winds. It was a tamed landscape. Like the wild horses of the pampas this country had been broken, the different colours of the *paja y cielo* (grass and sky) disappearing into the deep red brown of cultivation. Pampa comes from an Indian word meaning 'space'. The word is all that remains of that vast inland sea or indeed of the people who named it.

A clump of buildings appeared on the horizon. There it is, the fair town of Traill, said Veronica. As we drew nearer I saw an arch over the main road which read, '*1892 Traill 1992*'.

The centenary was a very big thing here, said Veronica.

The town or to be more accurate the pueblo of Traill consists of a couple of streets running parallel to the railway line that connects Buenos Aires and Santa Fé. The muddy thoroughfare of the main street is flanked by a once fine collection of civic buildings with intricate white stucco fronts, their uses visible from the signs that can still be read over the doors: a police station, a post office, a library, a school.

The library is meant to be open on Tuesdays, said Veronica, but whenever I go it's always closed.

On the next street there were five bars including the Tintoria de Traill, which at four in the afternoon appeared to be full. Only five years ago Traill had a population of about two hundred people, most of whom worked at the *tambo* (dairy) which made cheese. But the man who owned the factory fell in love with one of the workers and ran off with her and all the factory's profits to Buenos Aires. So the *tambo* is now closed and the inhabitants of Traill have dwindled from two hundred to sixty. At least half of the male population of Traill were in the bar that afternoon.

All the houses in Traill had a temporary look. Broken windows had been replaced by snagged polythene sheeting, a family was sitting outside on cardboard boxes eating lunch, a man was taking a crate of chickens out of the back of a Model T Ford circa 1925. Along the street there were holes here and there where a house had been pulled down, like gaps in a row of teeth. When people leave Traill to look for work they demolish their homes and take all the bricks and timbers with them to build a new place somewhere else.

When the Traill brothers founded the town in 1892, they were hoping to profit from the railway and the tide of immigrants which it was bringing into the countryside. They donated the land for the *comuna* and built the school and the library in the hope that they would be able to sell off the surrounding plots to would-be town dwellers.

But the Brothers Traill did not prosper as property developers. They did not know the importance of bribing the right official at the Cartography Society. As a result the new town of Traill was not officially marked on the map until 1905, by which time all the hard-working, desirable immigrants had passed through on their way to somewhere else.

Everything in Argentina had a key but the Traills could never find it.

The commune of Traill clusters round its station. But no trains stop there now; the occasional freight train is all that is left of the Central Argentine Railway, once the most profitable line in South America.

The empty platform felt oddly familiar. I recognized the wrought-iron pillars, the gingerbread-house edging to the roof. It was more or less the same station as the one in Swanage. The station where as a little girl I would wait for trains that would take me away from my mother.

After the last train stopped in Traill, the stationmaster was allowed to turn the buildings into his home, so that now the platforms bustle with hanging baskets and pots. The signal box has become a greenhouse, the switching levers are green with the tendrils of runner beans. His children play in the gentlemen's waiting room and his wife's clothes hang behind the ticket counter. In a niche where the mail-bags were kept, someone has made a shrine to the Madonna. Only the sign saying Traill has been left unadorned, the maroon letters stark against the yellow paint. The sign itself was clearly of a more recent vintage than the rest of the station. There was a reason for this. In 1949 Perón decided to nationalize the railways: 'Argentina is a country that must make its own future without foreign interference.' Argentina's position as an unofficial colony of the British Empire, which had suited the oligarchy of landowners and generals who had ruled the country for decades, was not acceptable to the Peronists. Resentment against the badges of the British influence ran high; the Buenos Aires Cricket and Rugby Club pavilion was burnt to the ground, the English Club had its windows broken so often that a special window sub was demanded from members. In Traill the local librarian wrote to the Ministry of the Interior and suggested that his town's name be changed as '*a patriotic gesture*'. He hoped that it would be possible to rename the town after the First Lady of Argentina who it was rumoured was fatally ill. Permission was granted and the town was officially renamed Evita in June 1952. The former Eva Duarte was in the last stages of terminal cancer but a note hand-written in green ink was sent to the citizens of the town to express her gratitude for the honour. When the woman who the Congress had designated as the *Jefa Espiritual de la Nación* (Spiritual Leader of the Nation) died on 26 July, the town that was now known as Evita went into mourning. It was the thirty-third town in Argentina to lose its namesake. The residents of the town clubbed together to buy a pastel-tinted oleograph of the nation's spiritual leader to place on the town hall. A special train was arranged so that the residents could pay their last respects. The librarian was elected mayor.

The town's new identity did not last long, though. In 1955 Perón was deposed in a military coup. Shortly afterwards the librarian-turned-mayor left Evita never to return. The new mayor was a butcher called Diego Theakston, whose grandfather had come from Norfolk to work for the Traills. His first act on taking office was to change the town's name. It was the same for Evita-villes all over the country. Nobody wanted to proclaim their connection to the old regime. In the town formerly known as Traill, the plaque of Evita looking like the Virgin Mary was taken down and the flower bed spelling her name was allowed to run to seed. Some of the townspeople wanted to call the town San Martín after the general who had liberated Argentina from the Spanish but Diego Theakston was firm: '*In a country like ours where we have so little history we must not forget the men who founded our community.*' In

January 1956 the town was officially renamed Traill. The original town sign had 'disappeared' so a new one was installed; the yellow-and-maroon colour scheme was chosen by Diego Theakston in reference perhaps to the colours of the now defunct Central Argentine Railway.

In 1992 Traill celebrated its centenary. A dais was erected in the station and the entire population of Traill and all the Traill descendants living in the area gathered round to hear speeches made by the mayor and by Dinny Harvey, Edmund Traill's granddaughter. Another plaque was put up, a handsome brass affair with Art Nouveau lettering which reads:

> *PUEBLO y COLONIA de TRAILL*
> *En Homenaje a sus fundadores*
> *EDMONDO y ROBERTO TRAILL*
> *Y primeros pobladores en el dia*
> *Del centenario de su fundacion*
> *27.9.92*

It seemed fitting that the only official commemoration of my Traill forebears should be in a language they had never bothered to learn.

In the street we passed a group of little boys playing football. One of them was wearing the Number 8 strip of Simeone, the player who had provoked David Beckham's petulant kick in the World Cup. Football was another British import that the Argentines had nationalized. I asked one of the boys what he thought of the English team. 'They do not play with their hearts,' he said.

Veronica told me that three of the white stucco buildings along the main street were for sale, 'only six hundred pesos', about three hundred and fifty pounds. There was one in particular that appealed to me: its pillared doorway and wrought-iron gates had a scaled-down belle-epoque sumptuousness that chimed with my childhood vision of the Traills. The front door was locked but there was a verandah at the back where the door could be opened easily enough. The house must have been built for someone substantial: the ceilings were high, there were elegant mouldings around the ceilings and door. Two large square rooms opened off the central corridor, and in one of them hung a grimy chandelier that every so often would catch the light, sending diamond spots flitting round the room. I pictured myself living in this pocket-sized mansion looking at the reassuring British-made bulk of the station from the front windows and then walking through the house to the verandah to face the blank horizon. Buying the house had a narrative appeal. It was a way of reconciling the past with the present. I could have my own Argentina. But as I looked west from the verandah as the bruise-like colours of the sunset seeped into the sky, across the land that had once belonged to the Traills, I felt the menace of that unbroken horizon.

The British thought that they could have the best of Argentina without getting involved; they did not understand that this was a country that needed to be loved. In 1899 an Argentine writer remarked of the English in Argentina that *'The Briton in Argentina is not of Argentina. He always looks forward to returning some day to his northern isles to end his days among the associations of his youth.'*

The British could not appreciate the resentment that their indifference provoked. The passion that the Malvinas provokes in even the most liberal-seeming Argentine has as much to do with this collective memory of British coolness as it has to do with territorial pride. Even today, when Britain's influence is just a ghostly trace of what it was, its very existence is as annoying as that of an ex-husband.

*   *   *

I asked Veronica to take a picture of me by the station sign. She was surprised. The idea of Traill held no glamour for her. But she gamely limped across the tracks to get 'the most flattering angle'. When I told her that as a child I had made Traill my middle name she was astonished. But there is nothing special about the Traills, she said, polo was the only thing they were good at . . . and drinking, of course.

Veronica looked tired. She may have been thinking about her father and his peculiarly Traill end. None of the Traills, past or present, seem to have been satisfactory fathers. My grandmother very rarely mentioned her father Bob but she did tell one story of his ignominious return to the Argentine after the family had been ruined by the Baring's Bank collapse. It ended with Robert, Bob's father, not recognizing his son when he got off the train. I was standing on the platform where this scene must have taken place. It didn't seem so very remote. I had stood on this platform's replica many times wondering if my mother would remember I was coming to visit. She always did remember but the doubt was still there.

The train which took Bob from Buenos Aires north to Traill in late May was unbearably hot. It was the last stage of the journey that had begun in a snowstorm in Cambridge. Bob sweated in his travelling ulster that he dared not remove because of the dust. The man sitting opposite him had been tinted sepia; when he took out his hunter the gold case gleamed against the matt background. This was Bob's second day on the train. Officially the journey to Carlos Pellegrini was only eighteen hours but the south-west wind that was blowing the dust into the carriage was slowing the train down. An Englishman who had left the train at Rosario told Bob that he had once spent four days making the same journey. The view from the window had barely changed in the last eight hours. Only the noise of the train made the idea of forward motion credible. For the first few hours after leaving Buenos Aires, the landscape had been more docile: there had been wheat fields and water towers, and clumps of poplars shading the houses. But after Rosario, the landscape lost this veneer of grooming. All Bob could see through the swirling dust was the occasional ombu tree and clumps of cattle gathered round a watering hole. The carriage, at least, was familiar, being of the same size and layout as the carriages on the trains between London and Cambridge. Screwed to the wall was a glass-framed picture of a flat landscape, which could have been the Fens. Bob wondered if he should have another drink. But his money was nearly gone. He had spent fifty pesos buying a lottery ticket in Entre Ríos from a man who had convinced him in English that this was the ticket for the *gran premio*. Bob had spent the last night on the train dreaming of what it would be like to arrive home with enough money to solve all the family's financial problems, but when he woke in the morning, this rosy future had evaporated. It was hard to believe in good or bad luck in this country without variation, where every mile just brought more of the same.

Bob was wondering whether Trinity would ever send on the oar from the university boat, when the train juddered and dropped speed. The carriage shook with the shriek of the train whistle and the steam escaping from the valve billowed into the carriage and made the dust run in fine brown trickles down Bob's face. He could see nothing at first as he leant out of the window – the view ahead was obscured by clouds of steam and dust – but above the scream of the whistle he could hear a higher note of agony. Now he could see shapes rearing and twisting around the carriages. He immediately thought of Indians, the menace of his childhood, but he had heard no shots. He realized that it must be a *tropilla*, a troop of wild horses, which had somehow wondered onto the track in this land without fences. He waited for the train to stop so that the guards could get out and drive away the horses, which must have panicked when the driver blew his whistle and let out that great hiss of steam. But the train did not stop. Bob realized with amazement that the driver was intending to plough straight through the herd. Bob saw a horse's leg fly past the open window, drops of blood spattering the inside of the carriage. He felt something warm and sticky fall on his hand. Salty bile was rising at the back of his throat. He fought his way through the crowds of people lining the windows to the front of the train. He could see the engineer throwing shovel after shovel of wood into the fire. He opened his mouth to speak: what was the word for stop? '*Más despacio*,' (more slowly) he screamed, grabbing the engineer by the shoulder and staring straight into his eyes. The engineer simply shrugged. It was not his fault that the train was slowing down; couldn't the gringo see that he was doing his best? A horse's head landed on the floor of the cab, and the engineer kicked it away with his foot. Bob was filled with panic: somehow he must stop this, why did the man not understand him? In desperation he snatched the shovel from the man's hand and threw it away. He felt the crack of the man's fist before his head hit the carriage floor. Struggling to his feet he jumped off the train into the screaming mass of horses. He tried to push them away from the train with his bare hands but they were wild horses that found the man as terrifying as the hissing monster on the track. All he could see were flashes of white from the horses' eyes. A hoof hit him in the ribs. There was nothing he could do, nothing that would stop the horses rushing headlong at this iron snake. He staggered back to the train which was still moving slowly enough for him to pull himself back on board. A man in uniform, the conductor, yelled something at him in Spanish, '*gringo loco*,' but Bob was too spent to reply. He just wanted to be left alone. He took off his ulster which was wet with blood and sweat and threw it out of the window. It was only then that he remembered the lottery ticket in the pocket. When, thirty years later, he told my grandmother this story, he said, 'I could have been a millionaire if it hadn't been for those damn-fool horses. Can't think what I was doing.'

My grandmother, when she told this story, used to finish the scene with the train at Traill station, the engine's cowcatcher covered in flesh and blood 'like an abattoir'. Robert, who was waiting at the station, did not recognize the limping figure with a black eye who got off the train as his son, and Bob, who had not seen his father for five years, walked straight past him. Only when all the other people had got off the train and dispersed did realization dawn. 'I don't think either liked the look of the other very much,' my grandmother used to say with relish.

Father and son had a difficult relationship. Bob had spent the last ten years of his life training to be an English country gentleman, or at the very least a barrister or an army officer. Now he spent his days rounding up horses and cattle, working alongside gauchos who performed these tasks far more competently than he did. Even his nine-year-old brother Johnny could throw a lassoo better than him. He felt humiliated daily and he blamed his father.

It was customary on British-run estancias for the sons of the family to work as major-domos on other camps before returning to run the family estate. It was a way of avoiding the inevitable tension that arose between fathers and sons working together. But Robert could not afford to replace his sons with paid workers, he needed all the free labour he could muster. Even Basil worked in the fields as a peon, strapped to the saddle in a special harness.

Bob's only escape was polo. It was a game that cost him almost nothing to play as he bred all the horses himself, and if he went to play in clubs like the Hurlingham outside Buenos Aires, he sold his ponies there to finance the trip home.

Bob was an eight at polo, better than most English players but never as good as his youngest brother. He and his brothers Ned and Johnny played together for years but there is no evidence that the team spirit extended beyond the polo field.

In England, as the eldest son, Bob would have inherited the bulk of his father's estate, leaving the younger brothers to make their own way in the world as indeed Robert and Edmund had done. But under Argentina's legal system, the surviving spouse and all the children inherit equally. None of the Traills, of course, were Argentine citizens, but the country's inheritance laws still applied to them. The only discretion allowed when making a will is that before dividing the estate between spouse and children you may leave a fifth to whoever you choose, but Robert had chosen not to exercise this in favour of his oldest son. It was yet another reason for Bob to feel that he had lost his birthright. If they had stayed in England he would have inherited Long Stratton and the status that went with it. But as it was, Bob was living in the Argentine running an estate of which he would inherit only one-seventh.

It must have increased Bob's feelings of resentment when his brothers began to find ways of escaping Las Limpias.

Among the Traill papers collected by Derek, I found a discharge certificate for a Sergeant E. Traill from the South African Irregular Forces dated 31 October 1900. Ned Traill was one of the 250 Britons from Argentina who enlisted in Kitchener's army. He joined the Horse Corps on 5 February 1900 right after the siege of Mafeking, when it looked as if Britain might lose the war to the Boers.

The discharge certificate is interesting. Like Robert and Alice's wedding certificate it anchors the family history in physical fact – Ned was twenty-five when he left the army, five foot ten inches tall with blue eyes, fair hair and complexion, and no marks or scars on face or body – and yet it hints at so many unanswered questions. Why was Ned only a sergeant? A polo-playing ex-public-school boy would normally have joined as an officer. Maybe he thought it would be easier to leave the ranks if he changed his mind. It may or may not be a coincidence that Ned joined up at the end of the polo season in Argentina and that he was discharged nine months later, '*at his own request*' as it says on the certificate, just in time for the start of the next polo season. Ned was with Kitchener's army for all the major British victories including the capture of Pretoria. The discharge certificate notes his conduct as being '*most exemplary*'. Ned had joined the army out of a sense of schoolboy patriotism, sharpened perhaps by a desire to affirm his true nationality. Once the glorious part of the campaign was over and the British army appeared to be settling in for what turned out to be years of guerrilla warfare with the Boers, it was time to return to the polo.

Back in the Argentine though, Ned may have regretted leaving the army. With his discharge certificate there was a letter from the War Office addressed to Mr E. Traill at

Las Limpias and dated March 1903. It informed '*Mr E. Traill that with reference to his application dated 17th October last, the Queen's South African War Medal due in his case was despatched to Mr L.I. Wasey, 30 Donninton Square, Newbury, Berks on the 26th Ultimo.*' Lionel Wasey was married to Ned's sister Edith – another member of the Traill family who had escaped Las Limpias. Why was Ned so anxious to get hold of his medal? Presumably because it was his only mark of distinction, a tangible reminder that there was more to life than branding cattle and mending fences. (Johnny complains in *The Long Chukker* that his father expected him to do the work of a peon, and Ned's lot would have been similar.) Maybe Ned needed the medal to show his resentful older brother Bob that his absence from Las Limpias had been worthwhile. Or did Ned want to taunt his brother for staying on the estancia while he was getting medals? Probably. Bitter sibling rivalry seems to be endemic in my mother's family. My mother and her siblings still watch each other with narrowed eyes, vigilant in case one of them is getting a bigger slice of the cake. And as for my grandmother, she could barely mention her sisters without pointing out that she had the best legs.

In the end Ned escaped Las Limpias for good. In 1905 he went to England to play polo with his two brothers and his cousin Joe. The Wild Horse Team as they were known played brilliantly, defeating the Duke of Westminster's team three times. Halfway through the season they got a telegram from Las Limpias. Foot and mouth had broken out among the herds, help was needed. Somebody had to go back. It was decided that as Ned had the lowest handicap (that season spent fighting for his country had affected his average), he should be the one to go. It was not a decision that could be questioned, there was more at stake here than just polo. Ned took the next train to Southampton to catch the express boat to Buenos Aires.

Ned appeared to be enjoying the voyage, settling down for a bridge game every night after dinner with the other men in his cabin.

One night, about two hundred miles off the coast of Brazil, the usual game was in progress. It was a sultry night with only the smallest breeze. No one thought anything of it when it was Ned's turn to be dummy and he announced that he was going out on deck to get some air. He never came back.

I heard about the jump from my mother, but the macabre bridge-game detail is unmistakably my grandmother's. It was part of her repertoire of unhappy endings. The reason why Ned might have disappeared was never mentioned, it would have spoilt the clean lines of the story.

Ned's death was not officially a suicide. In Johnny's memoir it simply says that he died young. The version of the story I heard from my mother was ambiguous, always ending with the words 'he never came back'. He might have jumped or he might have fallen or he might have been pushed; I think the ambiguity was intentional. I have no doubt that he jumped, but I wonder, in those seconds before the water filled his lungs, whether he wanted his life back – or did the impulse that pushed him off the boat carry him right through to the end? I hope so.

The ambiguity of his ending made it easier for his family. They kept the question mark at the end of the story, making it a mystery not a tragedy. For Bob in particular as the one who had summoned his brother back, that room for doubt must have been all important.

*   *   *

Life at Las Limpias must have been particularly lonely for Bob after Ned's death. His sisters had married and moved away, May and Edith to England, Blanche to another estancia. Johnny had decided to stay in England to play polo, and to relieve his 'gastritis'. Only Basil remained, but his epilepsy was a constant cause for concern: once he fell off his horse in the middle of a fit and was lost for two days. Alice and Robert were in their sixties, Alice by now an alcoholic, and Robert more interested in racing than running the estate.

In 1906 Bob married Evelyn Miles in Rosario. He was thirty-six, she was twenty-two. He was one of 120 British men to marry in the Argentine that year, more than three-quarters of them like Robert marrying their fellow country-women. Marrying a 'native' was rare especially in camp. Evelyn was the daughter of a manager of the London and River Plate Bank and a woman called Edith Shakespeare who was born in Naini Tal, India. Eileen, my grandmother, liked to stress the Shakespeare connection, which according to her could be traced directly back to Stratford. I wonder though, looking at photographs of Evelyn as a young woman, whether the Shakespeare connection may have been concealing something else. Could it have been to distract attention from what my grandmother would have called 'a touch of the tar brush'? Evelyn had very dark eyes and hair, colouring I have inherited from her. In Argentina she could easily have passed for a *criollo* woman. But neither of her parents was born in Argentina. Was it possible that her mother was a Eurasian who had come to this unofficial end of empire to escape the contempt of the British memsahibs in India? Edith Shakespeare's father was a soldier in the Indian army and might well have married or at least had children with an Indian woman. It is a notion that would fit the story, but there is no evidence beyond those early photographs of Evelyn with her glittering dark eyes.

Bob and Evelyn did not have a long courtship. Bob proposed to her within three weeks of meeting her at the North Santa Fé Races. He was attracted to her vitality and strength, qualities that his mother had always lacked. He had found a woman who seemed to be proof against the depression that lingered at Las Limpias. It is surprising perhaps that after all those years of bachelorhood he should move so fast but he had to act quickly, as single girls of British families were in short supply in camp where men outnumbered women by eight to one. An attractive girl like Evelyn would have had no shortage of suitors. I wonder if Evelyn was in love with Bob or whether he was simply a good 'catch'. The Traill fortunes might have been in decline but they must have seemed substantial enough to the bank manager's daughter. Bob, judging by his photographs, was handsome enough too: blond with deep blue eyes, and tall. This last would have been important to Evelyn as she was over five foot ten. In three weeks she would not have had time to notice the darker side to Bob's character. She probably would not have wondered why it had taken him so long to get married.

I think that Bob's decision to propose to Evelyn was a result of Ned's death. Whether he believed in the accident or not, Bob knew the reasons for the fall. Before his brother's death Bob had always thought that he might one day go 'home'. Now that was no longer a possibility. Marrying Evelyn was an act of commitment, or resignation.

Robert Traill Senior was delighted with his daughter-in-law. I think he must have found her attractive. He insisted on teaching her to shoot, placing his arm round her shoulders as he showed her the correct way to hold a gun. He must have been an attentive teacher as she became a crack shot. There is no record of what Alice felt about Evelyn. My guess is that she was rather frightened of her competent, dominating daughter-in-law, who was acceptable in all the ways she was not.

Evelyn became pregnant immediately, giving birth to her eldest daughter, Daphne, nine months after the wedding. The following year Bob went to England for the polo and Evelyn had her second daughter, Alice Eileen, my grandmother, in Newbury. They went back to the Argentine and Evelyn had three more children, Claire, Dick and Roy, in the next four years. Another wing was built onto Las Limpias. Beef prices reached a record high. For the first time in Bob's adult life it looked as if things might get better, not worse.

The land that was sold during the Baring crisis was lost for ever but there was still enough to support a sizeable herd. Now that Robert was in his seventies, he had at last retired, and so Bob was able to introduce some changes in the way Las Limpias was run. He bought some new bulls, which meant they could command much higher prices for their meat. Beef from the native longhorn cattle was considered too tough and rank for European tastes, it had to be sweetened with livestock that had come from grassy English meadows. Bob had wanted to introduce this change for years, but a decent bull was so expensive – costing upwards of a thousand pesos – that his father had baulked at the price.

Bob might have respected this decision if his father had not been spending hundreds of pesos a month betting on horses. Even after his son Ned's death when the herds had been decimated by foot and mouth, Robert had spent eight hundred pesos on having one of his best mares covered by a thoroughbred stallion. Robert had never given up an idea that one day he might return to England and race at Newmarket again. It was an aspiration that infuriated his son.

But Robert did not care what his son thought; breeding horses and betting on them was his only hope of getting back what he had lost. When cash was really short, races would be run for land or stock. Robert had once won two thousand *hectáreas* in a *dos cuadras* (two-league race). It made little difference to him that he had lost the same amount several times over. Every race was to him the chance of a fresh start.

The races themselves were among the few occasions when the old Argentina of the gauchos mixed with the new fenced-in world of the Anglo-Argentine camp. Sometimes the horses were ridden by gringos but for the big races, owners like Robert always employed gaucho jockeys. The gringos might play a passable game of polo but everyone knew that the gauchos were the better riders. The races were as much tests of nerves as they were of speed. There were no starting pistols: each race would start when both horses were at the starting line and one of the jockeys would shout '*Vamos*,' (Let's go), but if the other rider did not feel ready he pulled up and both riders would dismount and go back to the starting line. Most of these races, or *canchas*, would have five or six false starts, each jockey trying to unnerve the other and confuse the horses so much that they would be unable to run. This was a particular danger for Robert's horses as they were thoroughly inbred and more excitable than the *criollo* ponies. Too many false starts and these highly strung animals would be no good for racing.

In his retirement he entered more and more of these *canchas* for the highest stakes he could. On the morning of

12 March 1914 he had a wager with a neighbouring landowner, William Staunton, for a thousand *hectáreas* or a thousand head of cattle on the outcome of the *dos cuadras* at 2 p.m. After six false starts, Robert's horse was rolling its eyes and refusing to go anywhere near the starting line. In desperation Robert jumped on the horse and pulled it up to the starting line himself. This time the race started properly. Robert watched without hope: there was no way that his horse could pull through now, its back and quarters were flecked with foam, and he doubted whether it would even last the course. But the horse's frenzy was so intense that it kept neck and neck with its rival, finally pulling ahead in the last seconds. Robert lifted his arms in victory and the blood clot circulating round his body finally reached his brain.

'Of course the land he won was a swamp,' said Derek when he told me this story, 'but at least he was happy before he went under. Shame it took him such a bloody long time to die.'

EIGHTEEN

Robert remained alive but paralysed until June 1916. His will left all his property divided equally between his wife and children. He did not leave a discretionary fifth to any of his children, not even his oldest son. Bob who had spent thirty years running the estate was left with no more than his sister Edith who had spent her whole married life in England. It was a vicious legacy.

Argentine estancieros managed to keep their estates together despite the inheritance laws. It was not uncommon for three or four brothers to live together in the same house. J. A. Hammerton, an English traveller in the Argentine at around this time, commented on this system with amazement in his book *The Argentine through English Eyes*:

> To Britishers especially, it is a surprising fact that there are brethren in the world who can dwell together in harmony, to whom propinquity does not lead to family bickerings. That would be notoriously impossible in Great Britain. Our nature prompts to the

independent life and an early goodbye to the parental roof. Surely, then, there must be something radically different in the Argentine character which can enable half-a-dozen or more inter-related families to live harmoniously in the same house. Of course each family unit has its own particular quarters, but they have common dining rooms and sitting rooms, the women folk passing practically all their time in each other's company. As a people they must either be abnormally good natured, family affection must be developed beyond anything familiar among us, or their racial inclination to indolence makes them so tolerant of one another that they do not have the spirit to quarrel.

Robert's children were British enough to spend many years squabbling about their inheritance. Here was another instance where the Traills might have prospered if they had gone 'native'. The law favoured large extended families with a common purpose but the Traills could not see beyond their individual destinies, with fragmentation the inevitable result.

Johnny, who was in the Argentine when his father died, ostensibly because he did not want to stay in England and be '*one more mouth to feed*' but also because he may have wanted to secure his inheritance, insisted on dividing off his portion immediately. He and his wife and baby son could have lived quite comfortably at Las Limpias but he was determined to separate himself from the rest of his family, so he lived in a *puestero* (shack) with a dirt floor while he built the estancia house at La Esterlina, the house where Veronica still lives. He spent several thousand pesos putting up fences to divide his land from that of his brothers. In the end, he lived in the house for only a couple of years. As soon as the war was over he went back to live in England on account of his 'gastritis', leaving the place in the hands of a major-domo. He might of course have left the lands joined to the Limpias estate and have received the same income from them, perhaps even more as his overheads would have been lower, but it seems that he did not trust his brother. It was the same story with two of Bob's sisters who asked their cousin Joe, Edmund's son, to oversee their part of the estate. It was a deliberate snub to their older brother.

Only Basil and Blanche, whose husband Geoffrey was killed in the Somme, trusted Bob with their inheritance. Basil still lived at Las Limpias with Alice, and Blanche came back there when she was widowed. My grandmother remembered another room being built at Las Limpias for 'poor Aunt Blanche', who took five years to drink herself to death.

It was, typically, the worst time to be breaking up the estate. Argentina had recovered from the speculative crises of the 1890s and its economy was booming. The value of land was rising exponentially. Beef and grain prices had never been higher. If the Traills had stayed together as a family unit in the Argentine manner they might have regained something of their lost fortunes. Between them they still owned enough land to be one of the biggest estates in the province of Santa Fé. They could all have lived in some style, but none of them could bring themselves to commit to the Argentine or to each other. Edmund and Gertrude went to live in England as soon as their son Joe was deemed old enough to run the estate, taking the rest of their children with them. They never returned but a large part of the income of Chirù was spent supporting them in their retirement. This meant that Joe Traill, instead of expanding the estancia when the going was so good, was forced in Derek's phrase, 'to farm with one hand behind his back', all the profits going directly to England instead of being reinvested in the property. To give an idea of just how valuable the land was: in 1908 the Traill brothers mortgaged 8,183 *hectáreas* in favour of a Mr Henry Coffin in guarantee of a loan of one hundred thousand pesos at 7½ per cent interest. In today's money the loan was worth about a quarter of a million pounds. The Traills had bought land when it was cheap and they had an asset that was appreciating in value all the time but instead of letting their investment grow, they burdened the property with enormous mortgages so that they could live in England. Evidently any price was worth paying not to live in the Argentine.

I wonder if the Traills' preoccupation with going home was a form of collective agoraphobia. It was not so much about being in England as it was about getting away from the Argentine. The flat empty plains of the pampas scared them, not just because of the dangers that lay on the horizon but also because of the way in which the landscape magnified their failings, stretched them into attitudes of despair. Edmund, who was the more considered of the Traill brothers, left as soon as he could. Robert for whatever reasons would not go back; perhaps having had a taste of the grand life, he did not want to retire to England in a modest villa as his brother did. Edmund's children all led useful, respectable lives in England as doctors, solicitors, vets. None of them as far as I know committed suicide or drank themselves to death. But the lives of Robert's children all end in tragedy, the melancholy side of their nature finding no boundaries on this endless plain.

*　　*　　*

I knew how it could happen. All the time I was in Argentina I felt the grey weight of the sky pressing on me waiting for something to give. A fissure would quickly accelerate into a canyon. I held my return ticket like a talisman: I was only visiting. All the time the edges of the picture were blurred by glimpses of unbearable melancholy. Everywhere I went I heard the unmistakable blue notes of despair. Staying at Robin's house I could feel the currents that had pushed so many Traills over the edge. I knew that if I stayed there much longer I would start to wake up earlier and earlier.

A month or two more and I would have reached that point where the past and the future seem equally unbearable, the point where the only exit is to jump sideways.

At various times in my life I have visited all the stations of depression, felt all the gradations on the Beaufort scale of despair from the light rustlings of small sadnesses to the furious howl of hopelessness.

Once, about a year after my daughter's birth, I found myself at the bottom of a smooth-sided pit with no way of pulling myself out. I was in mental agony, unable to find any relief from the despair that was wounding me. The escape routes I had used before were all useless: for the first time in my life I could not read. I would go through the same page again and again, the words refusing to form themselves into sense. I drank. I remember walking into an off-licence to buy a bottle of wine and the man behind the counter offering to open it for me on the spot when he saw my face, but the alcohol just evaporated, burnt off by the heat of my unhappiness. I took all kinds of pills, but their various spells wore off so quickly. At the bottom of that pit I could see no relief, no possible end to my misery. Taking my own life stopped being an adolescent 'and then they'll be sorry' fantasy. For the first and I hope the only time it became a logical choice. Existence was unbearable and at the bottom of my pit there was no hope that things would ever get better. Time had become an endless loop. All tomorrow offered was more of the same.

I remember waking up at five one morning and thinking of the Traills who had jumped. When I had first heard the story, it seemed just that: a story with these long-dead relatives behaving like characters from some magical realist novel. It seemed to have the neatness of fiction. They were a throwaway line by a swimming pool. But that morning the story came back to me and I felt its reality, I felt the weight of their despair. I did not know what had pushed them there, but I knew how the thoughts whirled round their heads sweeping away their reasons to live. I found a kind of perverse comfort in these tragic genes: perhaps the pit I was in was not of my own making but a carefully concealed heffalump trap that one day, if I took the wrong turning, I was bound to stumble into. The pain I was feeling had come bundled up with my DNA.

As a child I had imagined ancestors who fitted the person I wanted to be at the time. Now I had found them. The jumping Traills took up space in my head, little patches of colour in the blackness. I began to wonder about them, to imagine their lives. For the first time in months I spent whole moments thinking of something other than myself. I felt the tiny pricks of curiosity. It was the beginning of my recovery.

NINETEEN

Two hundred thousand *hectáreas* was the size of the Traill estates at their apex. A *hectárea* is a little less than an acre, but as I was city bred an acre means little to me as a unit. To make topographical sense of this collection of noughts I translated the area in terms of the London Underground, going east on the Central Line from Shepherd's Bush and finding myself somewhere between Epping and Ongar. Most of the best land got sold off in the various financial crises, leaving unwanted pockets here and there for future generations to inherit. My oldest living Traill relative lived in one such pocket at least two hours' drive from where Derek lived at Las Limpias Two. Two scraps of former swamp linked by the man who sold off all the sweet farming land in between.

Gertie Traill was Edmund's granddaughter. As she was almost a contemporary of my grandmother's I thought she might remember something about Eileen's childhood, some clue to the precise sweet-and-sour flavour of her character.

Derek agreed to drive me there. I knew I would never find my way through the country with no landmarks, no familiar red Tube stops. The drive took longer than it should have done; the roads were muddy after a recent rainstorm and once we had to wait for a herd of cattle about a thousand strong to be manoeuvred across the road by men on trailbikes. 'Why anybody would want to ride a contraption like that instead of a decent horse is beyond me,' said Derek, 'but they've all got them now.'

In 1910 a British visitor to the Argentine wrote a best-selling book about his travels in the pampas, which thrilled Edwardian readers with its descriptions of the gauchos as *'more savage than the Arabs, only a step advanced beyond the Indians; tall, lean, long haired and thievish; born almost on their horses, sitting them like centaurs, living amongst them, talking and thinking but of them, and shying when they shied, as if they had been one flesh.'*

These new men on their 750cc Hondas with their electronic cattle prods were all that remained of the gauchos. Only the poorest ride horses now.

We arrived at Gertie's house at five o'clock exactly. It was still hot, the air heavy with rain. The building was low and comfortless; there was only one tree to shade it from the sun. There was a verandah at the front of the house but despite the heat all the windows were shut and the terrace itself was empty of chairs or any of the trappings of conversation. A maid opened the door and we followed her down a dark corridor. As I stepped into the *sala* a voice called out.

'There you are. Have you had tea?'

I could not immediately see where it was coming from, but the voice itself was one I had known all my life. It was pitched a tone or two higher but it could have been my grandmother speaking.

'No, not yet.'

'We have tea at four o'clock. It's five past five now. We hardly expected you at this time.'

Gertie was in the far corner of the room, a small humped shape swathed despite the heat in layers of plaid blankets. As I approached her I saw that the wraps were concealing a wheelchair. Her body, from what I could make out under the covers, had collapsed but the small head with its sharp nose and still-bright blue eyes looked alert and unmistakably hostile.

'Who are you anyway?'

I explained. Gertie said nothing. I saw her eyes flick to the Dick Francis novel on the little stand next to her chair.

At last she spoke. 'Well, I don't know what you want from me.'

I was wondering the same thing. But I stumbled on. 'I thought perhaps that you might remember my grandmother Eileen when she was growing up here in the Argentine.'

'Eileen, why would I know Eileen?'

Because she was your cousin and your nearest neighbour, I said to myself.

'She was much older than me.'

Gertie could not have been more than about three years younger than my grandmother. 'Can't say I remember anything about her at all.' Gertie was talking to me in a loud slow voice as if uncertain about the quality of my hearing.

'We never saw much of that side of the family. I went to England when I was ten. Remember landing on my tenth birthday. Father sent me to Sherborne – super school. But the war came so I couldn't come back. Only one of that family I can remember is Evelyn, no flies on her. Dead now, of course.'

262

I nodded.

'Well, if you don't want any tea I'm afraid you've come all this way for nothing.' Gertie turned her head and looked out of the window. It was a dismissal. Even looking out of the window was better than continuing this conversation.

But it had not been a wasted journey. Gertie's prickly solitude, the voice, the things that weren't said, all reminded me so strongly of my grandmother. This was definitely the place she had come from.

At the end of her life my grandmother lost things every day, her mind wandering the same paths continually, missing steps here and there. But sometimes she would come across a new memory, producing it like a shiny coin, turning it round and round until it grew dull from use. When she was still the Dragon Lady of Essex bridge parties and amateur dramatics, she rarely talked about her childhood, the dead donkey story apart. But as the crisp edges of her mind began to wilt with age so did the barrier that had kept that part of her life packed away.

'I told her by the dunny [privy]. That's where we went when we wanted to be private. You couldn't have a secret anywhere else, people could always hear. Ma didn't want to come. I don't like all this whispering, she said, but I made her. When we got there I didn't know how to say what had happened with Uncle Basil, but she made me tell her how he interfered with me. Then she asked Daphne and Claire and he had interfered with them too. Ma was livid, such a commotion.'

I heard the chorus of the story myself but there were parts I got second-hand from my mother and aunts. Sometimes the story would be the same, sometimes different, with so many unreliable narrators the ground kept slipping away. It was significant though, that the main focus of the story was always the moment when Eileen told her mother, rather than the encounter itself. The interference itself, the fumble, the grope, the glimpse of skin, was buried by what came next. Evelyn did not hesitate after hearing Eileen's story.

'Ma was very tough about it.' She confronted Basil and told him he had to leave at once, and when Alice protested that Basil could not look after himself, Evelyn suggested that her mother-in-law should go with him. My grandmother said, 'They had to go and stay with people for the rest of their lives.' But neither survived for long. After a year spent moving from estancia to estancia, Alice came back to Las Limpias to die. As Evelyn still refused to have Basil in the house it was decided that he should go to England.

But the boat taking him back to England ran into some rough water outside the Cape Verde islands and Basil, who had managed to get away from the man who had been paid to look after him, was swept overboard by a wave. His 'too short' arms made it impossible for him to stop himself from falling into the ocean.

It seems almost incredible that Basil should have been lost in identical circumstances to his brother, but perhaps he could think of no better way to die. It seems unlikely that it was an accident. Even if he did not throw himself overboard, he went on deck in the middle of a storm, and waited for a wave to make the decision for him. All he remembered of England was the misery of his schooldays. He knew that he would never see the only person who loved him, his mother, ever again. What reason did he have to stay alive?

The death was recorded as an accident. By the time the telegram reached Las Limpias, Alice had been dead for a week. She was buried in the garden. The nearest Protestant cemetery was in Rosario. Nobody considered the Catholic cemetery. The only people who knew Alice was Catholic were dead. In the end there were no priests of any kind to commit Alice's body to the earth. The camp chaplain, the peripatetic clergyman who visited every three months, had been and gone a month ago. There was no point in sending after him, it had started to rain and the roads would soon be impassable. It took hours to dig the grave, the hole kept filling up with water.

'When they put the coffin in, it floated. They had a terrible time trying to get it to stay down,' was the detail my grandmother remembered about her grandmother's funeral. 'We were meant to sprinkle dust on the coffin, ashes to ashes, dust to dust, but it was so wet that we had to throw great big clumps of clay down. Horrible noise.'

Looking at my daughter, I can well imagine Evelyn's rage when the eight-year-old Eileen told her what Uncle Basil had been up to. It is interesting though that she acted upon it so decisively. Revulsion against paedophilia seems such a modern phenomenon – the impression is always given that it had been tacitly acknowledged – and yet here was my great-grandmother sending the perpetrator, and the woman who had turned a blind eye to his problem, into exile. Evelyn clearly put her children's interests before those of her husband's family, or indeed those of her husband. Four years after banishing Basil and Alice from Las Limpias, Evelyn decided to take all her children to England to be educated. Bob stayed behind to run the estancia, but Evelyn never lived at Las Limpias again.

Why did Evelyn decide to go to England? Ostensibly she went so that her children could have a decent education: she settled in Bedford which had two good and cheap private day schools for girls and boys. But the children could equally well have gone to boarding schools like St George's or St Hilda's in Buenos Aires. Indeed, the two oldest girls, Daphne and Eileen, went to Northlands, a school in Hurlingham, for a year before the move to England. Evelyn may have felt the need for English schools more when her sons, Dick and Roy, reached the relevant age, but the boys could have gone 'home' to boarding school without the whole family being uprooted.

I think the move to England was about more than education, it was Evelyn's bid to save her children, to save them from Argentina. Evelyn could see what life at Las Limpias had done to her husband's generation of Traills. There was his alcoholic sister Blanche, his difficult younger brother Johnny, the two sisters in England still griping about their inheritance, not to mention the two brothers who had 'fallen' off ships into the Atlantic. Even if she believed that two of Bob's brothers had been washed overboard in tragic 'accidents', her husband's melancholia was impossible to explain away.

Bob had always been reserved, withdrawn, but now his silence became a barrier. He hated to be touched, flinching away from even the lightest contact. He would often spend all day out in the fields rounding up the remotest cattle, work that was usually done by the peons. Occasionally his mood would lift and he would give one of his rare smiles: his son-in-law later described his smile as 'a break in the clouds'. But these moments of lightness grew further and further apart. As Bob grew more and more silent, Evelyn's resolve to go to England grew stronger.

It was not a formal separation. Bob and Evelyn remained married, and lived together as a couple in the rare periods when they were in the same place at the same time. It was a rational arrangement. Bob stayed at Las Limpias running the estates and sending enough money home so that Evelyn and the children could live in comfort in Bedford. Perhaps Bob was consoled by the thought that his children would have the Cambridge education that he had been denied. But it was a separation nonetheless, with the same side effects. When he visited his family in England, the children found his presence disturbing. On one occasion, my grandmother walked into a room and found him with his shirt off; sixty years later she remembered how 'hairy and white he was all over, just like a polar bear'.

Looked at from this distance it seems clear that Evelyn was leaving the marriage fifteen years and five children later; but the circumstances of the time allowed the reality to be disguised. No one could blame Evelyn for wanting to educate her children in England. Nor could there be anything strange about Bob remaining in the Argentine, somebody had to pay the school fees.

Joe, Bob's cousin, sent all his children including the terrifying Gertie to boarding school in England, but his wife Audrey did not go with them, she stayed in the Argentine with her husband. Evelyn claimed that sending the children to boarding school would be too expensive: not wanting to be parted from them was evidently not a good enough excuse. But Evelyn had no intention of remaining at Las Limpias alone with her husband.

According to Derek, 'Once Evelyn had decided to educate the children in England there was no stopping her.' It was she who decided on Bedford as the ideal location because of its excellent high schools. She bought a large Edwardian villa at 19 Lansdowne Road, a spacious house with a conservatory and two bathrooms. It was a stark contrast to Las Limpias, which had no gas, electricity or running water. Two years after the move Evelyn was Chairwoman of the St Matthew's Church Bazaar Committee and actively involved in voluntary work of all kinds. Supremely competent, she appears to have had no problems adjusting to her new life.

The speed with which Evelyn settled in is surprising, given the fact that, until she married Bob, she had never been to England. It was only 'home' to her in the metaphorical sense. But neither did Evelyn feel at 'home' in camp. Although Argentine born and bred, she had grown up in a villa in Rosario, already quite a sizeable town with a large English community. Moving to Las Limpias, where the nearest neighbours were a day's ride away, where religion (Evelyn was a fervent Protestant) consisted of quarterly visits from the camp chaplain and where the only other women were both alcoholics, must have been quite an adjustment. Bedford, with its bustling provincial atmosphere, its church committees and tennis tournaments, must have seemed less strange to her than the isolation of life in camp. Bedford was a landscape she could dominate, Las Limpias was a place that threatened her.

But in saving herself and her children, Evelyn sacrificed her husband. At Robin's house I found a pile of papers that had once belonged to Bob Traill. Land deeds, mortgage papers, birth certificates – Daphne is described as a '*niña blanca*' – passports. From 1920 Bob had to have two, British and Argentine; the Argentine government were tightening the rules on foreign nationals being landowners. In 1928 he applied for a passport from the Argentine consulate in London, concerned that he would not get back into the country without one. He was sixty years old. His height was recorded as 1.77m and his eyes as '*claros medios*'; the Argentine authorities were particular about recording the exact shade of blue. In the passport picture his face is hardly visible under the thatch of white hair around his mouth and chin, but his eyes of medium blue look frozen, like a man who does not want to see into the future.

It was his last visit to England. Although he lived for another ten years, he never went to the house in Bedford again. Whether by choice or by circumstance he remained in the Argentine. It was a solitary life: his nearest neighbour was his cousin Joe who lived a day's ride away at Edmund's old estancia Chirù. At weekends Bob would ride over there and spend Saturday night. Dinny, Joe's daughter, remembers that he would rarely say more than ten words in the entire visit. He had got out of the habit of speaking aloud.

There is one more snapshot before the last freeze frame. Among my grandmother's papers is an account written by her husband Paul Innes, my grandfather, of his first visit to the Argentine in 1937. Given that it was written for family consumption and is annotated all the way through with cross little pencil marks from my grandmother (surely not!) the account must be read as much for what it does not say as for what is actually committed to paper. Paul arrived in the Argentine from China where he was working for Shell Oil. He was surprised by the primitive conditions of camp life: '*Decidedly the simple life it seemed to me after the relative comforts of a foreigner's life in China. So far removed are most estancias from civilisation that electricity (and of course, refrigerators), water mains and telephone are unobtainable. For letters, papers and kitchen requirements, a car journey of 20 miles to the nearest village is needed. A dinner invitation may mean going 50 miles – they talk of leagues, so great are the distances.'*

At the time of their visit Paul and Eileen were living in a compound for foreign workers on the west coast of China, not in the sophistication of 1930s Shanghai. Paul was used to life on the fringes of empire, but he was struck by the separateness of the British community in the Argentine: *'The Argentine government brings increasing pressure on these settlers to become Argentine or get out, but so far they have succeeded, to a far greater extent than we have in the East, in remaining completely English.'* He notes that for the English estancia families, *'the game of polo is almost their only recreation.'* For Paul, who did not ride, it must have seemed a barren life, after the bridge tournaments and tennis championships of the Shell compound.

At the time of their visit Paul and Eileen had been married for nearly five years and had been engaged for five years before that and yet Paul had never met his father-in-law. That simple fact underlines more clearly than anything the distances in the Traill family. Paul's description of his father-in-law is circumspect, but then it was written after the old man's death.

'Don Roberto' as Bob Traill was called by all the peons, was *'a tall man, close on 80. He was immensely dignified, quite apart from his patriarchal white beard.'* Eileen and Paul organized a sukiyaki party in the camp, at which Eileen and the Chinese amah cooked over an open fire (a sukiyaki party for Anglo-Argentines in the pampas!) and Paul taught his father-in-law some of the Japanese finger games which are *'an essential part of the ritual'*.

The loser in these games had to drink a cup of sake.

> *Believe it or not these games are really skilled and a skilled player will always win . . . Eileen's father vastly enjoyed trying to put his juniors under the table. It is a pleasure trying to see a naturally dignified man unbend. Reminds one of Disraeli's remark, 'There are few faces that can afford to smile. A smile is sometimes bewitching, in general vapid, often a contortion. But the bewitching smile usually beams from the grave face. It is then irresistible.'*

Reading this makes me think that Paul is perhaps protesting too much. The description of the smile, complete with casually thrown in quote, suggests a determination to accentuate the positive. Reading between the neatly typed lines it is possible to decipher another meaning – Paul found his father-in-law so depressed and withdrawn, a state which he euphemistically describes as dignified, that a smile, even a drunken one, is worth writing about.

The memory of the smile is a coat of whitewash slapped over an altogether grimmer reality. Paul does not mention Evelyn at all. Perhaps the reality of Bob and Evelyn's marriage was too dangerous to describe; this account was, after all, being read by Eileen and was intended for posterity. Better not to stray too far into dangerous territory. Paul clearly felt on safer ground writing about his father-in-law's driving.

> *Don Roberto had a new car and for the first time in his life showed an interest in driving. He drove it furiously round a field in the estancia – always in top gear because gear changing seemed to him an unnecessary frill for the fussy – and even on the vague*

tracks which pass for roads in this country. But the family united in deciding that he was not a safe driver and should not drive.

At this point Eileen has added a pencil comment '*only on main roads*'; perhaps in view of what came later she did not want to be associated with restricting her father. Paul goes on in this doggedly light-hearted vein:

The autocrat apparently accepted the decision and allowed himself to be chauffeured by one of the others. But one morning when we were all in the hills the car was found in the drive considerably bent. Eventually the mystery was solved when he confessed that he had got up early to outwit the critics, had managed to get the car out of the garage, but then when he was set to go he had put the gear into reverse instead of top and charged a tree. His smile at being caught out was irresistible.

Paul makes the incident sound like spirited high jinks by a madcap old man, rather at odds with the dignified patriarch with the white beard he was portraying earlier. But this seemingly jolly anecdote conceals a darker truth. The locking up of the new car and the decision that he should not drive (despite Eileen's disclaimer) sounds as if the family were trying to control Don Roberto in what must have been a manic episode. He bought a car on an upswing: being unable to drive was not a deterrent. He probably thought he could fly. At this distance the whole thing sounds less jolly than desperate with Don Roberto as a Lear-like figure being restrained by his increasingly unsympathetic family. Through the transparent typing paper that Paul used, the edges of which are yellow with age like a treasure map, I can feel the hot restlessness of the old man as he waited for his family, his gaolers, to fall asleep so that he could drive the forbidden car.

Paul's remark that Bob's smile '*at being caught out was irresistible*' is charged with ambiguity. Was Don Roberto laughing because he had outwitted his family or was he laughing at a private joke inside his head, a joke he knew his family would never understand? As he was writing about the irresistible smile Paul knew that six months after the car-wrecking episode his father-in-law had jumped to his death.

The end of Don Roberto came just six months after the episode with the car. I have to call him Don Roberto here since the conclusion of his story is both English and Argentinian, and though it can be read in either way, I lean towards the Argentinian version.

The English version of my great-grandfather's death is that after my grandmother and her family went back to China, Bob stopped smiling his irresistible smile and fell back into his more usual state of melancholy. As the months went by he retreated further and further from the world; he could not bear to see or speak to anyone. All his meals had to be left on a tray outside his bedroom door. After three months of watching her husband's self-imprisonment, Evelyn felt it was time to intervene. She went to La Cumbre in Córdoba, an Anglo-Argentine enclave with half-timbered villas ranged around a central golf course. La Cumbre was known as a town for the very young or the very old, full of schools and nursing homes, built in the hills of Córdoba away from the heat and glare of the pampas. Evelyn found what she felt to be a suitable establishment for her husband, a home called the Pines where all the staff were English.

The matron of the Pines had a place for Mrs Traill's husband. She showed Evelyn a very nice room on the third floor with a lovely view of the golf course and the hills beyond. As this was a convalescent home there were no bars on the windows.

Two weeks later Evelyn returned with her husband after a three-day journey. Evelyn drove. Unlike him she was an excellent driver. Now in her early fifties, Evelyn still relished new challenges like learning to drive. She did not allow her husband to take the wheel. Evelyn talked to him, extolling La Cumbre and the benefits of living there. She thought they might take a house there when Bob was feeling better, he was getting too old to run Las Limpias. Living in La Cumbre would be so much better than living in camp. Evelyn began to feel quite hopeful as she outlined the future: really it would be quite like living in Bedford. Her husband, though, did not break his wrappings of silence.

The matron could not have been pleasanter when the Traills arrived at the Pines. She showed husband and wife around the establishment without appearing to notice the husband's lack of interest in the tennis courts, the well-stocked library, the lovely grounds; as the matron remarked, 'standing by one of those borders you could almost fancy yourself in England'.

Evelyn thought the room that had been reserved for her husband was even nicer than she remembered. She stood at the window and looked out at the green swell of the Córdoba hills; as she said, it was so refreshing to get away from the flatness of camp. The matron suggested that they might like to have some tea. Evelyn accepted gratefully, she felt hot and dusty after the journey – the tweed of her skirt was scratchy against the backs of her legs. Bob looked exactly the same as he had when they left Las Limpias, apart from his stiff white collar, which was beginning to show a grimy edge around the neck. Evelyn also noticed a sharp rather acrid smell. She wondered if Bob had remembered to change his shirt. After the tea Evelyn was impatient to be off. Bob had come round before, he would come round again. A place like the Pines would be just what was needed to take his mind off things. Evelyn was going to stay with an old friend from Rosario who was now living near the golf course, and they were having dinner at the club. Bob had finished his cup of tea which Evelyn felt must be a good sign. He was standing at the window with his back to her. He did not turn around as she said goodbye. Evelyn walked down the linoleum corridor, down the wide marble steps and onto the gravel of the forecourt and stepped into her car. Like her husband, she did not look back.

In this version of the story the call from Matron Roberts came about a fortnight later. Evelyn was still staying with the schoolfriend from Rosario and had just come in from church when the maid told her that the English nurse was on the phone. Evelyn did not hurry, she had no feelings of foreboding. The matron was probably ringing about the bridge game they had talked about.

Even when Evelyn heard the word 'accident' she did not connect it with her husband. 'A tragic mishap', the matron called it. The window had been open, he must have leant out a little too far. It was most unfortunate. Evelyn thought about sending telegrams to her children but rejected the idea on the grounds of cost. Bob was after all in his seventies, his death would hardly come as a shock to any of them. Evelyn did not really believe that her husband's death was an accident but she felt that it was inevitable and she saw no point in indulging in regrets. You could hardly call a seventy-one-year-old man falling out of a window a suicide.

But there is another version of the death of Don Roberto, one that must have seeped through Evelyn's authorized version. I heard this story from my mother, who even as she told me the end, must have heard Evelyn's voice in her head because she finished with the disclaimer, 'Of course it probably didn't happen that way at all.'

In her story, the Pines was not a convalescent home but something much closer to a lunatic asylum. Evelyn had her husband committed there as she could no longer bear to live with his silent hostility. On 3 September 1939 she went to the Pines to visit her husband as she did every month. As usual Don Roberto said nothing while Evelyn talked. After an hour she got up to leave. 'Goodbye then, Bob, I'll see you again next month.'

There was no physical contact. Evelyn did not look up as she walked out of the Pines towards her car, so she did not see her husband climb onto the window ledge and step, his arms outstretched, into the air. She heard the moan though and the black thud as her husband's body hit the ground two feet behind her. There is a suggestion in this version of the story that Don Roberto may have intended to fall on top of Evelyn but he had forgotten how swiftly his wife walked. The day ended with the announcement on the wireless that Britain had declared war on Germany.

The truth of Don Roberto's death lies somewhere between Evelyn's version and the story that emerged later, the story my mother told me. Even as she described Don Roberto's final jump, she shrugged, 'It sounds a bit unlikely, doesn't it?' And yet this florid ending with its final Latin flourish has an emotional validity that Evelyn's buttoned-up version does not. Did Don Roberto try to obliterate himself and his wife with his final jump? His death certificate gives nothing away: the cause of death is recorded as heart failure, a bureaucratically convenient way of describing the end result. But while Evelyn may have controlled the official version of her husband's death, she could not stop this story pushing out from under the slabs of repression like a weed. Someone in the family, my grandmother perhaps, needed to add another layer of meaning to the story. No one could actually say that Evelyn had behaved heartlessly by shutting her husband away, that she had driven him to his death, but the story makes the point neatly. As for the date, the death certificate confirms that Don Roberto did indeed die on the day that the Second World War was declared, but the detail is included by the anonymous storyteller to reinforce the sense of an era ending.

When Don Roberto died Las Limpias was divided up and the house itself was sold; Evelyn had no desire to go on living there. Daphne, who was the only one of Don Roberto's children to settle in the Argentine, preferred to rent another house: the estancia house at Las Limpias had unhappy memories for her too.

The Second World War marked the end of an era in other ways too. The autonomy of the Anglo-Argentine community could not survive a war in which the Argentine government, though officially neutral, was unofficially pro-Axis or held the anti-British sentiments of Perón. The war in Europe also wiped out a generation of Traills. Three years after Don Roberto jumped from the window, both his sons were dead.

Having been to Las Limpias and felt the pressure of the uninterrupted sky I can supply another reason for the manner of my great-grandfather's death. After a lifetime spent unwillingly in flatness, the possibilities of that third-floor window were irresistible. His perspective had changed. Living in camp, Don Roberto spent his life at ground level, occasionally rising a few feet to get on his horse. He never climbed onto the roof of his house: there were no Indians to watch for any more. But in the Pines he was offered a view, and with it a choice. His family had locked up his car on account of his dangerous driving, but now his wife was leaving him in a room sixty feet up. The jump was an opportunity not an ending, an escape not an exit. And as he watched his wife walk briskly towards the car she had forbidden him to drive, he felt that this was his last chance to bend the straight lines that had shaped his life. For a moment he felt exhilarated, giddy with the sense of possibility, the weight of his depression lifted; he had been trapped, but now at the third-floor window he was free.

TWENTY

The day before I was due to leave the Argentine, Derek held an *asado* in my honour, to which he invited all the Traill descendants living in the area. There was sad Veronica and her *porteño* husband, a sprightly lady in tweeds called Dinny who was Edmund Traill's granddaughter, her son Michael, his wife and their eight-year-old son; Derek's daughter Helen who had come to the Argentine with her three daughters to get away from her Canadian husband, Derek of course, and me. Robin claimed to have an unbreakable appointment with his tailor. Fifteen or so people living on three different continents all bound by a fragile wisp of DNA to the Rector of Skull.

We ate outside on Derek's shadeless terrace, cramming the food into our mouths before the black flies that plagued this part of the pampas could settle on our plates. The conversation was staccato, barks between mouthfuls.

'Bloody flies,' said Derek, 'that's what you get if you live in swampy ground like this. No wonder the Traills couldn't get rid of this land. Who'd want to live here.'

'I must say, I've never regretted moving to the pueblo,'

said Dinny, who though in her seventies still looked and sounded like the captain of the lacrosse team. Dinny used to live in Chirù, the estancia built by Edmund in the 1870s; but after her husband's death she sold up and bought herself a large house in the pueblo San Jorge, complete with American-style kitchen and cocktail bar.

Her friends had thought this was a daring move, most widows in her position either struggled on alone in the estancia or moved to Buenos Aires. Living in the pueblo was considered rather déclassé. Dinny said, 'I went back the other day to see what they had done to Chirù. They had bought all the furniture from Buenos Aires, brand new, imagine! But the garden was a mess, the man looked at me oh so ruefully and said, I'm sorry, *señora*, the garden is not so good. But I didn't really expect them to keep it up, they don't really understand about gardens.' She had moved to the pueblo to be closer to her son who had sold his crumb of the Traill land to buy a mobile-phone franchise. The meal was constantly being interrupted by the cheeps of his three phones. Michael was unembarrassed. As he told me, 'Argentina is the land of opportunity for digital telecommunications. Out here on the pampas we have the best reception in the world.' Michael's wife looked less than thrilled by the digital future. Life here in camp was simply not civilized: like most *porteños* she regarded living anywhere other than Buenos Aires as living in exile. She was trying to persuade Michael to move, but though he was more Argentine than English he still found the city too foreign.

The conversation turned to the original Traills, Robert and Edmund. Derek was still complaining about their lamentable property choices. 'Worst piece of land in the whole of Santa Fé. But maybe it looked good compared to an Irish bog.'

Veronica looked puzzled.

'But if those Traills came from Ireland does that mean we are English or Irish?'

I said that Robert and Edmund came from a Scottish Protestant family who had been encouraged to settle in Catholic Ireland by Oliver Cromwell, so it was debatable whether they were Scottish or Irish or simply British. This conversation was in English and was being translated piece-meal to the two Spanish-speaking spouses. The translation must have caught up because Rafi, Veronica's husband, suddenly rounded on his wife in Spanish, 'How can you say that, how can you even ask that question? You were born in the Argentine . . . You are Argentinian, not British or Irish. Argentinian.' He slammed his fist down on the table, displacing a swarm of flies.

Veronica winced. The fist on the table was about more than the question of her nationality. Or rather Veronica's Britishness represented all the aspects of their life that her husband hated – having to live in the camp, her preoccupation with horses, her dowdy clothes and unmade-up face. But Rafi's anger soon subsided into his usual moroseness and he said, 'That's the trouble with us Argentines, we have no sense of identity.'

No one round the table disagreed. Only Raul, Michael's chubby eight-year-old son, who was wearing a Boca Juniors strip, was untroubled by the idea of how to define *argentinidad*.

The party began to break up. Rafi's outburst had made everyone feel self-conscious. Dinny was going to play golf with the mayor of San Jorge, Michael had phones to sell, Rafi said he had to go to town on 'business'.

Veronica lingered after her husband left; she had a tape

she wanted to show me of her daughters playing polo. As we watched the two blonde girls hurtle round the polo field, their straight lines distorted by the wavy video tape, she said, 'One thing about the Traills, they must have been brave. Like my daughters . . . They are completely fearless in everything. I envy them, I was brave when I was riding, and now . . .' She looked down at her stiff leg. 'If they don't like something they just get up and go.' She stood up and limped over to the jeep. 'Maybe one day, I will come and see you in England . . .' She smiled faintly. 'I would like to see where my grandfather played polo.' We both knew that she would never come. It was not just her leg that was holding her back.

I watched as she got into the jeep and drove away along the dirt track past the town of Traill to La Esterlina: the house her grandfather had built to get away from his family, the house where her father had shot himself. I wondered if Veronica would ever jump.

Later, when the sun had begun its nightly lurch towards the horizon before dipping quite suddenly out of sight, Derek appeared from his bedroom holding a battered leather box.

'I'd completely forgotten about this. I was looking for my sorghum quotas and I found this stuffed underneath the bed. It's full of Ma's old photographs and letters. I don't know whether any of this is of any use to you, but you might as well have a look through before you go.'

I took the box a little reluctantly. I was tired after the *asado*, I felt as if I had had enough of the past and its repercussions, all these broken lives. I wanted to get back to my present, to move on. Compared to the big-picture disasters that had broken the Traills, the small sadnesses of my childhood were insubstantial. My mother had left me, that was all; it was not much compared to the Potato Famines, Indian raids, freak snowstorms, Baring crises, World Wars, unsavoury uncles, and suicides that had afflicted the Traills. I had been depressed but I had recovered, my life now was comfortable and safe. Unlike my mother, my grandmother and the two generations of Traills before that, I live in the same country, in the same city even, that I was born in. When I take my daughter to school I see women I was at school with, dropping off their children. I am part of a cohort securely anchored in time and space. There are no plagues of locusts in my life, only vague worries about pesticides and global warming. I have never been in real danger, I have never been poor. I was fortunate in that I had nothing more to worry about than an unreliable mother.

I looked around me at the fragile polystyrene walls and the sagging armchairs and I thought of Daphne living here all alone, going to sleep every night with an axe within easy reach under the bed. I had never lived on my own: there had always been someone, a father, a boyfriend, a husband, to keep the murderers at bay. I could afford to be sensitive, I had not had years of hardship toughening my skin.

My mother told me that once when she sat on a wasp in her grandmother's house, Evelyn had told her to get over it quick as much worse things were going to happen to her in her life. After seeing Veronica limp round her paddock talking to the horses she might never ride again, I felt that maybe it was time for me to get over my particular wasp sting. I had my own daughter to bring up.

And yet. The moment, after I became a mother, when I realized what it meant for a mother to leave her child, still smarted. Until I had my daughter I had managed to believe that it didn't really matter, but after she was born I began to swell with rage. How could any mother leave her child, if she felt a fraction of what I felt for my daughter? How could my mother leave me? There were moments when my daughter was a baby when I would find myself crying tears of love mixed with self-pity. As she grew older there were days when I found myself unable to leave her to go to work; the expression on her face as I prepared to go brought back such sharp memories of all the partings of my childhood. She managed without me well enough, it was I who could not deal with the pain of separation. My anger with my mother grew inside me like a bitter cancer spreading, multiplying, distorting my take on the world, until it finally evaporated in depression. At the bottom of my pit the only person I could hate was myself. As my misery receded, the anger was replaced by a need for explanation. I could now understand what it was like to be forced to the edge, but what was it that had pushed my mother? My need to know had brought me here to Argentina, I had found a narrative which almost worked, although I still had to figure out the ending.

Sitting in the shadows that November evening, with Derek's box on my lap, listening to him swear as he dropped the ice for the gintonics on the sticky lino floor, I felt strangely reluctant to continue. Was there perhaps a part of me that did not want to know the ending? Did I want my mother to be innocent or guilty? And if I found her innocent, what then?

'One finger or two?' said Derek, holding up the gin bottle.

'Two,' I said. Strong measures of mother's ruin were what I needed.

'Nice box, isn't it? My father used to keep his revolver

in there. Never allowed to touch that box when I was a child. Absolutely forbidden. And now . . .' Derek lifted his glass. 'Mud in your eye. I must say it's a pleasure to meet such a well-organized, competent adult. You are not, I have to say, your mother's daughter.'

As he said that I saw myself as the solid, critical little girl who had stared at my mother's gaudy life with disapproval. The child who had enraged Joe Fame. The child who read Fox's *Book of Martyrs* with relish. I remembered my father telling me how once, when he was still married to my mother, he had put potatoes in all her discarded boots and shoes. Weeks later when she came to wear them my mother found herself plunging her feet into slime and putrescence. I think at the time I thought it served her right but now I am older and messier my allegiance has changed. I am not sure I am, or even want to be, a person who has all her footwear in serried ranks.

The gin began to take effect, deadening some of the doubts whirling round my head. I opened the box.

The first picture was a rectangular studio photograph of a woman in her late forties or early fifties who I took to be Evelyn. Judging from the marcelled waves in her hair, the portrait was taken in the 1930s. It is hard to tell from the picture whether it was taken before or after Evelyn became a widow. Her smile is playful and the hoop earrings a little roguish so I think this picture must date from Evelyn's golden years living in Bedford without her husband. She looks like a woman in the prime of life. One of Eileen's beaus from the thirties still remembered Evelyn as 'such an attractive woman, so vital', sixty-five years later.

The hoop earrings, only one of which is visible, don't quite match the gentility of the bow at her neck or the neat waves in her hair. They hint at something more exotic than the Bedford Women's Institute. They are the sort of earrings I remember my mother wearing when I was a child. Earrings that would sway and pitch as my mother threw herself around the room to Wilson Pickett's 'In the Midnight Hour'. I used to hate it when my mother danced. I found it subversive. It was definitely breaking the mother rules. Without knowing why exactly, I knew that the music, and the gyration that went with it, was a threat. My brother and I used to cover our eyes and hide under the kitchen table until all the hip-wriggling and hand-clapping had finished. But my mother, I think, rather enjoyed our disapproval. One quality my mother inherited from her grandmother was a sense that children should not be indulged.

The portrait looks as though it should be in a frame, and yet judging from the discolouration round the edges it has always lain here in the old revolver box. Perhaps Daphne, who was closest to her father, did not like the way her mother smiled in the photograph

Underneath the stiff sepia-tinted image of Evelyn were some leaves from a photograph album, black-and-white snapshots restrained on the black card by crackly adhesive corners. The photos are tiny, haphazardly framed but with the images recorded through the lens of some Box Brownie still sharp as miniatures. There are pictures of girls in drop-waisted dresses and shingled haircuts playing tennis, and of boys in flannels drinking pop or boys in scout uniform building fires. Each picture is annotated with a child's careful handwriting, '*Daphne playing tennis 1927*', '*Mother resting*', '*Sparky at the nets*'. One photo entitled '*Famaly* [sic] *group 1929*' has three girls and two boys arranged like a chorus line in order of size. My grandmother is second from the left; although her eyes are closed her cheekbones are unmistakable. She is holding a dog. This photograph must have been taken when Eileen was in her second year at Girton, where she had won a scholarship to read modern languages. Although higher education for women was no longer as exceptional as it had been for say Vera Brittain fifteen years earlier, it was still uncommon for a girl to go to Cambridge.

I wonder if that scholarship was earned to please the father she never saw. Eileen is flanked by her sisters Claire and Daphne who have less sharply modelled faces but broader smiles. Neither of them went to university. Evelyn sent them back to the Argentine to find husbands.

To the right of the picture stand Eileen's brothers Dick and Roy. Roy athletic, muscular and blond, Dick tall and gangly with thick horn-rimmed glasses. They stand with their hands on each other's shoulders as if about to set off on a conga line. At the time of the photograph Roy was in his first year at Cambridge reading law and Dick was still at school in Bedford. After university Roy went into the RAF and Dick became a schoolmaster. Neither of them returned to the Argentine to work on the Traill estancia. Their cousins all went back after being sent to school in England, and yet Dick and Roy seem to have gone back to visit the Traill estates only once. Their parents colluded in this even though for different reasons; Bob wanted his sons to have the English life he had been denied, while Evelyn worried they might go the way of their Traill uncles.

The girls would be all right, they had inherited Evelyn's toughness, but she did not want her boys to be yet more casualties of estancia life, frozen into melancholy like her husband.

There is only one picture in the album of '*Daddy*'. Taken in 1928, the year Bob returned to the Argentine for good, '*Daddy*' is at the edge of another '*famaly* [sic] *group*'. He stands with his weight on one leg, his hands in his pockets, and even though his face is hidden by his moustache and beard, it is clear that he is making no attempt to smile for the camera.

Underneath the album was an envelope with '*Eileen's wedding*' written on it in spidery italic writing. Inside were six postcard-size pictures of my grandmother's wedding in 1933. The first picture is of my grandmother getting out of a car with her brother Roy. The wedding dress, which I am sure my grandmother made herself, is a simple satin column with a train that she is carefully holding up with one hand. The veil is a wisp of tulle held back from my grandmother's face by a twist of pearls. The beautiful cheekbones, the smooth expanse of her forehead, are framed by the carefully crimped dark hair. I remember my grandmother as angular, sharp, formidable but in this picture she looks tender, exposed, anxiously stepping into a new life. On the back of the photograph someone has written, '*Roy and Eileen arriving at the church, Mr Smith's top hat that only perched on the crown of his head. Gerald Parson's spats – coat and trousers belonged to the man below his rooms at Cambridge.*'

Roy looks uncomfortable in his borrowed clothes. It took me a while to figure out why, but then it dawned on me – he was nervous because in the absence of his father it had fallen to him to give his sister away. Why did Daddy not show up at his daughter's wedding? What prevented him from leading Eileen down the aisle? At the time I assumed that he had simply retreated too far into melancholy to travel halfway across the world for a wedding, but later I discovered there was another reason, one that had strange echoes of an earlier marriage. Bob had refused to come to his daughter's wedding because the man she was marrying was a Catholic. Bob could not object to Paul Innes, Eileen's fiancé, personally, as they had never met, but the fact that he was Catholic was enough to keep Bob away from his daughter's wedding. In England in the mid-1930s for a Protestant to marry a Catholic was little more than a curiosity. But for Bob Traill whose Protestantism was part of his Anglo-Argentine identity, a foundation stone of his inherent superiority over the 'natives', his daughter's decision to marry a Catholic was an unacceptable loss of caste.

Evelyn was not pleased with her prospective son-in-law's religion either, but living in England must have softened her prejudices because there is a picture of her resplendent in a fox stole on the way to the wedding. Only the apprehensive look on her face undercuts the image of a radiant mother of the bride. Once again she is wearing a spectacularly gaudy pair of earrings.

A picture of the bridegroom, splendidly dapper in his morning coat, striped bags, white spats and silk top hat. His head is turned to reveal his aquiline profile, the only thing about him that I recognize. My grandfather scared me as a child; by the time I knew him he had gone deaf and communicated with the world in an angry roar. The house which he and my grandmother lived in was full of no-go areas, the chair where my grandfather sat, the study where he wrote angry letters. My grandfather's face was the colour of a child's painting: blue eyes, flushed red cheeks and a purple nose. The same nose that looks sharp and youthful in this photograph. Beside him in the picture is a man wearing a dog collar with a suit which looks a little small for him. The outfit is completed with a soft felt trilby. On the back of the photograph someone has written '*Paul Innes and his brother*'. Paul's brother was a monk at Downside; presumably he was wearing civilian clothes out of deference to the bride's family's Protestant sensibilities – a Catholic bridegroom was bad enough but a tonsured monk would have thrown them completely.

I know little about my grandfather's family. My grandmother, who was the family's narrator, naturally leant towards the Traills for her raw material. It was only recently that I discovered that his surname, Innes, was an assumed one. Paul's father, a Yorkshireman whose original name had been Tatchell, had changed it by deed poll in order to escape his creditors after one of his frequent bankruptcies. Innes senior had been born a Protestant but had converted on his marriage to Paul's mother who was a Catholic. Somehow they had managed to scrape together enough money to send their sons to Downside.

Paul's Catholicism was a defining feature of his life. As a child I remember the doors slamming on Sunday mornings and the crunch of gravel as my grandfather drove off to early-morning mass. Although my grandmother refused to convert herself, she had to agree to bring her children up as Catholics. But even if she had to bring up her children in the faith, she did not have to approve of its indulgences; I can still remember her saying acidly, 'Oh, Paul's gone to confession, he always feels the need to go after one of our bridge evenings.'

The constancy of Paul's faith reflected the uncertainties of his childhood; his surname might have been an assumed one, but at least his religion could be relied on. I remember a friend of my grandparents describing Paul as a Cavalier and Eileen as a Roundhead. It was a distinction that I found hard to understand aged eleven, but in retrospect it makes sense: Paul passionately, romantically Catholic, Eileen a cool, sceptical Protestant. Paul had a warmth, an optimism, a conviction that Eileen had not found in her father.

A picture of them outside the church, married, dusted with confetti. My grandmother is smiling, a joyful, unequivocal smile; she is holding out her skirt like a little girl showing off her new party dress. She looks softer than I ever remember seeing her and radiantly happy. Having grown up with my mother and her siblings constantly tracing the origins of their own dissolving marriages to their parents' unhappiness, it comes as a shock to see my grandparents looking so happily united. There has always been a whisper that my grandmother somehow married beneath her, but here she looks radiant with relief.

It had been a long engagement. They had met at Cambridge, when Eileen was in her first year and Paul was in his third. Paul proposed to Eileen just before setting off for China where he was going to work for Shell. She accepted even though she knew they would not be able to marry for more than three years (each tour of duty was three and a half years and Paul had to sign a contract promising that he would remain unmarried for the duration). That is a long time to be separated from the man you love when you are only twenty. But the lovers wrote to each other every day, even twice a day; letters that sometimes took months to cross the world. All my grandmother's letters to Paul have survived; he had them bound together in a series of calf-leather books with marble endpapers with the initials A.E.T. and the dates of the correspondence on the spine.

Reading them after her death, I understood why he kept them so carefully. They have all my grandmother's tart powers of description, her eye for the macabre detail, but they also have an innocence and a strength of feeling that is irresistible. In one letter written a year after his departure she writes:

> *I am wearing your mandarin coat – you can't imagine how quaint it looks between a voluminous night gown and a night cap – I'm sitting up in bed and I think I can hear a knock at the door – you come in your dressing gown, and you sit on the edge of the bed quite still at first and then you take my hand and push up my sleeves till your arms are right round me, and mine around you, and then darling I pull your head into my shoulder and rock you to and fro just like my baby. Your chin would be all bristly – but I wish you were here all the same. I would suffer it in silence for once.*

It is a chaste little fantasy, to rock your lover in your arms like a baby; perhaps the incident with Uncle Basil all those years ago made it hard for her to think of what would happen next. But the comment about his bristly chin is pure Eileen, tart and tender at the same time. Typically, she did not keep his letters to her, but we can imagine the tone of them from a rather crisp passage in one of Eileen's to him:

> *My Dearest, I've just had two letters from you and I've come to the conclusion that you spoil them by trying too hard. I think the ideal style in letter writing should be natural and totally unaffected, and you fail seriously in both respects. I can't think Paul, how*

> *you can have so little self criticism – your letters are*
> *so pretentious, they're either pompous or pseudo-*
> *poetical, mostly the latter. I'd much rather have*
> *straight narrative than an endless treatise on love.*

I can quite imagine my grandmother reading even her love letters with one eyebrow raised in criticism. She never shirked the truth as she saw it. When I was a child she never hesitated to tell me the sartorial truth: 'That colour makes you very sallow, darling.' But here she is not just being spiky. In her letter to Paul, ostensibly criticizing his writing style, she was really railing against what she suspected might be insincerity. How carefully she must have gone through his letters, in those long years of separation, combing them for signs that his love might be waning. I think the sharp tone of her letter was a form of pre-emptive strike – better to reject than be rejected. In another letter she writes about the differences between her family and his:

> *I think our family is far more reserved about affec-*
> *tions than you are, but I think that Mother knows*
> *there is a very strong bond of appreciation between*
> *us all – except perhaps with Daddy. He has always*
> *been too shy with us, and we have always been a bit*
> *afraid of him so that now he is rather a pathetic*
> *figure – I feel that he wants our love but doesn't*
> *know how to ask for it – and it is the same on our*
> *side.*

I find it hard to read this passage without feeling a twinge of pain. I know that as a child I found my grandmother alarming; it was difficult for me to love her in the way that I had loved my father's mother. I don't remember ever sitting on Eileen's lap. And yet Eileen wanted my love – she spent hours making up dresses for me from designs that I had scribbled on bits of paper – but neither of us knew how to break through the barriers of awkwardness; she was 'too shy to ask' and I had no way of translating her abrupt acts of kindness into love. Looking at these photographs, reading these letters makes me wish urgently that I had known how to speak my grandmother's language, that I had understood what she was trying to tell me with those carefully embroidered princesses' costumes.

The week before, in Buenos Aires, Robin had told me how, when Eileen visited the Argentine in 1985, she had boasted about me. 'She made you sound like a paragon of every conceivable virtue.' When he told me I dismissed it as politeness – it was hardly likely that my acid-tongued grandmother would be boasting about me – and yet now, deciphering her spiky italic scrawl, I can see that I have misread her. What I took for coldness was simply shyness; she had learnt from her father only too well how to put distance between herself and the things she cared about.

When Paul returned from China after being away for three and a half years, they decided to consummate their relationship to see if they were really 'suited'; an idea they picked up from their favourite book, *The Good Companions* by J. B. Priestley. They duly checked into the Royal Midland Hotel as Mr and Mrs Huxley. But the experiment was a failure. Paul, when it came to it, could not overcome his Catholic scruples and found himself impotent. After so much waiting and expectation Eileen was devastated and humiliated. Even though Paul tried to reassure her that the problem was not hers, her self-confidence was shattered.

There was no chance to put things straight, Paul had to leave again on another tour of duty. Eileen had planned to move to London and work there till Paul came back, but after the fiasco in the Royal Midland Hotel she decided to stay in Bedford with her mother, teaching at the school where she had been a pupil, a wounded animal returning to its lair.

But worse was to come: five months later Paul wrote to her from Shanghai announcing that his physical '*difficulties*' were at an end – an experienced widow had put him out of his misery. Dearest Eileen would be relieved to know that he was able to perform normally.

Paul was amazed when he received a letter from her breaking off their engagement. He had approached the whole business of losing his virginity in a scientific manner; he was simply not prepared for Eileen's jealous rage. It did not occur to him that she would be doubly humiliated by the fact that not only had he slept with another woman but that the other woman (Paul had described her as '*older and more sophisticated than you are my darling*') had succeeded where she had failed. Letters, their only form of communication, failed them here: the six weeks it took for the mails to travel between Shanghai and London was an unbearable length of time to wait for a reply that could change everything. Paul had to finish this tour of duty before he could come home and talk to Eileen. They could not even end their engagement officially as *The Times* required both parties to be present before agreeing to publish a 'Marriage Will Not Take Place' announcement (a requirement designed to avoid breach-of-promise actions). Eileen was left in limbo. She could not forgive Paul but neither could she make a clean break until he came back to England.

In the meantime, she did not answer Paul's letters and began a flirtation with an army officer called Lyndon, a man who was everything that Paul was not: light, sophisticated, witty, sensitive. Lyndon flattered Eileen and made her feel desirable. For such a beautiful woman, Eileen had not had a chance to become blasé about male admiration.

The photographs show that Eileen was perfectly made, elegant from the tilt of her jutting cheekbones to her neat ankles. She has the face of a heroine of a 1930s' screwball comedy – a Myrna Loy, or a Katharine Hepburn – and yet her eyes lack their pert self-assurance. Eileen needed to be loved.

The flirtation with Lyndon was enjoyable but limited. He never pushed it further than a goodnight kiss. After a while Eileen began to wonder why their relationship did not progress any further. She assumed that Lyndon was waiting until her engagement was officially at an end, so she did everything she could to let him know that her relationship with Paul was over, but still he did nothing except flirt. She found herself once again unable to provoke the right response from a man. Of course she blamed herself. It was not until the end of her life, when she met Lyndon again after fifty-odd years, that she discovered the reason for his reticence. All the time that he had been flirting with Eileen in Bedford, Lyndon had been having an affair with a married woman. The affair had to be kept secret, as Lyndon's career in the army would have been ruined if he had been named as co-respondent. He regarded his relationship with Eileen as a diversion, a way of passing the time until the future was settled. He assumed that Eileen with her outward sophistication, her brittle drawing-room-comedy face would understand the rules of the game. He did not understand how innocent Eileen was underneath, or if he did he preferred to ignore it.

Eileen did not discover Lyndon's secret at the time

because Paul arrived back from China six months earlier than expected. They arranged to meet at the offices of *The Times* so that they could hand in the official notice ending their engagement. After they had both signed their names to the notice in the presence of the editor, whom Eileen later remembered as needing a handkerchief, Paul offered to take his now ex-fiancée to lunch. The lunch, entered into without expectations, proved decisive. Overwhelmed by Paul's physical presence and his need for her, Eileen changed her mind. After the lunch they went back to the newspaper office – 'The man wasn't a bit surprised, apparently it happened all the time' – and cancelled the 'Marriage Will Not Take Place' notice. Four months later in July 1933 they were married.

After a two-week honeymoon in Europe, Eileen and Paul set off for China, arriving in Nanking in November. In an account Paul wrote of the first years of their marriage (a kind of résumé of their life for English friends who they had lost touch with during the war) he describes Eileen as '*settling down energetically to house-keeping, gardening and learning Chinese. She also did some book reviewing for the* North China Daily News *and the very inferior novels they received gave her full scope for some amusingly sharp notices.*'

But that early rift set the tone for their marriage which in the early years was full of misunderstandings and reconciliations. Eileen's letters to Paul in the first years of their marriage are passionate. She writes to him from the Argentine the day after he catches the boat to China, '*I wish time would fly my darling until I am in your arms again, I yearn to melt in my bed at night, when I think of you my nipples are two little tingling spots reaching for you, which sounds odd but it's true.*'

But after a few more days of absence, doubts begin to creep in again; her husband is going back to China alone. She realizes that he will be surrounded by the kind of sophisticated older women that had led him astray before, so in a rather challenging way she writes, '*My dearest I've never had any fear of your three women friends, I wouldn't laugh about them if I really took them seriously. I must admit though that I heartily dislike packing and unpacking your sentimental baggage. I believe I've quarantined it all in one small case now, which will be left to moulder unopened.*' Paul must have said something about saying goodbye to one of his old flames to which Eileen replies, '*Though I can sympathise with your desire to make your last meeting a joyful thing for both of you, I would blame you if sentiment made you try to quicken cold love again – my dear I am sombre today – it's raining outside and we're all collected in the drawing room round the ruins of a very small fire.*' I like the unintentional(?) metaphor at the end: Paul is warned not to quicken cold love while his wife and two children sit round a too-small fire.

Another small sepia snapshot. My grandmother looking like Mrs Simpson, sitting next to a small child who is holding a cake. On the cake is written '*For the Sweetheart of the compound*' in icing and there are three candles. The child's face is screwed up as if ready to cry; my grandmother is looking uncomfortable, and she is not touching the little girl. Eileen does not know why the little girl, who I realize must be my mother, is crying; Eileen would like her to stop and smile for the camera but she does not know how to make it happen. She turns her head away from my mother, looking perhaps for the Chinese amah who could make sense of this contrary child. Reading the picture now I am reminded of the phrase Eileen used about her father, about wanting love but being too shy to ask for it. Other photographs of Eileen and my mother as a child, all show my grandmother looking puzzled and apprehensive as if she is holding a small wild creature who might bite.

Underneath the stamp-sized photos of my mother as a little girl are a few pages of almost transparent writing paper that have held the same creases for fifty years. The pages are typed on both sides, no spaces between the closely packed lines. As I smooth out the paper, hoping that it does not fall apart along the ancient folds, I can hear the fierce clack of my grandmother's Underwood portable typewriter, the machine she carried from Cambridge to China and back to the farm in Essex where I stayed with her as a child. The first letter is dated '*17/2/41*', the address at the top is '*Tsingtao China*'. The letter starts with a brief paragraph about the imminence of war: '*Nobody knows what would happen here if there was trouble . . . The worst would be an internment camp, and I have arranged to get rid of the children to some Italians. However I am getting sick of discussing evacuations. People are pretty sensible here and anyway we are all so bored with discussing the chances of getting berths etc. that we refuse to talk about it any more.*' Eileen's flippancy about the future seems incredible now; but it is possible that in Tsingtao at the beginning of 1941 the war in Europe seemed unimaginably remote. And yet only eight months after Eileen's letter the Japanese bombed Pearl Harbor.

But Eileen's world of Red Cross dinner dances and golf tournaments was to be interrupted even sooner. Interleaved between the first and second letters were two telegrams dated 14 March and 21 March 1941. These papers I realized were more than a random selection of stuff, they were an organized chronology of a family tragedy. The first telegram read, ROY KILLED 12TH FLYING ACCIDENT BABY EXPECTED SEPTEMBER MOTHER TRAILL. The second telegram, the strips of type worn and crinkled against the yellowing paper of TRANSRADIO INTERNACIONAL, is starker still: DICK KILLED 13TH EVELYN TRAILL. In one of those bleak coincidences that seem typically Traill, Eileen's two brothers died on successive days.

Roy was killed on his way back from Ireland to see his wife who had just told him she was pregnant. The plane he got a lift in crashed into a mountain. Dick was in a hospital tent near Cairo having a septic finger dressed when a shell went off accidentally, killing everyone inside.

Under the telegrams is another letter from Eileen dated 26 April. She deals with the tragedy in the first paragraph:

It is such a waste, such a pitiable waste. I always felt that Roy couldn't possibly survive, but somehow Dick was never meant to be a soldier and I thought that would possibly help him. I didn't know that Betty [Roy's wife] was going to have a baby till I got your letter. I am very glad. I hope it's a boy. I don't know why one should wish one's family name to survive. Heaven knows our family hasn't anything to distinguish it particularly, just good chaps in their way.*

The rest of the letter – Eileen always covered both sides – deals with their growing financial difficulties, '*the exchange is so much against us that we can't afford to live on Paul's pay*', the imminence of war, Eileen's difficulties with her gardener, her unsuccessful attempts at making marmalade and the difficulties of finding decent clothes for the children, '*I haven't bought anything new for them since we've been here and I'm very busy cutting up all my old clothes for them. I don't know what I shall do when my stock gives out.'* She does not mention the double tragedy again.

Reading Eileen's letter by the harsh light of Derek's standard lamp, I was taken aback by its briskness. Was there another one that I had missed which expressed the real grief that Eileen must have felt on losing both her brothers in the same week? But the sheaf of letters was clearly dated and Eileen prefaces the letter by saying that she had put off writing it after receiving those awful telegrams from Ma. I read the letter again trying to unearth emotion buried beneath the talk of golf handicaps and exchange rates – it must I felt be there somewhere. What kind of woman writes about the death of her brothers on the same page as marmalade that refuses to set? Could Eileen really be as pragmatic as this letter suggests, or was she simply unable to express her feelings? And yet her letters to Paul are vivid enough. I can only imagine that Eileen had been rendered numb to tragedy by the circumstances of her childhood; sudden deaths were too much part of the fabric of her life to arouse special comment. There is something odd about her phrase, *'I always felt that Roy couldn't possibly survive.'* It is almost as if she knew somehow that her brothers were doomed, that this was a tragedy that she had been preparing for all her life. I remembered the story of the dead donkey, my grandmother's precise description of the feel of decomposing flesh, the relish with which she unveiled the unhappy ending. Eileen had not expected her brothers to live. The war had only accelerated the inevitable.

Derek came in to find me looking at the telegrams. 'Bloody typical that, all those Traills rushing to join up and they all get themselves killed, without going near the enemy. All of them bought it in stupid accidents. Roy gets killed hitching a lift home from his air base in Ireland so he could go and see Betty who was having a baby. He'd flown that route hundreds of times himself so he must have known the hill was coming but because he was sitting in front in the gunner's seat he had no way of warning the pilot. Sat there facing his own death, poor sod. And then there was Tom Traill, Joe's son, Spitfire pilot, flying home from a mission, gave the wrong signal, shot down by his own side. And Tony Traill who was in the navy was standing on the prow of his ship having his photograph taken. When the photographer looked up he'd been washed overboard by a freak wave, couldn't swim, poor bugger. And my Dad, wasn't able to join up till '44, everyone said he was too old. He was delighted when he got a job in the air force auxiliary, but two months later his plane collided with another one when it was taking off. Damn difficult for Ma, couldn't even say her husband had been killed in action.'

Two hundred and thirty Anglo-Argentines enlisted in the British Services in the Second World War. Eleven of them were Traills or Traills by marriage. Only one, Jack Traill, sad Veronica's father, survived. Perhaps that generation of Traill men would, had they survived, have gone on to lead happy and contented lives with no thought of jumping. But Jack's post-war career did not augur well for the rest of the Traills had they survived: his life followed the familiar Traill pattern of drink, depression and then a final act of oblivion. Jack did not jump, he simply pulled a trigger. He had survived a direct hit on the tank he had been driving in France in 1944, but life in the pampas defeated him.

He was a casualty of a different kind of battle.

Derek switched on the television, suddenly impatient with all this distant sadness. Striking metalworkers had stormed the governor's residence in Jujuy province; President Menem had frozen teachers' salaries all over the country; Chapaleufu had won the Argentine Open. I watched for a while trying to guess the tenor of the news from Derek's exclamations, but the present was no distraction for me then, I had to get to the end of the box. I was nearly at the end of my journey.

TWENTY-ONE

Derek drove me to Rosario the next day, where I would catch a plane to Buenos Aires and then home. I had wanted to go by train to get a real sense in my mind of all those Traill comings and goings but the trains only carried freight these days. It took us two hours to drive to Rosario along one of those straight Argentinian roads that ended in a shimmering blur, a pool of quicksilver that we never quite reached. Derek was quiet, I think he wanted to get back to his sorghum. I tried to thank him for his hospitality but he shrugged it off, embarrassed in true Traill fashion by sentiment. At the airport he said, 'I hope you got what you came for. I had a helluva time making sense of it all, but I'm sure you won't find it so hard, you know what you're looking for.' It was an oddly intimate remark for Derek to make but I think in that moment he sensed almost before I did that I had found my story.

The night before I had taken the box into my room. I was tired but I knew that I would not sleep for hours, there were too many stories banging in my head like unsecured shutters in a storm. I found a picture of my mother aged about twelve, her hair in plaits, her face shining. The background is indeterminate; she could be in Cairo where the family spent the last years of the war and where my mother went to a convent school run by Coptic nuns, or in Bedford where my mother was sent to the same school that Eileen had attended. My mother's face is eager and vivid, she looks familiar but also strange, there is something I don't quite recognize. I realize that she is looking straight to camera; nowadays my mother rarely looks anyone or anything directly in the eye. I wonder when she lost that frankness. I know that after the war Eileen, having put her three eldest children in boarding school, went back to China to be with Paul. In the holidays my mother, her sister and brother were dispatched to a seaside boarding house where they were sent out after breakfast and expected to amuse themselves until teatime. My mother did not see either of her parents for two years. It was not so unusual at the time – there certainly would have been no social censure attached to my grandmother's actions – but I wonder how that separation affected my mother. She had spent the last five or so years buffeted from Asia, to Australia and then Africa by the war but always at her mother's side; now she was being left in an unfamiliar country with only her siblings for company. There was no appeal possible. Eileen presented this decision as a fait accompli, and my mother as the eldest was expected to implement her orders.

I wonder whether Eileen agonized about abandoning her children for two years or whether the dislocated circumstances of her own childhood had left her unable to sympathize with the feelings of her own children. Unconsciously Eileen was reproducing the familiar Traill pattern of parents and children 'too shy' to express their feelings for one another.

I think she rationalized leaving her children behind as the 'best thing' for them, but underneath the sensible explanations I think she felt that it was all right to leave them because they did not really need her. She had taught her children the virtues of toughness, but she had forgotten that they had only learnt not to cry. The tears were still there. I suspect that when Eileen was reunited with her children, my mother did not look her in the eye, it was too painful to connect.

I knew in a corner of my mind as I studied these photographs looking for the narrative thread that bound them together, that I was in the process of building a legend, creating a well-turned story around a slew of possibly unconnected facts, looking for clues where none might exist. And yet as I connected the various jumps that my family had made, as I bound them together in a seamless chain of cause and effect, I knew that it was a story that made sense to me. I had found here in Argentina a way to explain why my mother had jumped away from me.

There was a picture right at the bottom of the gun box, a black-and-white snapshot of two people in their twenties, sitting on a bench playing with a dog. My mother I recognize straight away, I can date the picture by her Julie Christie hairstyle. She is teasing a small dog with her foot. But it takes me a minute or two to realize that the man sitting next to her with his arm lightly round her shoulders is my father. I find myself blinking back tears, unwished-for sentimental tears, because this is the first picture I have ever seen of my parents together. They look happy, at least my father does, but of course I cannot see my mother's eyes – as usual she is looking away from the camera. Photographs like this are part of the casualties of divorce – why would anyone keep these reminders of a relationship that failed – and yet that picture was to me priceless, a clue. My mother looking down, my father encircling her lightly but possessively with his arm. I grieve for my parents' marriage, crying for that sunny afternoon with a small dog. I want it to have worked out for them, but as I look at my mother's downcast eyes and twitching foot, I know that she is set on a course that will end in her getting on that bicycle away from me. Another picture of a fat anxious-looking baby, its face screwed up with worry, me. I can't be older than eighteen months and yet I look as if I know things are going to end badly. I also look very like my own daughter at that age and as I make that connection I wait for the familiar rush of indignant self-pity to course, hot and salty, round my head. The feeling that says how could my mother have left a child that she loved, how could she? *How could she?* But the feeling does not come, that tide has gone right out. I feel sad but I don't feel angry. I remember the picture of my mother as a shining-faced schoolgirl looking candidly into the future and I know that I am not the only one who has been damaged. I remember the picture of my grandmother in her wedding dress holding onto her brother's arm because her father will not come to her wedding. I remember the way that Bob Traill looks away from the camera in the photograph of the North Santa Fé polo team, his expression hidden by his moustache. I think of Alice's unmarked grave and the careful stencilling on the crumbling plaster walls of the old estancia house at Las Limpias. I remember the picture of Ann Traill, the Rector of Skull's widow, the gallant curls concealing the lines left by a life filled with loss.

All these pictures lock together in my head, to form a cypher that decodes my mother's actions. At last I understand, and with that understanding comes relief. The tears are still falling but they are tears of release not sadness. A memory comes to me. The night that I went into labour with my daughter, anxiously pacing round the flat waiting for the contractions to come closer together so that I could go to hospital. My mother came over then and I remember her smell as she embraced me awkwardly because of the bump containing my daughter between us – a smell so sweet, so reassuring that my fear vanished. We did not need to talk, we communicated on another visceral level and on that level there could be no misunderstanding. Drinking in the scent of my mother that night I knew without doubt that she loved me and my fear of the ordeal ahead evaporated. I felt supported, euphoric, whole.

Later when that heightened sensory awareness had subsided, I forgot that smell and the peace it had given me. But now it came back to me. I had found a story that worked in my head and in my heart. I had been hurt it was true, but my mother could no more have avoided damaging me, than her mother could have been prevented from hurting her. A chain of hurt and misunderstanding had been uncurling through the generations. I thought of my own daughter and how after the first few days of this trip I had stopped phoning her despite the pleasure it gave me to hear her voice. I stopped because I could not bear the questions. When are you coming home, Mummy, when? How many more days? I could not bear the sound of my equivocal replies, Soon and Not long now. The shock of parting was still fresh enough for her to admit that things were not the same without me but I knew that if I did not come home soon there would be a point when I would ask her how she was and she would say, Fine, and I would be too shy to ask for more.

As the aeroplane took off from Rosario, I looked out

of the window to see the great grey channel of the Río de la Plata. As the plane went higher I could see how the straightforward force of the river was diverted and distressed into the growing pyramid of the delta. Obstacles that the river would have swept away further upstream were now respected, the sluggish water looking for the line of least resistance, turning these obdurate bits of grit into islands. In winter the delta flooded but when the waters retreated, the same pattern of islands came through, the now tamed river returning to its familiar course.

After weeks spent in the pampas, the height was exhilarating.

I felt free. Insulated from the responsibilities of my life by this carapace of aluminium, I looked down at the flatness and understood my mother's decision to jump. My mother did not stand on a windowsill like her grandfather and uncles, but like them she wanted to control her destiny, to escape the flatness.

She once told me that she felt she had no choice. At the time I thought it was an unsatisfactory answer, one that let her off the hook, but up here remembering all those frozen marriages and disappointed lives down on the plain, it began to make sense. The Rector of Skull had made a moral leap when he gave his life saving Catholics, Robert Traill jumped into a marriage and across continents, his sons jumped from windows, my mother had jumped into a life of her own invention; each generation had felt impelled to make its own leap. I remembered my own encounter with despair, that smooth-sided pit, and it was clear to me why they had needed to jump.

Below me the Silver River was pushing into the Atlantic, the clash of currents twisting into knots of surf. The mighty river was going to surrender its status without a fight. I thought about what there was in me of my jumping, leaping family. Their intimacy with despair certainly, their preoccupation with story definitely, but not their talent for jumping. I am not brave like them, I will never make that final glamorous leap, but perhaps it takes a different kind of courage to live with the flatness.

Two days later, landing in Gatwick airport on a grey November morning, I feel my daughter's arms go round my neck and smell her hot slightly sour breath. No one has been checking that she cleans her teeth. It was time that I came home. I am needed here.